SHAKESPEARE
PRESS

The memoir of Gerald Jaggard
completed by
ANDY JAGGARD

Published in the UK in 2023 by Shakespeare Press

Copyright © Andy Jaggard 2023

Andy Jaggard has asserted their right under
the Copyright, Designs and Patents Act, 1988,
to be identified as the author of this work.

All rights reserved. No part of this book may be reproduced, stored in a
retrieved system or transmitted, in any form or by any means, electronic,
mechanical, scanning, photocopying, recording or otherwise, without the
prior permission of the author and publisher.

Paperback ISBN 978-1-7393077-0-7
eBook ISBN 978-1-7393077-1-4

Cover design and typeset by SpiffingCovers

SHAKESPEARE
PRESS

The memoir of Gerald Jaggard
completed by
ANDY JAGGARD

Acknowledgements

My thanks to the many people who have helped to create this book – authors, book reviewers, photographers, family tree researchers and genealogists, and to my sister, Anthea for her enthusiastic support for this project.

Also to Chris, Susie, Jenni, and Moira who have been involved in our dramatized presentations of 'Walked Alone' and 'Gerald's Shakespeare Press' hosted by the Shakespeare Club and King Edward VI Shakespeare's School.

My special thanks to Alan Harry for his detailed family tree research and for introducing me to Helen Greenland née Jaggard who provided a crucial part of the story.

In 1964, (the same year that the "Shakespeare Press" bookshop closed its doors for the last time), the Baylis family arrived in Tiddington and soon were at the heart of our Dark Lane and School Lane community. Richard and Judith were both very fond of my father, Gerald. In 1981 they moved to London and later to Cornwall, where they still live, but they have remained friends for life and have taken a keen interest in this book.

"This is an authentic story, meticulously researched, from a bygone era."

Judith Baylis

Finally, thanks to my wife, Moira for her patience and her complete support over the last three years, not to mention far too many chapter-by-chapter reviews.

Author's note - the three voices

Our story involves three generations of Jaggards, myself Andy, my father, Gerald and my grandfather, Captain William Jaggard (known as "WJ" by the family). To avoid confusion between the three voices we use a typewriter font for Gerald's unfinished memoir and his letters, and a script font for WJ's letters and for his private papers.

Andy Jaggard - April 2023

**Captain William Jaggard in his Liverpool Bookshop, 1890s
Registered 'Shakespeare Press' in 1893
Founded 'Shakespeare Press' bookshop in Stratford-upon-Avon 1910**

"This title has been used by various firms, according to books in our possession, for the last two hundred years, but we were the first to record it officially (as ours, in 1893) and therefore it may no longer be used by anyone without our permission.

There is a certain appropriateness in this, as you will admit, seeing that our ancestor produced the first edition of Shakespeare.

We await your early reply before taking further steps."

*Yours truly,
Captain Wm Jaggard*

Contents

Chapter 1 'The Life And Death' 13

Chapter 2 The Shakespeare Press 22

Chapter 3 The First Folio And The
Shakespeare Industry 35

Chapter 4 The Sixth William 47

Chapter 5 "Bring It Over". 57

Chapter 6 A Farcical Tale 69

Chapter 7 William Jaggard Man Of Letters –
All 2,000 Of Them 77

Chapter 8 Piracy 88

Chapter 9 City Librarian Or Nothing 98

Chapter 10 Life At Home With WJ At 'Rose Bank' 107

Chapter 11 WJ's Missions And Making Enemies 113

Chapter 12 WJ In The First World War 125

Chapter 13 Gerald – Smitten By Shakespeare 135

Chapter 14 The Housekeeper's Story 148

Chapter 15 Gerald's 'Lost Years' 161

Chapter 16 A Voice From The Dead 170

Chapter 17 Forgery 176

Chapter 18 A Great Find 188

Chapter 19 He Walked Alone.. 198

Chapter 20 Gerald's 'Shakespeare Press' –
1947–1960.. 204

Chapter 21 Gerald's 'Shakespeare Press' – 1960–1964............ 225

Chapter 22 The Game Is Nearly Up... 237

Chapter 23 The Direct Descent.. 247

Postscript – Reflections On The Direct Descent....................... 265

Chapter 24 Loose Ends 268

Appendix – Contents... 275

Bibliography 300

Image Captions 313

CHAPTER 1 'THE LIFE AND DEATH' – *Andy Jaggard*

Perhaps if bookshops can be haunted, No. 4 Sheep Street can claim more ghosts than most.

That was his opening line.

In March 2002 I got an urgent message to call my older sister, Anthea. We hurried to a local Spanish bar which had a public phone. Anthea told me that our father, Gerald Quentin Jaggard, had died that afternoon. He had complained of feeling a little unwell that morning and had sat in his armchair all day, sipping a small brandy. Around 4pm, our mother, Diana, decided to call the doctor. By the time the doctor had arrived he had slipped away, still sitting in his armchair – they think his heart gave out. No medics, no fuss.

It was a shock. He was only 97. We fully expected him to get to his century. A week and a half earlier he had played out a tough game of chess with me, with a hard-earned draw.

I flew back to England to the family home in the village of Tiddington, near Stratford-upon-Avon. Diana was in shock. We had ten days to make the arrangements and prepare for the funeral. A couple of days later I was searching for an important document in Gerald's study. One of the drawers in his desk was jammed with just the corner of a typed document protruding. It caught my eye. There was a word count and a correction written in pencil, *No. 4 Sheep Street*. I forced the drawer open and, holding the document up to the light, realised that it was the manuscript of an unpublished book by my father. Gerald called it, *The Life and Death of a Stratford Bookshop*.

That day back in 2002, I sat down and immediately read *The Life and Death*.

Gerald had lived in Stratford for ninety-two years, since his arrival from Liverpool, aged five, with his eccentric father, Captain William Jaggard, who founded his 'Shakespeare Press' in Sheep Street. Gerald was part of the fabric of the town: educated at 'Shakespeare's' Grammar School, vice-president of the Shakespeare club, and well-known for running the iconic antiquarian bookshop in the centre of town.

(Growing up in Stratford-upon-Avon it's impossible to escape the Shakespeare connection. It <u>was</u> Shakespeare's home town. Following in my father's footsteps, I also went to the boys' Grammar School and true to the Shakespearean tradition, in my first year, I had to play one of the female roles, a shepherdess, sporting an ancient blonde wig.)

Gerald's funeral service was held in a small chapel, part of a country house estate a few miles from Stratford. Unable to face the ordeal of making a speech at the funeral, I decided I'd read an extract from his unpublished book instead.

I stood in front of the packed chapel, trying to hold myself together. After explaining the discovery of my father's manuscript a few days earlier, I read a section of Gerald's opening chapter.

Perhaps, if bookshops can be haunted, No. 4 Sheep Street, Stratford-upon-Avon, can claim more ghosts than most. Haunted certainly, by my father and by the generations of book lovers, notable and ordinary, who bought or browsed among its dusty shelves in the fifty years of its life …

There was some nice detail – the mummified mouse he had found behind a radiator, a beetle plopping onto an old print Gerald was showing to an American customer. Then I was able to return to my seat, the ordeal over.

An old friend of the family gave a 'proper' speech – a warm, funny and moving tribute to my father. There were so many stories to draw on – such as the occasion reported in the local paper when a burglar broke into the house and finding nothing of value downstairs tried his luck in Gerald's bedroom. As the baseball-capped youth pilfered £75 from his wallet, Gerald woke up. The youth mimed he should keep quiet, but Gerald, aged ninety-three, struck up a discussion with him, eventually agreeing the return of £50 after which he let the youth out of the front door.

The obituaries described Gerald Jaggard as *The Quintessential English Gentleman, lover of the written and spoken word ... his laconic, dignified, and witty style endeared him to all.*

But I cannot open this book without discussing my grandfather.

When Anthea and I were growing up in the 1950s, Gerald frequently entertained us with amusing stories of his father, Captain William Jaggard, *a difficult man who had fallen out with most of the important people in the town.* That was Gerald's way. He was a quiet man, not forceful, who made his point in subtle ways, through stories and witty observations.

Gerald and his father, Captain William Jaggard (or 'WJ' as the family called him), could not have been more different.

One of Gerald's memorable stories was of WJ's approach to teaching Gerald and his twin, Aubrey, how to swim. He took the two *delicate boys* down to the riverbanks (the town's 'swimming pool' was a murky, sectioned-off area of the River Avon), and threw them in. The twins crawled along the muddy bottom of the riverbed, and then gasping for breath, each climbed up one of his legs. Neither Aubrey nor Gerald ever did learn to swim.

Looking back, Gerald was still clearly preoccupied with his father, many years after Captain Jaggard had died, although to us as young children they were just funny stories. Was Gerald exaggerating or was our grandfather really such an extreme character?

A couple of weeks after the funeral, Anthea had *The Life and Death of a Stratford Bookshop* digitalised. Sadly, Gerald's book was unfinished. After a promising start, the book seems to lose its way, meandering into a chapter on 'The Art of Dyeing' (as in cloth) and finally a chapter on a local postman who loved flowers and who was a bit of a character. After which it ends abruptly. Why didn't he finish it? It promised so much. It was disappointing.

I went back and forth on what to do with it – publish it, do some writing of my own, or just shelve it?

Then the book was forgotten and put away in a drawer for almost twenty years. Until I heard from the American. The American changed everything.

In September 2020, the American scholar contacted me out of the blue. From his research he knew that Captain William Jaggard had owned a copy of *Holinshed's Chronicles*, back in the 1930s. Did I know if it was still in the family? As Shakespearean scholars will know, *Holinshed's Chronicles* is the famous source book for many of Shakespeare's plays, both for his plots and for entire passages of blank verse. The American believed that this particular copy, once owned by my grandfather, might contain Shakespeare's signature. It seemed a bit far-fetched, but I offered to help. Attempting to trace the copy of *Holinshed's Chronicles* required some research into the family papers, including looking back through *The Life and Death*.

The opening chapters are intriguing: Gerald's witty, very honest and highly critical observations on his father's character, excerpts from Captain Jaggard's superior and incredibly 'rude' letters,

Gerald's account of the rather comical family move from Liverpool to Stratford in 1910 and of how WJ was determined to 'make his mark' on Stratford, which was still a small sleepy parochial market town in the first decade of the 20th century.

Reading it again, twenty years after his death, although the story of the founding and eventual demise of the iconic Stratford bookshop is both charming and eccentric, it doesn't seem to be the book's raison d'être. Gerald had started writing the book aged seventy and the unfinished book is dominated by his boyhood memories of his father recalled as though it was yesterday. He seems to be exorcising his demons about their relationship, about his father's overbearing character and behaviour, and ultimately about the impact on the whole family.

What is noticeable for such a mild-mannered, polite and somewhat reserved man as Gerald, is his fierce antipathy to his father.

By coincidence, a few months before the enquiry from the American scholar, I had received the 'Jaggard Papers' passed down through the family and had started to browse through them and sort them into order: Captain William Jaggard's family descent research from over 100 years ago; memorabilia and newspapers from the 300th celebration of Shakespeare's First Folio in 1923; and various family letters.

One of Gerald's 'copy' letters describe the genesis of *The Life and Death*. He was writing to Eric Jaggard (WJ's youngest brother) who was living in Vancouver:

Gerald Jaggard 10th March 1972

Dear (Uncle) Eric

… I have become involved again with No. 4 Sheep Street (the old bookshop). Not that I intend to go in there again, but in another way. The BIRMINGHAM SKETCH is doing a feature on Sheep Street and have asked me to write about 3,000 words for their April number. As you can imagine, I jumped eagerly at the opportunity. I am still asked all over town why the place is still empty, and the Corporation find it hard to explain why they turned me out in such a hurry and then let it stand empty for 7 years …

When I sent him the script, the Editor was very kind about it; just what he wanted etc. and had I any more ideas for features. I immediately suggested the story of No. 4 and its connection to the Jaggards, and he very much liked the idea. I thought I could write this in instalments, starting off with the Jaggards of Tudor days, then the Liverpool bookshop, the transfer to Stratford, and the 54 years of bookselling in Sheep St. The line of descent that you have so kindly let me have will be tremendously useful …

Andy Jaggard The other dominant story from our childhood was the belief that we are directly descended from William and Isaac Jaggard – the famous Tudor Printers whose 1623 First Folio of William Shakespeare's Comedies, Tragedies, and Histories was directly responsible for saving around half of Shakespeare's 38 plays from oblivion.

Gerald was researching the family descent throughout our childhood, trying to complete the links. Captain William Jaggard had proudly promoted himself as 'the Sixth William' in the line of descent from his famous ancestor.

These threads (sorting through the Jaggard Papers, the American's strange enquiry and studying Gerald's brutally honest and emotional book) all took place between late 2019 and autumn 2020. I can't remember exactly when, but the idea began to form that perhaps we should attempt to find out what happened to Gerald and to the family that caused him so much angst. And then, if we could, complete his story on his behalf.

It wouldn't be just about the 'Life and Death of a Stratford Bookshop'.

The full story must include Gerald's story of his father: his Herculean achievements, his many battles, complete lack of tact, and his thirty-year mission to prove that he was the direct descendant of William and Isaac Jaggard, the Printers of Shakespeare's First Folio.

Our Jaggard family's 'direct descent' from William and Isaac Jaggard, would be a central issue. Was it true, or not? Did it matter?

My grandfather WJ was sure of it. My father Gerald had not been able to prove it in his lifetime. Some recent commentators have cast doubt on it. We would set out, to tell the truth, at last ... one way or another.

There were many other important family issues to unravel.

Why had Gerald waited until he was seventy before writing his story, telling the truth for the first time about how he felt about his father and about what had happened to the family? And why had he abandoned his half-written story?

The pandemic was underway with its series of lockdowns, the ideal time in many ways for some in-depth research but also fraught with difficulties with so many restrictions in place.

My father had been dead for twenty years, my grandfather for over seventy years. Many of the crucial events had taken place 100 years ago and more. One way or another, I was going to find out the truth, and finish what my father had begun. This book is that journey.

Gerald had started work on his book a year or so after his letter to Eric in 1972, so probably in 1974. The Preface to the book sets out the story he intends to tell, and is surprisingly hard-hitting and emotional:

The Life and Death of a Stratford Bookshop (Unpublished book) c.1974

Gerald Jaggard
Preface

The extinction of the bookshop brought a tremendous reaction from the local people and annual visitors. After ten years, they are still asking … Why?

As for myself, I ask the same question - how could the civic authorities of Shakespeare's town deliberately eliminate one of their greatest assets? Sadly, the answer must be to them it was just a property. Their vision was limited to the boundaries of the borough. What could they know of a bookshop in which hardly any of them had ever set foot?

But although No. 4 Sheep Street is gaunt and empty, it has a story to tell. It is a tale covering almost a century, when my father first set his sights on Stratford, and resolved to conquer it. By incredible industry and strength of purpose he achieved many of his targets; by vanity, overconfidence, and a complete lack of tact he made so many enemies on the way that his life ended in bitter failure.

I, too, can tell the story of running a Stratford bookshop for seventeen years on a shoestring, enjoying the hustle and fascination of the summer season, enduring the misery and anxieties of the winter months.

But above all, this book is dominated by the shop itself, by its 18,000 books, its yearly stream of customers, staid, scholarly, or eccentric, people of all classes, creeds, and colour - all drawn to that tiny shop by the fascination of its atmosphere, its structure, and its literary treasure. So here it is, the life and death of a Stratford bookshop …

CHAPTER 2 THE SHAKESPEARE PRESS

The Research Plan – Andy Jaggard
Naturally I started with Gerald's book. I sat down at my desk to decide how we should use his half-finished story. The old bookshop is the central theme that links the two men, but the real drama concerns my grandfather's overpowering impact on Gerald's life. With this in mind, I highlighted all those sections I thought we could use. There are some beautiful descriptive passages evocative of the age and his witty observations on my grandfather's character.

Gerald's book starts with the origins of my grandfather's 'three great missions in life'. *We will backtrack to this later but first we will start with the historic moment when my grandfather uprooted the family to make the move from Liverpool to Stratford-upon-Avon and founded his* 'Shakespeare Press' *in the Bard's home town.*

This also introduces us to five-year-old Gerald, an imaginative and respectful boy, who already seems to have the measure of his father, although he is embarrassed, even horrified, by WJ's behaviour. Later Gerald describes my grandfather's founding of the 'Shakespeare Press', *where WJ* 'bends the truth' *somewhat in the pursuit of commercial success.*

The Life and Death of a Stratford Bookshop (Unpublished book) c. 1974

Gerald Jaggard
'I Carried the Kettle'

My twin brother and I were at what is described as a tender age when the move was made from Liverpool to

Stratford. Geoffrey was two years older and had already attended a dame school in Liverpool, and so was broken into the idea of losing some of his freedom.

However, Stratford schooling was not in my mind as I stood in a strangely bare drawing room in our Canning Street home and waited for the call to set out for the station. There is always, of course, a tinge of sadness at leaving familiar surroundings, but to a child in the centre of a bustling city, the small orbit of his known surroundings is not so hard to leave. Instead, my mind reached out in excited surmise at what lay ahead. To me, the little Warwickshire town gleamed as a place of open meadows, small timbered houses, a church where a great poet was buried, and, more magical still, a little theatre set beside a river. Such were the fragments I had gleaned from my mother's description.

After even a few years in the city centre, it was difficult to believe that such a place was real.How could one compare a small church to the great Anglican cathedral now being slowly completed close to our home? How could one imagine a theatre standing all by itself instead of being a mere frontage wedged between shops and houses, as were the playhouses of Liverpool.

The meadows, too, the lanes and the hedges surrounding this fabulous place, how did they get the room to exist, and surely there must be uniformed men with whistles watching to see that you did not tread on the flowers or dig your heels into the turf?

Well, it was soon to be reality. The boxes had been packed and the furniture sent on, although one very important item had been left behind at my urgent request. I was determined to be of some use in the great exodus, and so I was entrusted with the tin kettle, to provide us with a cup of tea when we arrived at Paradise. From the moment when we stood on the platform in Liverpool waiting for my father to get the tickets to descending from the Great Western express at Stratford station, I clutched that kettle. The long delay before my father came back with the tickets was perhaps predictable. Still, we preferred the waiting to being present at the ticket office, listening to the fierce argument as my father disputed the price of the tickets, as he invariably challenged the cost of almost everything. He was a one-man Consumers' Association, but he carried his complaints to such lengths that sometimes we didn't know where to look.

Curiously enough, for a man so precise and particular in his business affairs, WJ often made a singular mess of his outside activities. The trouble was that he paid as little as possible for help, then expected first-class service. Our arrival in Stratford-upon-Avon was an example. He had taken a semi-detached house in the Shipston Road for our first abode, 'Rose Bank', was not to be built for two years. When we arrived there, somewhat weary after our journey, the house was empty except for a few cases packed with ornaments and crockery. No beds. I don't think we could even use the cherished kettle, because neither gas nor water had been turned on.

After listening to WJ's long and eloquent summing up of the failings of all removal firms, and these in particular, we had to seek help.

This came in generous measure from the Boydens, George and Kate, who lived in a large house in the same road, but nearer the town.

Mr Boyden, proprietor and editor of the local paper, the *Stratford-upon-Avon Herald* knew my father well, having given him hospitality on previous occasions, and published letters and articles from WJ's ever busy pen. Years later, when Mr Boyden's son Rupert succeeded him as editor, my brother and I were to have a long and happy association with the *Herald* as contributors of prose, verse and, for one season, as their drama critic at the Shakespeare Festival.

So we were put up for the night at the Boydens' house, 'The Sycamores'. Our missing beds and larger furniture arrived the next day, I believe, but that would not save the removers from having a sizable sum deducted from their account!

Boyhood days of endless summer

All this took place in the spring or summer of 1910; I cannot remember the exact season, but I know it was warm and sunny, a happy time of year to settle into our new surroundings.

Our house - 'Avonthwaite''- was almost the last house in the Shipston Road; there was just 'Broom Cottage', and after that the dusty and sinuous highway led to Shipston-on-Stour itself, to Long Compton, and eventually to Oxford. Opposite us, the view across the fields and farms was unhindered by buildings, behind us was the small embankment which carried the tram-way. Perhaps luckily for us, this former line to Shipston and Moreton-in-the-Marsh was derelict. As schoolboys, we scrambled over it with our friends, to explore the meadows beyond, and follow the brook which eventually ran into the River Avon just opposite the parish church.

Those boyhood days in the Shipston Road stand out as an endless summer. Such are the tricks of memory that I cannot remember the winter months, the wind or the rain; I can only recall the heavy sweet scent of the privet hedge that seemed to be perpetually in flower, the birds and insects that abounded in the garden (unconscious of the chemical age that was to decimate their descendants) and the clouds of dust that passing traffic, mostly carriages, aroused as they went past the front gate.

In those days, especially in the country, road accidents were chiefly caused by bolting horses and carriages overturning in ditches. Motor cars, of course, were quite plentiful, but the rigorous laws controlling their speed and general behaviour kept accidents to a minimum.

Soon after our arrival in Stratford, the owner of a farm within a mile of us was thrown from his trap when it was jolted over on a rough road and killed instantly.

Back in Liverpool, the perils of the highway had been somewhat different. I remember news being brought to our horrified ears that a child had been run over by a steamroller; an unlikely hazard on the face of it, but I suppose the clanking monster was in reverse by the street kerb, unaware of the victim playing in the gutter.

The grander houses in Shipston Road were mostly occupied by well-to-do gentlemen with thriving shops or businesses in the town. The lower strata usually lived over their premises, a situation which had both advantages and disadvantages. In our road were to be found Mr Jackson, who had a prosperous coal business in

Waterside, Mr Robert Cox (as Councillor Cox he became the first Roman Catholic mayor of the borough), Mr James Cheney, an insurance inspector, and, of course, the Boydens.

Mr George Boyden, a small white-haired gentleman, used to walk each morning to the *Herald* office dressed impeccably, if incongruously, in black coat with striped trousers carrying a pair of kid gloves. His route took him past the Swan's Nest Hotel on our side of the river, along a track to the Tram Bridge crossing the Avon, over the small wooden bridge at the canal lock, and into the Bancroft Gardens. This led to Sheep Street and turning right at the top brought him into High Street, where the *Herald* press was then operating.

This same route my twin brother and I were soon to use on our way to the preparatory section of King Edward VI School. As Mr Boyden was in the habit of arriving at his office at 9am sharp, and we had to get to school at the same time, our trails occasionally coincided. Then a happy little ceremony took place, during which a couple of sixpences found their way from the striped trousers to our hands, and we were instructed to buy some sweets. As the benefaction was something like double our pocket money for a week, we never crawled 'like snails, unwillingly to school' - we went with alacrity!

The Founding of the Shakespeare Press

I suppose, in a way, it was an historic moment - William Jaggard the Sixth* bringing his Shakespeare Press to Stratford-upon-Avon, the birth town of his Tudor ancestor's greatest client.

Of course, it was no lightning decision - it had been planned for years, and WJ, like all wise invaders, had prepared the ground and made friends in Stratford with great care.

*Andy Jaggard *WJ had been researching his direct lineal descent from his namesake, William Jaggard, the Printer of the First Folio, for many years. He was already sufficiently confident that he had proclaimed that he was 'the Sixth William' in the direct line from his famous ancestor.*

He corresponded continuously with Mr William Salt Brassington, the Memorial Theatre's lively and gifted librarian. Probably it was at his suggestion that Sheep Street was chosen. There were several old cottages available; in poor condition certainly, but who could grumble at £24 per annum!

Sheep Street forms part of a 'grill' of half-a-dozen old streets making up the centre of Stratford-upon-Avon, most of which still bore their ancient names. The earliest street plan of the town shows clearly that this grill has retained its shape and identity for two hundred years at least (the plan is dated 1768) and probably much longer. Linking the old Corn Market (now the Town Hall) to the grazing land of the Bank Croft, its gentle slope down to river level must have made the driving of flocks a simple task.

1. The Shop in Sheep Street

Andy Jaggard - Sheep Street taken around 1908. The Town Hall is on the right, and No. 4 Sheep Street is the building on the left. Gerald describes it as a cottage, but in this shot, it appears to be a fresh fish shop. Whichever, it is clearly before WJ gave it a Tudor makeover a couple of years later, with false beams and a small gable roof above the first-floor window.

Gerald Jaggard
No. 4 Sheep Street, which my father selected as the most suitable place for his Shakespeare Press and bookshop, must have looked somewhat unpromising when he first surveyed it. It was small, cold and damp, with a plain exterior and a narrow entrance. Certainly, its timbers were old, it had remnants of the wattle and daub dating back to about 1490. But this was no fit facade to contain a descendant of Shakespeare's printer, nor to tempt the eyes and cameras of Stratford's myriad visitors. So, he decided to give it a new face. A Tudor facelift might be a better description.

And so, it sprang to life, acquiring a plate glass window fronting the ground floor, a large window above and surmounting this a gable framed in modern oak beams bearing carved oak letters (old English of course) proclaiming its antiquity and ancestry. Over the shop window were more carved letters bearing the words 'Shakespeare Press'. For good value, he added an oaken sign relating how the Tudor Jaggard had founded in 1591 the Shakespeare Press which had brought forth the precious Folio of Shakespeare's plays.

I don't suppose it crossed his mind that the patrons of the bookshop would inevitably jump to the conclusion that the Sheep Street premises were the actual site of the original press. This, however, is what they certainly did, and when I took over the shop, I was continually explaining the truth of the matter, that the First Folio was undoubtedly printed by William Jaggard, but in London and not in the poet's home town. I was not always believed!

2. The lettering in black reads, restored 1910 by Wm Jaggard.

Andy Jaggard

I'm not sure whether Gerald was being naive ... or ironic when he states above, "I don't suppose it crossed his mind" etc. inferring that WJ's chosen name for his bookshop was more accident than design. Certainly, there are other examples from our research of Gerald taking his father's stories and assertions at face value. He was too accepting and trusting. This may have been because he was honest and straightforward himself and therefore expected that of others. My own experience of Gerald was that he was 'gentle', polite and respectful and much preferred to deal with any difficulties through humour and inference rather than through more direct methods. Faced with his father's aggressive and domineering approach, I imagine that Gerald as a boy simply retreated into his own inner world.

No. 4 Sheep Street is now a Grade 2 listed building, and this is an excerpt from the listing about a plaque that was discovered on the premises.

HISTORICAL NOTE: a plaque, now removed, stated that a press was **founded here** in 1591, and that the 1st edition of Shakespeare's works was **published here** in 1623. William Jaggard, the bibliographer of Shakespeare and said to be the descendant of the publisher of the 1st folio, lived here late C19 onwards and set up the Shakespeare Press. **Historical Buildings – Grade 2 Listing NGR: SP2016654834**

*WJ was a successful businessman, an innovator, an 'entrepreneur' and a self-publicist of the first order. If you look at WJ's oaken sign carefully you'll see it says Shakespeare Press **founded 1591**, it doesn't include the word **here** as stated in the historical listing.*

*My own take however is that WJ was being deliberately misleading, and he knew it. It was a great selling point – the original Shakespeare Press, now a bookshop in the Bard's home town, run by the direct descendant of **the** William Jaggard who printed Shakespeare's First Folio in 1623.*

Now back to Gerald dealing with the aftermath of his father's actions. It was to be a recurring theme throughout Gerald's life.

Gerald Jaggard
Another complication was that WJ had re-founded the Shakespeare Press in Liverpool in 1890 and re-established it in Stratford in 1910. Imagine explaining that to a bewildered German or a confused American! It was not easy, but it had to be done.

With the overseas visitors, the new face of No. 4 was a great success. In my seventeen years of occupancy of the shop, it must have been photographed from the street thousands of times, almost rivalling the Birthplace. The Americans, especially the ladies, thought it 'cute'. The only brickbat it got was in an English architectural journal, which pictured it as an outstandingly bad example of Tudor restoration!

WJ's tactics for dealing with criticism or advice

Probably WJ never saw this scathing comment, for had he done so I would certainly have found the journal and his blistering replies neatly filed and stowed away. Apart from his literary contributions, he was constantly writing to the editors of national and provincial newspapers on all sorts of topics.

Naturally, when a Shakespearean controversy cropped up, or an old argument was resurrected, he plunged in with banners flying. When the Tudor Jaggard who printed the First Folio was maligned, or even merely overlooked, WJ was there, and this time not only were the pennants flying, but the lance was poised to transfix his misguided opponents. Such correspondence went on and on until the long-suffering editor applied the closure 'This correspondence must now cease', and WJ made it a point of honour that this usually appeared under his last letter on the subject. The last word had to be his.

I can picture the letter he would have written to the architectural journal who dared to condemn his Sheep Street premises. The word 'ignorant' would undoubtedly have come into it. How, he would enquire, could mere architects set themselves up to judge the construction of an antiquarian bookshop? How could they presume to dictate to a bookseller and Shakespearean scholar whose very ancestor had owned a bookshop in St Paul's Churchyard? And finally (for the best form of defence is always attack) who anyway could respect the judgement of a profession that had perpetrated such monstrosities as … (and he would name a few glaring examples of architectural folly).

Such tactics WJ employed on many occasions during his career, never giving quarter and never accepting defeat … or advice!

Thus, the Tudorised frontage of No. 4 Sheep Street was left in peace for over fifty years, until the Stratford Corporation, owners of said property, suddenly saw visions of profitable development of their older premises, even that shabby, mouldering, well-loved and widely known shop in Sheep Street. However, that unhappy episode belongs to the end of my story, not to the beginning in 1910 when Sheep Street, until now somewhat sleepy, and, in parts, somewhat slummy, woke with a start to realise that it possessed a new and decidedly lively inhabitant. William the Sixth had come to stay.

CHAPTER 3 THE FIRST FOLIO AND THE SHAKESPEARE INDUSTRY

"...here's twenty plays by Shakespeare saved in the nick of time from oblivion" Capt. Wm Jaggard.

Andy Jaggard
Gerald in his letter to his uncle, Eric Jaggard, in 1972 had said of his planned book, "I thought I could write this in instalments, starting off with the Jaggards of Tudor days." Unfortunately, Gerald did not include a chapter on the Tudor Jaggards in The Life and Death.

One Thursday evening, when rain was lashing against the window, I made myself a mug of coffee, climbed the stairs to my study and resumed work on Gerald's book.

I was remembering my years at the grammar school in Stratford. Every year, on Shakespeare's Birthday (23rd April), the entire school took its place at the head of the procession of diplomats and dignitaries to march through the town to pay homage to 'the immortal Bard' at his resting place at the Holy Trinity Church.

I should mention, near the beginning of this book's journey, that although I was educated at 'Shakespeare's Grammar School' and have seen some wonderful plays at the Royal Shakespeare Theatre, I am no Shakespearean scholar. As I sat down to work on his book, my coffee going cold as I immersed myself in writing and editing, I realised that I must be clear about that.

This is at heart a family story of how my father dealt with, and survived, the disastrous impact my grandfather's actions had on his life. However, there was also a very significant backstory of *Shakespearean issues that I had to research, make sense of, and include if I was to discover the truth of the two men's very different lives.*

Just one example of this is my father's story from our childhood of how WJ at one time had owned a First Folio. He had apparently wired the details to an American oil millionaire called Henry Folger (an obsessive collector of surviving First Folios), who replied, "Bring it over!" and WJ went on an all-expenses-paid trip to New York, so that Folger could personally inspect the famous book.

The only trouble was we didn't have any of the details to authenticate the story.

First, I needed a far better understanding of the contribution the First Folio had made to the preservation of Shakespeare's plays.

A bonus were WJ's and Gerald's large collection of 'Treasures'. Gerald would have been nineteen at the time of the Tercentenary of the Printing of the First Folio in 1923. WJ preserved many of the newspapers of the day, pasted meticulously onto large sheets of card, commenting on the significance of that landmark. I decided that wherever possible we would use archive stories of the day to capture the spirit of the time:

The First Folio – the doyen of the world's books –
***Times Literary Supplement* of Thursday, 19th April 1923.**

The claim does not rest in its external beauty ... or upon its price in the market, for that is a fact of bibliopoly, not of literature; or upon its rarity, for at least a hundred and seventy-two copies exist out of an edition not likely to have exceeded a thousand.

But, after all, the primary function of a book is to make reading matter available; and here are twenty plays by Shakespeare, never before printed, and rescued in the First Folio from the chances of edacious time, to be the perpetual entertainment, instruction and consolation of mankind.

Gerald was a regular theatre goer to The Old Memorial Theatre in Stratford (before it burnt down in 1926). He had appeared as a schoolboy actor in Julius Caesar *and had also started writing and producing his own shows. He would have loved the following article by J. L. Garvin on 'The Great Improver' as well as Garvin's imagined scene of Shakespeare turning up at the theatre with his latest work.*

The First Folio Centenary – The Comedy of Doubt – Who Shakespeare was? The Observer – Sunday 22nd April 1923 – By J. L. Garvin

THE GREAT IMPROVER … had precisely the qualities of a great alchemist working from translations in the English tongue … Shakespeare, somehow, could turn out the stuff on any theme.

His manuscripts came to the theatre and necessarily were more or less knocked about in consultation with the management. We may wager that he got in more pure poetry than they liked, but as he was keen for the Company to pay – he made all reasonable concessions, and some flagrant ones to the crudity of the mob.

There is one wonderful thing about Shakespeare: he is what they call a cool customer; he works in a hurry … but he is serene and will not sweat, except perhaps on passages to please himself, like the great, difficult speeches in *Troilus and Cressida*. He borrows and plagiarises and transliterates like no man … but he does not worry about critics. He is not cynical; he is unconscious. He does just what he wants to do and is entirely himself. He may modify details for business reasons in acquiescence with the judgement of Burbage and Heminge, but in the main he knows that whenever he chooses … he can hit the crowd between wind and water or obliterate class distinctions by the wand of humanity and humour. Literal fact he despises. The imaginative interpretation of the spirit of life is his aim.

I had started reading up on Henry and Emily Folger, in particular through Andrea Mays' book The Millionaire and the Bard, *which describes many of Henry Folger's dealings in First Folios. I was hoping to strike gold with a reference, in Andrea Mays' book, to my grandfather's all-expenses-paid trip to America with a First Folio for Henry Folger. (Disappointingly there was no reference at all to WJ.) There was, however, some fascinating material describing the error-prone process of the printing of the First Folio that had such a dramatic impact on the value of surviving copies (selling for vastly escalating prices from the early years of the 20th century). I had also studied Peter Blayney's book,* The First Folio of Shakespeare.

Most modern-day readers would assume that the first edition copies of a published book would be identical. This, however, was very far from the case with the First Folio. To understand the reasons for the inconsistencies and flaws in different copies of the First Folio, and the huge effect this had on their value, it's vital to know something of the printing process in William Jaggard's workshop.

16TH CENTURY PRINTING SHOP

4. A print from WJ's collection of 'Treasures'.

William Jaggard's expectations for the First Folio were modest. If he printed too few copies, a couple of hundred say, the price would be too high. If he printed too many, a thousand or more, it might take years to sell enough copies to cover the costs. Scholars have estimated the print run at around 750 copies. The decision to print Shakespeare's plays in one complete, impressive and expensive volume demanded the folio format. Paper was expensive, the print run would require around 170,000 sheets. It would be imported from Normandy: good-quality rag paper.

Jaggard's workshop had two presses and half a dozen employees. The Folio would be typeset in well-worn type, two columns per page, with running titles at the top of each page. Skilled workmen called compositors set each individual letter into its place in the rectangular trench of the composing stick, the letter, then the word, then the sentence with spacers added. The line of type was lifted from the stick, placed on a wooden board then the next line of type added. To make the printed text read correctly from left to right the letters and words were composed backwards. Once two pages were set, they were placed on a flat surface with an iron frame, the 'chase', and tightened with screws or wooden wedges called quoins. Then all 750 copies of those two pages were printed before the type was thoroughly cleaned, dried and sorted, before the composition of the next two pages.

A proof was a single sheet that could be marked for corrections. Sheets were hung up to dry. The end result was that any particular page could exist in three states: the uncorrected page; a page containing corrections by hand; and a corrected page with the errors fixed that involved some re-setting of type. The high price of paper meant that proof sheets were not discarded but included in the finished book. The three-page states were intermingled, stacked, and collected into quires, four or six sheets of paper folded once and gathered together, then the workers sewed the gathered pages together. Pages were not printed in sequence, each quire of the printed book starting from the middle, and then working both towards the front and to the back of the book, requiring the compositor to make some estimation of the amount of text required for each page. This order of printing, and the process of making corrections during the printing process, explains the numerous errors in the book. In the 17th century, spelling was not standardised, words being spelled in several different ways. Compositor 'A' might spell or misspell the same words in the same ways, while Compositor 'B' also had his own unique way of spelling and misspelling, and the so-called 'teenage apprentice', for the First Folio, was a youth exceedingly prone to error.

Two men worked each press. One smeared ink onto two big soft inking balls. The ink was made of boiled oil and lampblack. It took some skills to ink the 'forme' properly. The other pressman, careful not to touch the ink, placed the clean sheet on the press, then pulled a bar attached to the screw and the plate was pressed against the paper.

The whole printing process was *part art and part industry*, a quiet process, powered by the muscle of the pressmen. It required flexibility and improvisation – with the inevitable consequences.

Heminge and Condell wanted to present Shakespeare's image as well as his plays. Other books had included author portraits but not as the central feature on the title page. They commissioned a twenty-two-year-old Flemish émigré artist, Martin Droeshout, to engrave their friend's image on a copper plate. As Shakespeare was dead and Droeshout had never met him, the actors presumably supplied him with a drawing or oil painting of their friend, now long since lost. The engraving, printed by another shop, left crisp images on the early impressions but the plate wore down over time and had to be re-touched or re-engraved.

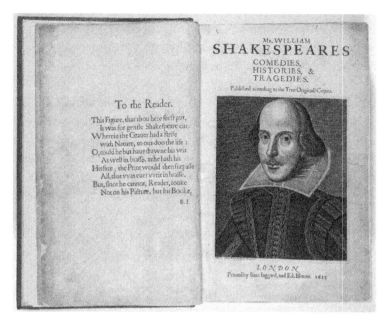

5. The First Folio.

When at last the printing was finished in the autumn of 1623, the First Folio was a physically impressive object. More than 900 pages, the tallest copies untrimmed measured 13½ by 8¾ inches. It had taken two years to print the massive First Folio. Publishing it had been an unprecedented, ambitious, complicated and risky project. Customers could buy it in unbound sheets and pay their own bookbinder to 'cloth' it. Alternatively, they could purchase it from Jaggard in one of three bindings: limp, cream white parchment; untanned calf or goatskin; or the most costly binding, which was light brown or mahogany in colour.

Andrea Mays' humorous account, in The Millionaire and the Bard *of what an accurate catalogue description of the day would have looked like makes amusing reading:*

'Each copy unique, some copies missing one play, pages miss-numbered, different copies containing portraits of the author in varying states, some copies with one page of crossed out text …

Spelling and punctuation haphazard ... printers ornaments worn and broken, inconsistent page numbering ... ready to take to your favourite binder to indulge your preferences at your expense.'

Despite the many defects, the most valuable copy of the First Folio, the most valuable book in the world, was sold for a record sum 280 years later in 1903. It was called the 'Vincent' copy (also known as The Jaggard Presentation Copy). A few months later I was to discover an amazing coincidence in relation to the sale of this 'Vincent/Jaggard Presentation First Folio'.

Andrea Mays describes the stages after Shakespeare's death that led to his growing reputation and to the foundation of the Shakespeare industry in Stratford.

Shakespeare's growing fame

Had it not been for the First Folio of 1623 a substantial part of Shakespeare's work might have been lost forever but it took over 140 years for Shakespeare to be acclaimed as one of the greatest writers in the English language. There were three distinct phases:

- The first forty years which were difficult for the theatre and for the performance of his plays.

- Shakespeare's growing reputation and his establishment as a pre-eminent literary figure and playwright by the middle of the 18th century.

- The foundation of the 'Shakespeare industry' whereby the man morphed into some kind of God-like figure and the embodiment of England.

By 1632, copies of Jaggard and Blount's First Folio had sold out. A second edition, the Second Folio, was published in that year. Essentially a reprint, it corrected some errors, but introduced others.

Shakespeare's collected plays were not printed again for another thirty-one years. First the London plague of 1636 closed down many theatres, then the English Civil War, 1642–1651, and the execution of Charles I led to a period of Puritan dominance and the banning of the performances of plays. It wasn't until the death of Cromwell, and the restoration of the monarchy, with the crowning of Charles II in 1661 that there was a revival of the theatre.

During the Restoration Period, plays were being staged again, although some of the plays were decidedly bizarre. *Romeo and Juliet* ended with a happy marriage and one theatre offered its audiences alternating tragic and romantic endings every other night.

The Third Folio was produced in 1663, with seven additional plays, unfortunately only one of them, *Pericles*, partially written by Shakespeare. Many of the copies of the Third Folio were lost in the Great Fire of London in 1666, so although not the most valuable of the Folios, it is the rarest. In the minds of many people, the Third Folio was thought to have superseded the First. Some libraries disposed of their old copies of the First Folio when they obtained the 'new' edition, including famously the Bodleian Library in Oxford.

What many did not realise at the time was that the text of the First Folio was superior to that of the Second, or Third, and the closest to Shakespeare, as Heminge and Condell intended (Shakespeare's fellow actors in the King's Men). Copies were dwindling and no one had yet realised the unique literary value of the First Folio.

The Fourth Folio was published in 1685. It included the seven new plays, six of them 'spurious', and perpetuated errors from the Second and Third Folios.

In 1709, Nicholas Rowe, published his edition of the plays in an entirely new format, a multi-volume octavo size based on the Fourth Folio text. Rowe became the first real 'editor' of Shakespeare, after Heminge and Condell. He added a list of dramatis personae, inserted act and scene divisions, and stage directions for actors' entrances and exits. This heralded the era of 'the editors' and of literary criticism. Rowe also attempted a biography of Shakespeare, by this time ninety years after his death. It was too late: no one who knew Shakespeare was still alive to provide their memories, their stories, and more details of the facts of his life.

Shakespeare's fame was on the rise. In Stratford, his Holy Trinity Church Monument was restored in 1748/9 and the first known performance of one of his plays was performed in the town.

During my research, I had come across a Stratfordian writer called Steve Newman who had been a regular customer of the Shakespeare Press bookshop during Gerald's tenure in the 1950s and 1960s. Steve has written a comprehensive internet article on 'Shakespeare's Legacy'. I have drawn on Steve's article including his amusing account of the Shakespeare Jubilee, organised by a famous 18th-century actor, which kick-started 'the Shakespeare industry' in Stratford-upon-Avon. Also, on Johanne M. Stockholm's book published in 1964 to coincide with the 400th anniversary of Shakespeare's birth, Garrick's Folly – The Shakespeare Jubilee of 1769 at Stratford and Drury Lane.

The Shakespeare Industry

In 1769 a famous Shakespearean actor, David Garrick, staged a grand (and disastrous) Shakespeare Jubilee, not in London, but in Stratford-upon-Avon. Garrick, born in 1717, was slight of build and short of stature, but he created a more natural style of delivering Shakespeare's lines. He had made the part of Richard III his own and was England's first modern-day stage star, a playwright and a businessman, with an ego to match. After a quarter of a century of fame he wanted to honour the man he dubbed, *the God of our Idolatry.*

An octagonal wooden rotunda was to be built, close to the site of the current RSC building, as a centrepiece for the celebration, as a theatre, banqueting hall, and ballroom, with space for a hundred-piece orchestra and a thousand guests. The local tradesmen refused to work with the Drury Lane craftsmen, the delivery of the timber was sabotaged, and the event had to be postponed from August to September.

A huge number of nobility, gentry and theatrical celebrities were to attend.

Spread over three days, each morning started with cannon fire and a lavish breakfast. There was to be horse racing, great lunches, grand balls and dinners followed by fireworks. The first day was sunny, but overnight it rained heavily, and it kept raining for the next two days. The river kept rising, one of the wooden walls collapsed, and the rotunda was soon surrounded by a large lake, requiring a causeway to be constructed for the guests attending the evening's masked ball.

6. The octagonal rotunda for Garrick's Shakespeare Jubilee 1769.

In the waterlogged ground the rotunda was slowly sinking and mud paralysed Stratford's unpaved streets. Garrick cancelled the third day, including what was to have been the high point, a pageant of characters with Garrick reciting *'the Ode'*, over a musical accompaniment.

There had been a good deal of drunkenness and bad behaviour. Garrick later described the Stratford folk as *inferior*. At the end of the three days not a single line of Shakespeare had been spoken and the jockey of the winning horse declared that he knew *nofink* about Shakespeare

It had cost £50,000 (several millions in today's terms) with a shortfall of £2,000, which Garrick offered to make up. However, it had brought a great deal of trade and money into the town. Garrick moved his pageant and entertainment called The Jubilee to Drury Lane where it ran for ninety-one nights. He was able to re-pay the shortfall from the healthy receipts.

David Garrick had launched the Shakespeare industry and the Bard had been transformed from a mortal man into an English god. Stratford capitalised on the idea by deciding to honour their most famous son every year on his birthday. The Bard's former homes became shrines and over time Stratford became an all-year-round tourist destination. These days there's even a couple of re-incarnated William Shakespeares doing the guided tours.

So I understood more about the significance of the First Folio in saving over half of Shakespeare Plays from oblivion. The error-prone printing process in William Jaggard's Tudor printing shop was responsible for huge variations in the quality, and therefore value of individual copies of the famous book. And my grandfather, with an eye on the main chance, had established his carefully named bookshop in Stratford-upon-Avon at the heart of the burgeoning Shakespeare industry.

The next section of Gerald's book would describe the origins of WJ's THREE GREAT MISSIONS in life. Gerald, it turned out, had been 'haunted by his father' in more ways than one.

CHAPTER 4 THE SIXTH WILLIAM

"I am thy father's spirit" Hamlet Act II Scene 2

Andy Jaggard

Back in 2002, after I had discovered Gerald's unfinished book, my mother Diana contacted the local paper who wrote an article on our discovery of the manuscript. We had several days before Gerald's funeral, and I asked Diana whether she knew about his book. She said she couldn't remember, but later recalled a time back in the 1970s when Gerald complained that all night, he had been 'haunted by his father'.

It was Easter Monday, Diana said, and she had already been down to Stratford on her trusty bike for hot cross buns, returning for mid-morning coffee with Gerald.

First there had been an argument about the new low-fat margarine (one of Diana's numerous free offers). Gerald hated it. 'SCRAPE' he called it and insisted on getting out the Lurpak from the pantry, cutting himself a thick slab for his hot cross bun.

In a better mood, Gerald had recounted the nature of his 'haunting':

"It was quite extraordinary, and so vivid, Diana ... my father in the magnificent reading room of the library of Warwick Castle. He was cataloguing a huge stack of Shakespearean books, they almost reached the chandeliers, WJ was cursing and muttering to himself, 'infuriating ... absolutely useless.' Then the Earl of Warwick himself entered and after the usual pleasantries made a quip about the Jaggard connection. WJ took that as his cue to launch into a long and very detailed account of the Jaggard

lineage of Cambridgeshire and Suffolk. He went on and on. The Earl started going red in the face, eventually interrupted, asking William, tetchily, whether he could 'venture a guess as to when he might complete the cataloguing of his collection".

"After that, it got far worse, WJ started lecturing the Earl about exactly how the cataloguing task should proceed and how impossible the job was without a proper reference book. I was cringing with embarrassment, helpless to step in and steer the conversation in another direction ... because I was asleep, of course. The Earl looked like he would explode, his face was puce. He turned on his heel as though to leave, then had a thought, turned back to WJ, and struggling to contain his anger said, 'Well, Master Jaggard, if the lack of a reference book is such a damned nuisance, perhaps you should complete your own Shakespeare Bibliography one fine day.'

"Then WJ was just sitting at a very large mahogany desk, as though in a trance, just staring at that beautiful edition – a First Folio, of course, the words it seemed, trying to jump off the page, 'Printed by Isaac Jaggard and Ed Blount'. JAGGARD, JAGGARD, JAGGARD, it was very hot, but perhaps that was the sun streaming through my bedroom window."

Diana could be quite vague on the day-to-day realities of life, but any good story from years before she could usually recall word for word.

It seems that Gerald started writing The Life and Death *in 1974 – in the Preface he states, "It's ten years, hard to believe I know, since the sad demise of the bookshop." (The bookshop closed in 1964.)*

I like to think that Gerald started work on his book very soon after describing to Diana how all night he had been 'haunted by his father', which gave him the book's opening line.

Shakespeare Press

The Life and Death of a Stratford Bookshop (Unpublished book) c. 1974

Gerald Jaggard
The Sixth William

Perhaps, if bookshops can be haunted, No. 4 Sheep Street, Stratford-upon-Avon, can claim more ghosts than most. Haunted certainly, by my father, and by the generations of book lovers, notable and ordinary, who bought or browsed among its dusty shelves in the fifty years of its life. Haunted, perhaps still inhabited, by other forms of life that lurked, mostly unseen, behind its battered shelves. Rats, mice, book worms, tapping beetles, all, like the denizens of an ancient oak tree, had found refuge and sustenance within its walls. The rats I never saw, but in earlier days they brought peanuts and brazils through holes from the neighbouring fruit shop, to consume at their leisure. I found a mummified mouse once behind a stove; an unusual form of death in premises which defied proper heating and could usually claim to be the largest refrigerator in town.

For bookworms - the silver fish - it was a paradise indeed. They were never short of food. The beetles inhabiting the old beams had a good time too. I always knew that spring had come to the world outside when their brisk Morse messages resounded through the still shop. They never worried me except on one occasion when a beetle became too excited and dropped plump on an old map I was showing to an American gentleman. I brushed it off hastily, although he made no comment. I think he bought the map, and probably would have liked me to have included the beetle as well.

My father had started his first bookshop in Liverpool, after being assistant, as a boy, to Simmons of Leamington Spa. The story goes that during his apprenticeship he studied the trade journals to discover which English city was most in need of literary sustenance, or, in other words, had the fewest bookshops. No doubt it took some courage, and limitless confidence in his own ability, to invade a city not renowned in those days for love of literature.

WJ's three great missions

It must have been at this point that my father started working firmly and relentlessly towards his three great missions.

The first was to produce a work in the Shakespearean field long needed by the scholars and libraries of the world. When in Leamington Spa he had helped catalogue the Shakespearean section at Warwick Castle and had realised then how urgent was the need for a complete bibliography of the poet's works.

His second mission arose out of the first. The title page of the precious first printed collection of the poet's plays states plainly enough "Printed by Isaac Jaggard, and Ed.Blount". Imagine my father's delight when handling this most famous product of the Jaggard Press, founded by his namesake, William Jaggard.

So, it must have been at Warwick that my father determined to trace the family descent, a task which was to occupy innumerable hours of research, travel and correspondence for the remaining sixty years of his life. He soon discovered and proclaimed that he was the sixth William descended from the original Tudor printer.

And his third great aim? That lay in the home town of the Warwickshire dramatist. The target seemed modest enough - to establish a bookshop in Stratford-upon-Avon, and to become either Custodian of the Birthplace, or Librarian of the Shakespeare Memorial Theatre.

Eventually he did achieve these three missions. His drive was dynamic, his industry tremendous, his patience inexhaustible. Such qualities overcame all obstacles in his work but eroded and finally destroyed his family life.

That endless patience necessary for indexing trade journals and preparing a bibliography was real enough in his bookshop but vanished before he got home. That is why, to this day, church bells depress me. They remind me only too vividly of those endless Sundays when the bells of the parish church came over on the breeze, and at our family home near the Clopton Bridge, the master of the house was at home - all day.

Andy Jaggard

This last paragraph describing how Gerald found it depressing to even be in his father's company was really striking. Aged seventy, he still associated the sound of church bells with those 'endless Sundays' when his father was at home 'all day'.

In May 2022 we had been invited to give a talk to the present-day Shakespeare Club in Stratford on 'the Jaggard Story'. We had met two of the club's officials, Susan Brock and Sylvia Morris, on a research trip in 2021. Gerald had been a long-standing member of the Shakespeare Club. What started as a talk with slides on Captain William Jaggard's life gradually developed into an entertainment performed by myself, my wife Moira and two friends, Chris and Susie Chaplin. Chris played WJ in the performance which we called 'WALKED ALONE'. I played myself, and Gerald, indicating when I was switching roles by donning his double-breasted blazer, kept on a dummy the rest of the time.

It was a very strange experience attempting to inhabit my father's character, using many of his words, including those above about the 'depressing' church bells. Moira could see I was struggling and gave me some coaching. I was "too loud and too forceful". "First, you need to speak properly" (my father wasn't 'posh' but he spoke clearly with good diction) "and second you need to be gentler." Even if he was saying something very critical, or sad, my father might cover it with an apologetic smile.

7. **Andy as Gerald – 'Walked Alone' for the Shakespeare club – May 2022.**

Tracing the ancestors

The work on the direct descent involved looking back on family trees constructed recently by various Jaggards. This also gave us some insight into my grandfather's family background.

Our Jaggard ancestors remained in a small area of rural Cambridgeshire for generation after generation, until Jesse Jaggard (1820–1898), WJ's grandfather, born in Dullingham, Cambridgeshire, moved to Berkshire. Jesse was an agricultural labourer and in his youth, as they used to say ... euphemistically ... "he was known to ROAM", *in his case the Bucklebury Manor Estates (now belonging to the Middletons).*

By 1857 it was recorded that, "... an old offender charged with setting wires on the Estate of W.H.H. Hartley esquire of Bucklebury on the 2nd instance, Jesse Jaggard, one of the keepers, deposed to catch the defendant in the act". *So, Jesse Jaggard was a poacher turned gamekeeper.*

Ancestry website 'memory'

8. Jesse Jaggard – 'Poacher turned Gamekeeper'.

Jesse's son, William Jesse Jaggard (1846–1913) was living in Theale in Berkshire, where WJ was born in 1867. William Jesse, with his wife Elizabeth Ada Puttock, had eleven children, nine of whom survived, several settling around the world.

It came as no surprise that WJ was the first-born, and he was three when his sister Florence was born, also in Theale, in 1870. By 1871 the family had moved to Leamington Spa, Warwickshire, a few miles from Stratford, where the rest of the children were born including the youngest, Eric Jesse in 1889. The family moved to Leamington so that William Jesse, WJ's father, could take up a role with The Great Western Company as a railway porter.

William Jesse had an interest in literature as reported in the Stratford Herald in 2005 – Handwriting Solves the Mystery of the Two William Jaggards, Mairi Macdonald, Shakespeare Centre Library and Archives. *(Mairi was also confused between WJ who was christened Jesse William, and his father William Jesse.)* *William Jesse was the owner of* 'The Catalogue of the Library of Warwickshire Literature', *he added his name Wm Jesse Jaggard to the cover, and had personalised the book by including another twenty-five items of literature he had chosen, to the 313 items already listed, even adding his own columns and notes describing the twenty-five new items.*

There was a comment in the article about 'William Jesse Jaggard, a Railway Porter, age fifty-three, on the face of it an unlikely candidate for the book collector'. *The date on the book was 1891, perhaps his father did encourage his interest in literature, despite being only a railway porter. He did however take WJ out of school before he had finished his grammar school education in order to have him start his apprenticeship with Simmons the booksellers of Leamington. (WJ always claimed he was educated at Leamington and Cambridge.)*

During his time in Liverpool, WJ often travelled to different parts of the country carrying out his very painstaking research into his ancestors, but he was already sufficiently confident of the line to proclaim that he was the SIXTH WILLIAM.

Ironically it turned out that WJ was christened Jesse William Jaggard. An old envelope sent to one of his Liverpool bookshops was addressed to J.W. Jaggard.

So, by my calculations, the Sixth William was actually the Third Jesse. WJ dropped the 'Jesse' for the rest of his life.

Identifying and validating the more recent ancestors was straightforward in our initial investigation of the direct descent. It would become increasingly difficult as we went back in time, although we had the work of others, including of course my larger-than-life grandfather's own research, as a strong starting point.

More significant, for now, was the picture that was beginning to form of my grandfather's character and the times he was living through. From humble beginnings, the eldest of a large family, he was clearly a very driven and determined individual who had the courage as a young man to establish his bookshop business in the city of Liverpool 'not renowned for its love of literature'. *He was bold, forthright and confident with a talent for self-promotion.*

WJ understood the significance of the First Folio and the commercial opportunities it offered, with the added bonus of the marvellous connection to our Jaggard family name, and the historic setting of Stratford-upon-Avon with its burgeoning Shakespeare industry. What's more, there was a growing interest in First Folios, particularly from American collectors, and this together with the idiosyncrasies of the original printing process and the wide range in quality of individual copies, was to result in vastly escalating prices during the early years of the 20th century.

It seemed likely that WJ, an ambitious young man, knowledgeable and experienced in the bookselling trade, would want to get in on the act.

And there was THAT story.

CHAPTER 5 "BRING IT OVER"

Andy Jaggard
I was in my study early one morning in 2020 trying to decide on the next move in our research plan. There was that family story, that both Anthea and I recalled from our childhood, of how WJ had once owned a First Folio, that he had taken over to America, all expenses paid, for the oil millionaire, Henry Folger, to personally inspect.

But was it even true?

I glanced up at my bookcase and spotted the yellow and black cover of Gerald's other book – **Stratford Mosaic – A Medley of Memories** *– which had been published in* 1960, *when Gerald was in his mid-fifties. I'd read it of course, but not for many years.*

Moira gave me a shout saying that the croissants were in the oven. I grabbed the copy and made my way down to breakfast.

I was flicking through the pages, explaining that this published book was, as the name suggests, a more general book with chapters on the Shakespeare Club, the birthday celebrations, 'the Mop' hiring fair and so on. I was quickly scanning the pages but couldn't find what I was looking for. Then I reached the final chapter on Stratford's famous characters. *There were several deferential pages on* Capt. William Jaggard Bibliographer of Shakespeare *starting appropriately with this heading from his obituary notice, and Gerald's opening line ...* "My father would have appreciated this crowning recognition of his chief labour, the great dictionary of Shakespearean Literature". *Finally, towards the end of the article I found it ...*

"YESss!" I said. "GOT IT!" *Then I read out Gerald's* 'Bring it Over' *story:*

Gerald Jaggard (Stratford Mosaic)

I suppose one of my father's greatest moments was when he tracked down a First Folio of the poet's works, and wired details to Mr Henry Clay Folger, the millionaire Standard Oil Chief, who was then building up his amazing collection of Shakespearean items now housed in Washington, USA. Mr Folger's reply was "Bring it over" and so my father duly crossed the Atlantic and made the personal acquaintance of the great collector. They became firm friends, and my father made several trips afterwards to lecture there and was indeed offered a post at the Folger establishment.

Andy Jaggard So, it was true. The details of WJ's 'all expenses paid' trip and some insights into the relationship between the two men would form a crucial part of our book.

It was a glowing testimony from Gerald. Folger and WJ became 'firm friends'; *WJ* 'made several trips to lecture there'; *WJ was* 'indeed offered a post at the Folger establishment'.

We contacted the Folger Institute in Washington to try to establish which of Folger's eighty-two First Folios was the one that WJ took over. Surely there would be information on the acquisition of each First Folio? Both the archivist and the assistant curator, Elizabeth DeBold, were very helpful: the problem was that this was at the height of the pandemic.

Not only that but the Institute was undergoing a major building restoration project, which meant that all of the archived material was in secure storage and couldn't be accessed, Beth thought, until at least July 2021. We knew from the online information that there was correspondence between WJ and Folger between 1909 and 1921. We could only hope that some of these letters would provide vital information. However, we were going to have to wait for over a year before this was even possible, very frustrating.

In the meantime, I continued my research on the Folgers, hoping this might provide some leads.

Henry Clay Folger worked for the Standard Oil Trust of John D. Rockefeller, starting in 1881 as a clerk. He quickly showed his prowess as a mathematician and statistician and in 1886 became the secretary of Standard Oil's manufacturing committee. In 1899, he was promoted to chairman of the manufacturing committee, and eventually he was elected in 1911 as the President of the Standard Oil Company of New York.

Folger was an avid collector of Shakespeareana, assembling the world's largest collection of First Folio editions of Shakespeare's plays. There are eighty-two First Folios in the collection today (from around 220 surviving First Folios). The first rare book Folger acquired was a 1685 copy of the Fourth Folio, purchased in 1889, for just over a hundred dollars. He purchased his first copy of a First Folio four years later. Folger favoured *imperfect* copies of rare volumes and his Folio collection is noted for its diversity in provenance and condition.

Henry and Emily first met through their love of Shakespeare. At an 1882 picnic held by the Irving Literary Circle, the two were asked to each give a toast; Emily quoted *Othello* and Henry from *As You Like It*. They married on 6th October 1885. Though the Folgers had no children, they considered their collection to be their descendants, and Henry was known to refer to his rare books as '*the boys*'.

The Folgers chose items to purchase from booksellers' catalogues, which were initially perused and marked up by Emily, before she passed them onto Henry, who kept an extensive and precise list of items he intended to bid on. If possible, he inspected an item personally before purchasing it. He also avoided consulting scholarly experts about rare volumes, preferring his own and Emily's expertise. Folger used professional booksellers as middlemen at auctions, believing that the concealment of his identity would keep prices low.

Folger financed a half-century of collecting with his Standard Oil salary and extensive investments in the company. His high placement at Standard Oil also allowed him to take out loans with his friend Charles Millard Pratt, John D. Rockefeller, and even his wife, to fund his purchases. He generally paid for items in cash, a strategy that was popular with many booksellers who preferred immediate funds.

Early in his career at Standard Oil and as a collector, Folger doubted that he would eventually have the funds to build a memorial or library for his growing collection, and in 1895 he offered to sell it to John D. Rockefeller, who refused.

Toward the end of World War I, Folger and his wife began searching for a location for his Shakespeare library. Among the sites he and Emily considered were the University of Chicago, New York City and Stratford-upon-Avon.

The Folgers settled on Washington DC, a site they discovered in 1918 during a stay-over in the city, while travelling to Hot Springs.

The cornerstone_of the library was laid in 1930, but Henry Folger died soon afterward. The bulk of his fortune was left in trust for the library. With additional funding from Emily Folger, the library opened in 1932 on 23rd April, the date traditionally believed to be Shakespeare's birthday. Folger's collection of Shakespearean works is considered one of the most important resources for scholars of the playwright.

Then I read Andrea May's comprehensive book, The Millionaire and the Bard. *Sadly there was no mention of WJ, but it was very helpful in describing the Folger's methods as collectors.*

I was surprised to read that Henry and Emily Folger lived in a rented house, rather than an impressive mansion.

Their vast and growing collection was stored in packing cases in all manner of secure warehouses. They were totally immersed in their passion, with the obsessive acquisition of First Folios the centrepiece of their life's work.

Andrea Mays describes how they became extremely knowledgeable, understanding all the bookseller's terms to assess the provenance and value of a particular copy. Some of these words retained their common usage, *faded, frayed, rust-hole, broken*, but others like *washed,* positive in normal life, were negative when applied to a book. A once popular process to remove unsightly stains, done too aggressively *washing* could turn warm age-toned pages unnaturally white and it could ruin the original crisp feel of the Normandy rag paper. In a similar way, where terms have the opposite meaning of what you might think, *unsophisticated,* was high praise, it meant that the book was as close to its original state as possible. At their height, Henry and Emily Folger were as skilled as the best dealers in the world in *flyspecking* and analysing a book.

Folger had many qualities: he was intelligent, a skilled mathematician, had a high work ethic, and his amiability and lack of pretension meant that he got on well with most people. He was also by nature highly secretive.

Folger tried wherever possible to keep his identity a secret in the interest of keeping prices at a reasonable level. Equally he didn't want people to know how many First Folios he owned. As Andrea Mays describes, he lived by three maxims: *"ONE, don't tell them what you've done; TWO, don't tell them what you're doing; THREE, don't tell them what you're going to do."*

Sidney Lee and his census of surviving First Folios

This extract was interesting. Sidney Lee was a Stratfordian and a renowned Shakespearean scholar. From Gerald's writing I already knew that WJ and Lee had a fractious relationship, they were 'at war' with each other as Gerald described "like the captains of two warring galleons".

Lee's work was important as it was the start of the process to document and describe in great detail surviving copies of the First Folio.

This might help me identify WJ's First Folio. It was also amusing, with more on Folger's highly secretive nature and his 'shopping list'.

At the turn of the century, Sidney Lee attempted to collect all available information on the surviving copies. He designed a questionnaire which he sent out with a letter to all known owners of First Folios. Lee located 156 First Folios and the *Lee Census* was published in 1902. When Lee's Census landed on Folger's desk, complete with a questionnaire for him to fill in, Folger was elated. Lee listed only *one copy* as belonging to Folger whereas he actually had *six*. He had no intention of completing Lee's questionnaire but annotated his copy of the census like a shopping list, which he would keep within reach for the rest of his life.

Sidney Lee went to his grave in 1926 never having had sight of Folger's collection, and not knowing how many copies it contained. There are three copies of Lee's questionnaire in the Folger archives – all blank, and an evasive letter from Folger's assistant, explaining why he had not yet replied.

Soon I discovered that two men, West and Rasmussen, had continued Lee's work with a massive volume published in 2012 with a detailed description of every surviving First Folio and recording all known historic owners. This led me to some very deep and time-consuming research again in the vain search for WJ's 'Bring it over' Folio. I was becoming obsessive, and the lack of progress was driving me mad.

The Vincent First Folio

Not only was Sidney Lee responsible for the first census of all surviving First Folios he was also famous for breaking the news of a great 'Find' in February 1899. My search for newspapers and periodicals in 2022 had unearthed the story of Lee's 'Find' in several newspapers of the day, the Dundee Evening Telegraph, the Hartlepool Northern Mail, *and in the newspaper of WJ's home town,* the Leamington Spa Courier. *By 1899 WJ was just thirty-two and building his successful bookshop business in Liverpool. I'm certain that WJ would have read about Lee's lecture. He would have been infuriated by Lee's criticism of William Jaggard's printing of the First Folio and, I suspect, jealous of Lee's amazing achievement.*

Leamington Spa Courier – 25th February 1899 – 'Shakespeare in Folio'

An exceedingly interesting lecture at the London Institution on Monday … The lecture was illustrated by Lantern Slides.

Lee started by describing the role of the actor managers who were the owners of the manuscripts of Shakespeare's plays. After which Lee had some stinging criticism of the printing of the First Folio (which was repeated word for word in many of the other papers, the Stockton Herald *for example).*

The First Folio was carelessly printed, and extant copies show many variations among themselves owing to the compositor's incapacity. The pagination is most irregular but in spite of all the mechanical defects, the First Folio is the most valuable contribution to literature that ever issued from a printing office.

Lee then described how "this country is being drained of its First Folios by the United States of America ... they thus get scarcer and dearer every year."

Then Lee showed the audience the great 'Find'.

Mr Lee exhibited to his audience one of the rarest copies known which, as far as he knew, had hitherto escaped the notice of bibliographers. It belonged to Mr Coningsby Sibthorp of Sudbrook House, Lincoln. It was a taller copy than any other that had come to light and the portrait on the title page was of unexampled freshness and clearness ... its most remarkable feature was an inscription on the title page in a contemporary hand, the authenticity of which was unhesitatingly admitted by the expert authorities at the British Museum.

I need to explain at this point that although Lee broke the news of this previously unrecorded First Folio in February 1899 it had actually been discovered in 1891. It had taken eight years for Sidney Lee and the other experts to 'de-code' the origins of the 'Vincent Copy' and authenticate that it was genuine.

In our entertainment to the Shakespeare Club, 'Walked alone', we dramatised the 1891 discovery of this 'Vincent' Folio, that had been lost for many years, and later the protracted negotiations between Coningsby Sibthorp and Henry Folger, who was desperate to own this most famous First Folio. This is at the end of the chapter, but first Lee's explanation of its origins:

The arms stamped in the binding, fragments of which were in the original state proved that Jaggard had given the book to Augustine Vincent, an officer of the Herald's College. Jaggard and Vincent were on friendly terms. Both had been furiously denounced by Ralph Brooke, a colleague of Vincent's at the College of Arms, who had also displayed hostility to Shakespeare by asserting that the poet had no right to the coat of arms granted by him to the heralds in 1599. Vincent in 1622 had published (and Jaggard had printed) a book exposing Brook's ignorance and *perverse temper* and Jaggard himself had inserted an amusingly caustic tirade against Brooke ("*Your own intolerable arrogance and pride of conceit ... your tongue gliding over no man's name, but that it left a slime behind it.*")

In 1623 Jaggard was to celebrate their silencing of Brooke by presenting his friend Vincent with one of the earliest impressions of the First Folio. The motto on the cover, "Vincenti Augusti", '*Proud things for a Conquerer*', is a *jeu de mots* on the name of Augustine Vincent. William Jaggard could not inscribe this presentation copy because the blind printer had died before the First Folio was completed. So Augustine Vincent inscribed the title page in his own hand:

The discovery of the Vincent copy and its sale to Henry Folger

In July 2021, Moira and I, and our friends Chris and Susie Chaplin, were staying in a pub in the pretty Warwickshire village of Tamworth-in-Arden a few miles from Stratford. I had brought along the first draft of 'Walked Alone'. It was a beautiful summer's evening and the pub garden had plenty of post-lockdown garden furniture. We planned a read-through after dinner with a couple of glasses of wine, and the help of torches to read our scripts, as the light started to fade.

This section of 'Walked Alone' used a dramatic device based on the real-life situation that Gerald was in during his last year at the grammar school, aged sixteen. Gerald loved the English and drama classes, but WJ was about to take Gerald out of school to work in the local bank. The English master had asked each of the boys to give a talk on Shakespeare's play scripts and Gerald, unsurprisingly, with the Jaggard connection, had been asked to do something on the First Folio.

He had devised a short entertainment to explain the Vincent feud to his classmates, his swansong if you like, before he became a bank clerk, ending with this scene of the discovery of the 'Vincent copy' in 1891 and the protracted negotiations for its sale between Coningsby Sibthorp, the English aristocrat and Henry Folger after Sidney Lee broke the news of this most famous First Folio in 1899.

'Walked Alone' First read through, pub garden, Tamworth-in-Arden, 21st July 2021

'Walked Alone'

Acting Edition – Gerald's drama

Susie: In 1891 a bookseller named Railton had been engaged to weed out worthless books and prepare a catalogue for the library of an old English aristocrat, Mr Coningsby Sibthorp of Canwick Hall in Lincolnshire.

*(**Gerald** as 'An old retainer' enters carrying a small pair of steps. He is overacting badly, shuffling in with a limp and arched back with a few moans and groans.)*

Susie: On top of a large case of old books were stacked a great number of old folios covered in dust.

(The old retainer slowly positions the steps which he eventually unsteadily starts to climb – Moira places the folio on 'the shelf' and the old retainer blows off the dust.)

The old retainer who lived on the estate spotted a folio lacking one of its covers, with many leaves in tatters, tightly bound with a rough piece of cord.

(The old retainer throws it down, it crashes onto the lower floor.)

(descending stairs) The old retainer shouted ...

O.R: That's no good, Sir, it is only old poetry. *(Exits SL)*

Susie: Railton untied the cord and discovered it was an unrecorded First Folio.

Moira: It took eight years, from 1891 to 1899 to prove the authenticity of the copy, requiring the combined skills of Sidney Lee and three eminent librarians from the British Museum, including Professor Alfred W. Pollard. They meticulously de-coded the feud, Vincent's support for Jaggard, and the play on words ... Laurels for a Conqueror.

Susie: Railton arranged for several of the missing leaves to be replaced from another incomplete copy.

(Climbs stairs) Then, in his letter to Henry Clay Folger in April 1899, eight years after its discovery, Railton said, *"I had it finally restored by a Mr Pratt as nearly as possible to the state in which it was originally presented by Jaggard the printer."*

Moira: Folger was open mouthed, "Presented by Jaggard". In nearly three centuries no presentation copy of the First Folio had ever been found. That made it special, but presented by Jaggard, the printer of the First Folio, that seemed too incredible to be true. From his first offer in 1899 of £5,000 until he finally secured the Vincent copy four years later in 1903, the negotiations between Folger and Coningsby Sibthorp were delicate and tortuous.

Susie: Sibthorp was an old-fashioned English aristocrat and a quixotic, temperamental and indecisive seller. Both sides took offence at various points at the other party's behaviour. Finally on 22nd January 1903, Folger instructed his book dealer, Sotheran, *buy without fail even at ten thousand cash.* On 27th January the cable from Sotheran confirmed that it had been bought.

Moira: As the most expensive book in the world at a price of £10,000 (almost $50,000) it was more expensive than the finest copy of the much rarer Gutenberg Bible with only fifty copies, printed on vellum. Folger's ownership of the Vincent copy remained a closely guarded secret for another five years.

Well, that was it. We had a lot of fun. It was very dark and quite late. I'd drunk a bit too much wine. I went to my room and decided for some reason to pick up my emails. It was 21st July 2021.

There was an email from Beth DeBold, the assistant curator at the Folger Institute.

I'd completely forgotten about her promise to try to access the correspondence between WJ and Folger by July 2021.

She had attached fourteen letters and documents.

Beth's first attachment was a letter written by WJ on 7th April 1903 from his Moorfields bookshop in Liverpool to Henry Folger in New York.

I read WJ's first letter and couldn't quite believe my eyes.

CHAPTER 6 A FARCICAL TALE

Andy Jaggard
When I woke up the next morning and opened Beth's attachment, I was relieved to find that WJ's letter to Folger was still there – I hadn't imagined it.

I was beginning to realise that whenever I made a new discovery about my grandfather the reality was usually stranger than anything I could have made up.

The first thing that surprised me was that his letter was written in April 1903, much earlier than I had expected. It was sent from his Moorfields bookshop in Liverpool (seven years before WJ made the move to Stratford).

He had a First Folio that he was offering to sell to Henry Folger.

These are his opening lines:

7th April 1903, 8 Moorfields, Liverpool

Dear Sir

First Folio Shakespeare

When I thought of selling the above a few years ago it was with the idea of buying a perfect copy, but the value has now reached Two Thousand pounds and is still advancing, so there is not much hope for me.

It was my great-great-grandfather's copy and for ought I know has never been out of the family since produced by my ancestors in the Barbican.

I stopped at this point to let WJ's claim sink in. He was saying 'for ought I know' *or as far as I know ... his First Folio* 'has never been out of the family since produced by my ancestors in the Barbican'. *The Barbican in London was where William Jaggard, the printer had his Jaggard Press which produced the First Folio in 1623. That would mean it had been in the Jaggard family for 280 years ...*

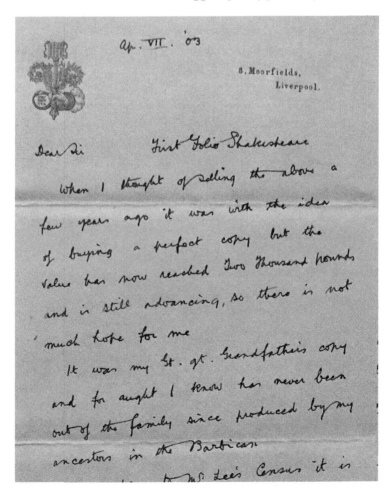

He was also claiming it had been his 'great-great-grandfather's copy'.

By July 2021 I had sound evidence of the line of descent from WJ – William Jesse, the railway porter, his father, then Jesse, the poacher turned gamekeeper, his grandfather, then John, his great-grandfather and then William Jaggard, his great-great-grandfather. William Jaggard was born in 1758 and lived around Dullingham in rural Cambridgeshire all of his life, worked on the land, and died in 1828.

How likely was it that this man would own a First Folio?

I read the rest of the WJ's letter.

According to the Lee Census it is one of the tallest and broadest copies known and if the few missing leaves could be obtained from some imperfect copy will make one of the finest. The price will be £500, but I am not anxious to sell even at this as I can never replace family heirlooms. I also have the Second, Third and Fourth Folios. Including the foregoing the price will be £850 for the set of four.

In selling them I deserve the curse that rests on the iconoclast.

Yours sincerely Wm Jaggard

(£500 may not seem much for a First Folio but it was a considerable amount of money in 1903. Ten years later in 1913 WJ had a very beautiful house built on the banks of the River Avon, in Stratford for £600.)

The Lee Census of 1902 was the first census of surviving First Folios and had information on WJ's First Folio.

The order of these chapters and the times when we made discoveries and breakthroughs don't always match. By this time, I already knew that WJ was at one time the owner of a First Folio (although I didn't know whether it was this one).

'The Shakespeare First Folio: A Descriptive Catalogue' (2012) by Eric Rasmussen and Anthony James West, updates and documents the historic owners and the condition of all the known surviving copies of the First Folio. West's Number 184, known as 'The John Hay Library Copy', displays a fair number of scars, torn corners and edges rather amateurishly repaired ... extra leaves inserted between the front cover and the text include a virtual scrapbook of owners' marks, notes and a few souvenirs.

After a couple of earlier owners in the 17th and 18th centuries, and then a gap of a century, this First Folio found its way to Shakespeare's birthplace, Stratford-upon-Avon, where it was first the property of the Rev. John Day Collis (1816–1879), vicar of Holy Trinity Church.

Later it was owned by Captain William Jaggard, possibly, but not provably (*it had not been proved*) a descendant of William Jaggard, the printer of the First Folio.

Was it this one? If it was, that would blow WJ's claims apart. Perhaps he had dealings in more than one First Folio?

There were several more letters between WJ and Henry Folger:

On 25th April 1903, three weeks after his first letter WJ had second thoughts and wrote again, "a slight difficulty has arisen between members of my family who claim joint ownership" so to settle the dispute the Second, Third and Fourth Folios were to be entered in the Sotheby's sale on 8th and 9th May.

On 16th May 1903 WJ replied to a letter from Folger. "The three Folios had not quite reached the reserve set for them by WJ's relatives, and the set was now intact again. *" The price was £850 for the set, but (now increased to) £650 for just the First Folio.*

On 3rd June 1903 Folger wrote back questioning the increase in price of the First Folio and with some very surprising news:

I am sorry you did not send to me the copy of the First when I acknowledged your letter as I am starting for London on the 13th, will you please forward by express to London, so that I may see it there during the week beginning the 21st of June, to me in care of Messrs. Henry Sotheran & Company, 140, Strand. *Folger wrote that if he* cared for it, provided it was only £500, he would pay cash immediately on receipt. If not sent to England, the Folio would need to be sent to Folger's Broadway office in New York any time after 6th July.

At this point the penny dropped and I realised what was going on. 1903, OF COURSE. Folger had finally bought the Vincent Copy for £10,000 on 22nd January of that year just a couple of months before WJ's first letter, and now in June of 1903 the Folgers were going to collect it. It's all detailed in Andrea Mays' book.

What an amazing coincidence. Two 'Jaggard' First Folios for sale in the same year.

Henry and Emily Folger sailed to England to pick up their £10,000 Vincent First Folio. They collected their prize from Sotheran & Company in London, then made their first visit to Shakespeare's birthplace in Stratford returning to New York by ocean liner famously carrying the book in Emily's suitcase.

The reason for their visit to England would be a closely guarded secret. WJ would have been completely ignorant of what was going on. In fact, it wasn't until five years later in 1908 that Folger finally admitted, in an article, that he was the owner of the Vincent copy.

The rest of the saga was farcical:

WJ had missed Folger's letter of 3rd June requesting that his First Folio be sent to Sotheran & Company in London by 21st June so ...

On 27th June 1903, he wrote to Folger saying, "due to his absence in the South he was now forwarding to your Broadway office, in New York, direct." *He also invoiced for £500* "although the price is <u>too low</u>".

On 31st July 1903 WJ wrote again saying he had received no news.

Folger must have decided that he did 'not care for it' *and he returned it in September. WJ's Folio had travelled across the Atlantic and back while the Folgers had travelled in the opposite direction.*

I'm now sure that the First Folio WJ attempted to sell to Folger was the John Hay Library copy.

Several months earlier after studying Anthony West's work on the sale prices of First Folios, I had emailed him to see if he knew anything of the Folio WJ delivered to Folger in the 'Bring it over' story. Anthony West was kind enough to reply and said he only knew of my grandfather's ownership of one First Folio – the John Hay Library Copy, No. 184 (Lee 111) and he wished me luck with the book.

I asked Beth DeBold what she thought. She said she believes Number 184 – 'The John Hay Library Copy' was the Folio that WJ tried to sell to Folger in 1903. *WJ remained the owner for several years until it was eventually sold in America in 1928.*

So, what is the explanation of Gerald's 'Bring it over' story?

My belief is that it's simply not true.

WJ probably conflated some real and some made-up information so that it sounded more impressive than the reality that Folger rejected his own rather poor First Folio. The Folio went across the seas to New York and back, but not accompanied by WJ.

I don't blame Gerald; he wasn't a dishonest man. The problem may have been his source. It may also say something about Gerald's accepting and trusting nature, taking WJ's story at face value.

I had been on a wild goose case for many months, but I had learnt a lot about my grandfather's character. He was shameless in spinning stories and making audacious claims which he believed would help him to achieve his end goals.

My suspicions about my grandfather's character, motivation and behaviour were developing, the more I discovered. I could understand why WJ had such an acrimonious relationship with Sidney Lee, (later Sir Sidney) the impressive Shakespearean scholar, who was also a man who didn't 'mince his words'. WJ's propensity for conflict and his obsessive letter-writing habit is covered in the next chapter.

But there was more to ponder:

Sidney Lee's impressive lecture in 1899 had also included the exhibition of a famous Second Folio. This Second Folio was at one time owned by Lewis Theobald, the inspired textual critic of Shakespeare and many manuscript notes by Theobald were found on the margins. The copy had afterwards passed into the hands of Dr Johnson and then Samuel Ireland. Ireland's name is chiefly remembered in connection with the Ireland forgeries.

That set me, and possibly WJ, thinking. How to really make your mark in the world?

A great Shakespearean 'Find', previously owned by a well-known figure, some handwritten notes in the margins, validation of its authenticity by experts from the British Museum ... and then a dramatic 'reveal' in a leading newspaper.

If only you could chance on such a lucky find.

CHAPTER 7 WILLIAM JAGGARD MAN OF LETTERS – ALL 2,000 OF THEM

" *'Tis a tale full of sound and fury ...* " Macbeth Act V Scene 5

Andy Jaggard
After Gerald's death in 2002, our mother Diana lived alone for a few years at Greensleeves. After a fall and a spell in hospital she needed more suitable accommodation and moved into a rented converted chapel nearby, still in the village of Tiddington. The family home was eventually sold and, when the house was cleared, some of Gerald's papers were donated to the Shakespeare Birthplace Trust.

Bob Bearman, an expert on Stratford's historic buildings, wrote this article on one of the items that had been donated – an office letter book.

I remember reading Bob's article back in 2005 when I had been both amused and shocked by my grandfather's 'unique' style of letter writing.

Now that I was digging deeper into WJ's life, these copy letters would provide some more insights into WJ's eccentric, domineering character, his feuds and his propensity for engaging in conflict. Bob kindly agreed that I could use a section of his article to open this chapter.

It describes WJ's very extensive letter writing habit in the two years before his move to Stratford in 1910.

Robert Bearman – Shakespeare Birthplace Trust Records Office – William Jaggard, Man of Letters all 2,000 of them – Stratford-upon-Avon Herald 2005

Anybody who believes that letter writing is a dying art will have their worst fears confirmed by one of the most recent additions to our collections.

It is what is known as an office letter book in which outgoing letters could be pressed between its flimsy leaves to provide a copy. This particular volume has a thousand of them, around two copy-letters a day for the period November 1907 to June 1909 and these are no ordinary letters. They were written by William Jaggard (1867–1947), a remarkable, if controversial figure …

Convinced that he was a descendant of the famous William Jaggard, who in 1623 had printed Shakespeare's First Folio, his ambition was to establish a bookshop and set up a printing press in the poet's native town of Stratford. This he achieved in 1910, when he opened his 'Shakespeare Press' at 4 Sheep Street …

Jaggard undoubtedly knew a lot about books, and about Shakespeare in particular, but he had very strong opinions and did not suffer fools gladly; nor it seems anyone else who disagreed with him. The letters document several long-running feuds; a very entertaining one was with the Liverpool branch of the Dickens Fellowship, whom he accused of indulging in "frivolous pursuits" when it should have been discussing the work of a great English novelist …

Another involved the Woolton Library Committee, whose library he catalogued in 1908. His final letter to its unfortunate chairman, the Rev. Lisle Carr, concludes: "I have formed an estimate of your character for which the dictionary supplies no polite term, but which is engraved on my memory."

One of the oddest letters is one to Scotland Yard, in which he proffered the name of a man he suspected of murdering Mrs Caroline Luard, an infamous crime which the police never solved.

Andy Jaggard
Gerald had a very large collection of WJ's letters, some also covering the period before the move to Stratford. They are by turns, opinionated, superior, amusing and rude.

First, he reflects on how WJ had 'invaded' Liverpool in 1890 and was 'alone' before he met and married Emma Frances shortly after his arrival in the city. It is also the first mention that Gerald makes of his mother, there is only one more in the whole of Life and Death.

The Life and Death of a Stratford Bookshop (Unpublished book) c. 1974

Gerald Jaggard
When he 'invaded' Liverpool in 1890, armed only with a lively pen and a deep knowledge of books, my father was alone. Somehow, he managed to secure a small shop in Moorfields, and later opened up another one at 92 Dale Street. Rents in those days must have been modest, to get a foothold in such important and busy areas. He did take on partners in later years, one to manage the philatelic department, stamps being a profitable line. However, such partnerships were brief, culminating in a thundering row after which the participants split up, remaining the worst of friends.

However, he did take a partner whose help he could rely upon at difficult times, and who, in addition to running his household, became an unpaid assistant. This, of course, was my mother, Emma Frances Cook, whom he married soon after his arrival in the city. WJ had begun work upon his great bibliography of Shakespeare, and mother was set to work upon the 'slips'. This was the tedious and mechanical process of copying items from catalogues on to slips of paper - author, title, page and line. There were thousands of them. The same task had to be undertaken when indexing ten years' issues of 'BOOK PRICES CURRENT'. After that little job, my father declared that he was some £200 out of pocket, extra time involved in putting right numerous errors he found in BPC.

WJ was putting out short pamphlets on various subjects, operating as THE SHAKESPEARE PRESS, a title which he duly registered. Somebody else dared to use the title, and WJ pounced like a puma. There began an acrimonious correspondence, the forerunner of so many similar skirmishes.

The offenders in this case were a Birmingham author and his printers. They received this letter:

> *Dear Sirs,*
> *Our attention has been drawn to the fact that you are using upon a book entitled 'Book Makers of Old Birmingham' our registered title 'The Shakespeare Press' and we are at once writing to ask whether this was an oversight or done purposely. If, as we prefer to believe, it was an unintentional oversight we presume you will at once do your best to rectify the error.*
> *Awaiting your early explanation.*
> *Yours truly,*
> *Jaggard & Co.*

The recipients of this letter digested it for a fortnight, then replied that they had been using the title since 1876. This did not help them one iota:

Dear Sir,

In reply to your letter of 23rd Nov. unless we are greatly mistaken you appear to be labouring under a delusion. The mere use of the title 'Shakespeare Press' from 1876 onwards, presuming your assertion is correct, does not make the title yours unless you registered it prior to 1893, and it is assumed you did not so register it, or

(1) We should have discovered the fact in that year – and

(2) You would mention it under the circumstances that have now arisen.

Further we should like to make it clear that this title has been used by various firms, according to books in our possession, for the last two hundred years, but we were the first to record it officially (as ours) and therefore it may no longer be used by anyone without our permission.

There is a certain appropriateness in this, as you will admit, seeing that our ancestor produced the first edition of Shakespeare.

We await your early reply before taking further steps.

Yours truly,

Jaggard & Co.

What 'further steps' my father took in this matter I do not know. There was apparently no further correspondence on the matter. I doubt very much if legal action was taken. WJ had a horror of putting money into lawyers' pockets, as he was, so to speak, a law unto himself.

This episode occurred in 1907, a year in which he was strengthening his ties with Stratford-upon-Avon. Besides contributing articles to the *Stratford-upon-Avon Herald* he made frequent visits to the town, dropping in at the Shakespeare Memorial Library to consult its records, and often staying for a night with his friend Mr George Boyden, editor of *The Herald*.

At the Shakespeare Memorial Theatre, Mr F. R. Benson was directing the annual Shakespeare Festivals, as he had done since 1886. The Stratford Festivals were short in those days, the 1907 celebration lasting but three weeks. However, in that period he managed to present *Love's Labour's Lost* as the Birthday play, together with eleven other Shakespearean plays. *David Garrick, The Country Girl* and *Don Quixote*. You got your money's worth back then: Benson himself played Biron in the Birthday production, with Mrs Benson as Rosaline and George Weir as Costard.

WJ was still working busily on his research into the Jaggard family history. In November 1907 he was writing on the subject to a distant bearer of the name - Mr Josiah Jaggard, at Rockhampton, Queensland, Australia:

As you may guess, I am a very busy man, and regret that so many valuable hours have to be wasted in sleep. If only the working hours were 20 instead of 12 or 14 one might accomplish all one's private hobbies. I have several great tasks on hand, and have completed one huge one since writing last, an Index ('Book Prices Current') of rare books containing 100,000 titles.

I am now at work on a Shakespeare Index (The Shakespeare Bibliography) of some 21,000 entries (see circular) and when that is done, I hope to complete the Jaggard family history, of which I have a great sheaf of material ready.

It is highly amusing (and would perhaps be flattering if compliment lay in imitation) to hear some American Jaggard now proposes to do what I am engaged on. If he meets with the same amount of discouragement from the race that I have met with it will be interesting to know where he will get the material from. I have been at it many years on and off and have to search old wills, registers, libraries, and personally different Jaggards all over the kingdom to get my records. Even

then it required special knowledge to be able to get same.
How on earth will he accomplish this?
I trust you are well and prospering. Your over-zealous Tariff
reformers have roused a very bitter storm of indignation against
Australia in this country. Perhaps they will learn a little sense
in time and revise that tariff.
With kind regards,
Yours sincerely
W Jaggard

With his eyes ever upon Stratford-upon-Avon, WJ was now looking for customers in that town. To the two leading estate agents he offered:

Inwood – Table of Interest & Mortality for the purchase of
Estates and Valuation of Properties (cost 8/- net) price 4/6
quite new & a great time and trouble saver.

To Messrs Bolland in Guild Street he quoted:

Hasluck (Paul) The Automobile: A Practical Treatise on the
Instruction of modern Motor Cars – steam, petrol, electric –
with over 800 illustrations – large vol. handsomely bound (cost
37/6 net) price 18/6 - quite new. Cassell & Co 1907.

Even more ambitiously, he was trying to select a new vicar for Stratford, obviously being a non-runner for the post himself. He wrote to the Rev C. Lisle Carr of Woolton (where WJ had catalogued the library), adding as a postscript:

By the way, the living of Stratford-upon-Avon will be vacant
next Easter, Mr Arbuthnot having just been promoted
Archdeacon of Coventry, to the intense satisfaction of the
townspeople. He has been a kind of 'square peg in a round hole'
there, for although scholarly and clever, he is devoid of tact. So,

if you are not firmly fixed at Woolton and think it would be a beneficial change, pray let me know and I will do my best for you with 'the powers that be' down there, with whom I have some influence.

They are mostly a nice warm-hearted people around Stratford, and I am convinced you are the kind of man who would adorn such a prominent post. The official income is not very fat, but there are other assets which help it. The old families, many of them titled, are the best around in England, and it is a fashionable church for marriage.

The Stratford Shakespeare Club had been founded by twelve townsmen in 1824 and, after a lapse in activity, had been re-founded in 1874. Eminent speakers were invited to address its members. In its hands, also, was the task of staging each year a fitting celebration of Shakespeare's birthday, 23rd April, with luncheons and elaborate displays of street decoration.

In November of 1907, WJ was invited to read a paper upon 'Witchcraft in Macbeth' during which he 'cleared up' a mysterious passage in the witches' scene.

At the same meeting a letter was read from Mr F. R. Benson urging the Committee to make an immediate start upon their preparations for the 1908 Festival. WJ was promptly placed upon the Committee dealing with this matter. Returning to Liverpool, he gave immediate thought to the affair - naturally, he was brimming over with ideas. He wrote to Mr Ellis, secretary of the Stratford Shakespeare Club with a long and very detailed list of suggestions. Not many of WJ's suggestions were adopted. As 23rd April 1908, drew nearer, WJ wrote to the Committee, apologising for not being able to attend the January meeting, and with a few more suggestions for them to digest:

As I stated at the last meeting, I should greatly like to see better marshalling of this procession, with greater comfort and security to ladies taking part. Without proper order and precautions a procession runs perilously near becoming a rabble, because outsiders will quickly take advantage of weak arrangements.

A little careful forethought on the part of those who have had some military training of infantry, or those accustomed to handle large crowds will prevent all that disgraceful pushing, crowding and unseemly behaviour which to my amazement occurred outside and inside the church ...

P.S. Marshals should be provided with white wands (about 7ft long)

WJ's respect for military training arose from his own experience of having served for two years in the Liverpool Volunteers. It was a queer combination - bookselling and part-time soldiering - but the experience was to be extremely useful to him when the First World War came along. Unfortunately, it had an adverse effect as well, reinforcing the dominant side of his character, the desire to bend everybody else to his own dictates, regardless of their desires or feelings.

One certain way to arouse his greatest ire was to ask for money that he did not owe. On such occasions the average person is tempted to reply with annoyance, or a little gentle sarcasm. Not so WJ, he opened fire with all guns blazing, and fired salvo after salvo into the offending craft. Such an incident occurred with the producers of the 'PUBLISHERS CIRCULAR' to which he subscribed from his several establishments:

In reply to your p.c. of yesterday – may we ask whether any bookkeeping whatsoever is done in your office? If so, it must be of the most slovenly and lazy description. If your clerks are 'tired' why not replace them with some of the hundreds of poor devils out of work, who would be only too glad of the chance to earn a salary?

We are now requested to pay our 'Dale Street' subscription which expired in November last and was promptly paid (for which we hold your receipt). This is by no means the first instance of this kind of request, which might bear an uglier significance to those unaccustomed to the lack of proper management in your place.

Game, set and match to WJ (he played a keen and blustering game of tennis, too).

WJ held the view, and often expressed it, that 'all book dealers are scoundrels'. He referred, presumably, to those gentry with no special love of books who bought job lots at auctions and hawked them round the booksellers for a quick sale. To one such optimist he wrote:

We beg to return your list of books and regret we cannot purchase them at present being unusually full of stock.
We may add that honourable booksellers, among whom we include ourselves, never think of offering second-hand books as new, when once they have been used. **However, Welsh and English morals differ.**
Yours faithfully, Jaggard & Co.

Andy Jaggard
WJ certainly didn't hold back in speaking his mind and dishing out his fierce judgements of the actions and character traits of others. He clearly had a talent for coining an insulting, and sometimes amusing, turn of phrase – as well as making free with his prejudices.

There was one subject on which he was on the defensive himself. He had aligned himself wholeheartedly with his famous ancestor and namesake, William Jaggard. Although the Tudor printer was a highly successful and experienced businessman, he was also guilty of two infamous acts of literary piracy against none other than William Shakespeare.

CHAPTER 8 PIRACY

"Alas ...this is not my writing

Though I confess, much like the character" Twelth Night Act V Scene 1

Andy Jaggard

WJ was enormously proud of his 'direct lineal descent' from his namesake William Jaggard, the architect of the First Folio. He saw it as his duty to ensure his famous ancestor received sufficient recognition for his 'priceless service to literature' *and to defend his reputation against his critics.*

This presented a real challenge for my passionately biased grandfather for, on the face of it, the Tudor Printer Jaggard was a most unlikely choice as the printer of the First Folio.

William Jaggard (1568–1623), is best remembered as a printer of the First Folio of Shakespeare. Printing was completed in October or early November 1623, about the time of his death. Although a successful printer and bookseller, he was also known for unethical practices. In particular these involved two notable acts of literary PIRACY against none other than William Shakespeare.

The first involved an anthology of poems called The Passionate Pilgrim. *The second involved a quarto of ten plays by or attributed to Shakespeare, printed with false dates.*

I needed to understand these two acts of piracy, but also how WJ and my father would each deal with the stain on Jaggard's reputation and the criticism of their revered ancestor. They both had 'skin in the game' as direct descendants of the famous printer.

I had my grandfather's large collection of essays and research notes in preparation for his many lectures and Gerald's draft chapter on the Printer, written in the 1970s in which he attempts to describe the piracy of The Passionate Pilgrim.

Their very different approaches revealed a great deal about their respective characters.

But first I'm relying on Stanley Wells – Biography of William Jaggard *for a short and more objective explanation of his first act of piracy,* The Passionate Pilgrim.

Jaggard rapidly became a successful businessman. Ill feeling followed his publication in 1599 of *The Passionate Pilgrim.* Ascribed to Shakespeare, this poetical anthology includes versions of sonnets 138 and 144, three extracts from *Love's Labour's Lost,* and other short poems, some by writers other than Shakespeare, others of unknown edition ownership. In a third edition of 1612 Jaggard added without authority nine poems from *Troia Britannica* (1609) by Thomas Heywood. In his apology for actors (1612) Heywood protested and declared Shakespeare "much offended with Mr Jaggard (that altogether unknown to him) presumed to make bold with his name". The original title page was replaced with one that did not mention Shakespeare's name.

WJ writing in his 'Jaggard family jottings', some private papers, written during the years of the First World War, is typically forthright employing his fierce defence and attack strategy:

> *Jaggard opened in Fleet Street, on his own account, in one of the shops forming the frontage of St Dunstan's Church, where he issued in 1599 Shakespeare's The Passionate Pilgrim. Much fatuous criticism has been levelled at him since, all*

because he failed to state that this little anthology was by Shakespeare and others. Now most of these purblind critics have written a so-called 'Life of Shakespeare'. If the same rigid rule were applied they would state, to be meticulous, that their said 'Life' is actually written by Nicholas Rowe and J. O. Halliwell-Phillipps (the two real biographers).

Andy Jaggard

And so, it goes on, first dismissing the criticism of Jaggard the printer with a few of *WJ's choice phrases* – fatuous criticism … purblind critics. *Then attempting to draw a parallel between literary piracy and the biographers of Shakespeare, reliant on the* real biographers.

Gerald writing his draft chapter on the printer in the 1970s was more conflicted. I'm not sure whether this chapter was intended for The Life and Death *or for an earlier project. In any case, this was over twenty years after WJ's death, but I imagine Gerald was still keenly aware of his father's presence in his study as he typed:*

THE JAGGARD STORY – (Gerald's Draft Manuscript)

When my father, William Jaggard, installed himself in the small Sheep Street bookshop some sixty years ago, it was perhaps natural that he should step up his research into the family pedigree …

Gerald continued, describing how Dr John Jaggard had 'migrated' in 1569 to London and set up as a barber-surgeon and then apprenticed his two sons, William and John to printing and publishing. Soon he was recounting William Jaggard's early career as a Freeman of the City of London and as a member of the Stationers' Company:

… from here he issued sundry publications, the most notable of which was Shakespeare's *The Passionate Pilgrim* in 1599.

Then Gerald, perhaps with a heavy heart, started a new paragraph:

Perhaps I should describe this publication as notorious
rather than notable for Jaggard had omitted to say …

(there were some more words about … literary scorn pointed
at the printer ever since by Collier, Hazlitt and
Swinburne *(three of Jaggard's fiercest critics).*

*Gerald had clearly stopped typing, picked up his pen, and crossed
out the first line of this offending paragraph. Then more carefully
and to ensure nothing could be read he more thoroughly crossed
out the complete paragraph.*

~~Perhaps I should describe this publication as notorious rather than~~
~~notable, for Jaggard omitted Shakespeare's name from the title page.~~ ~~He was~~
~~content to state~~ ~~publication as notorious rather than~~
~~notable, for Jaggard~~ ~~He~~
~~content to state~~
'The Passionate Pilgrim' was a charming anthology of verse, ~~and~~ but

Then, deciding to be more 'upbeat' he typed a new sentence:

The Passionate Pilgrim was a charming anthology of
verse but for some reason Jaggard failed to state that
Shakespeare was not the only contributor. For this
'heinous' offence, the Elizabethan printer was labelled
a literary pirate.

Andy Jaggard

*It seems to me that Gerald in his mid-sixties was still under the
sway of his father's overpowering influence and was feeling guilty
about his disloyalty to his ancestor.*

*And the second act of piracy? In 1907 there was an amazing
discovery as the result of some brilliant bibliographical detective
work by Professor Alfred Pollard, Sir W.W, Gregg and others. This*

was in relation to the Pavier Quartos sometimes referred to as the False Folio affair.

Professor Alfred Pollard himself writing in The Sphere *on 26th May 1923, during the celebrations for* The Tercentenary *of the First Folio Shakespeare looked back on some of the evidence of his discovery, the fraud established in 1907 and the likely sequence of events.*

The Mysterious 'Volume of 1619'

In 1619 these three men (W. Jaggard, N. Butter, T. Pavier) with Arthur Johnson who owned the pirated *Merry Wives of Windsor* brought out a set of editions, closely alike in form of ten plays, five by Shakespeare (two in bad texts) one perhaps partly by him, two he may have re-handled, and two which he can never have touched, attributing them all to him. The volume was conceived as a collection to which a general title page was to be attached but ended in a fraudulent use of earlier dates, probably to enable it to be sold in the country as a 'remainder' of previous editions. This Mysterious 'Volume of 1619' has caused great confusion in Shakespeare bibliography, and its history now is still not fully worked out. It seems probable, however, that the readiness of this enterprising William Jaggard and the three publishers to risk their money on such a venture shamed Shakespeare's friends to begin active preparations for the First Folio. Probably Jaggard, who was brought into frequent contact with the players by holding (from the Stationers' Company) a monopoly for printing their bills, offered to print such an edition on easy terms.

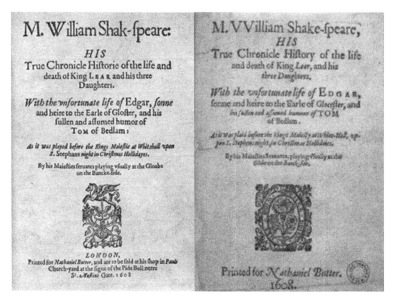

11. King Lear – showing the genuine 1608 original on the left, and the 'False Folio' also dated 1608, but actually printed in 1619 – on the right.

Printing and Publishing in the Elizabethan Age

To understand how William Jaggard, despite these acts of piracy, came to be the printer of Shakespeare's First Folio, it's helpful to understand a little of the printing and publishing trade of that time.

It was a time of mighty religious and political struggle. In this context, the enforcement of the censorship of books, particularly those expressing opposing religious views, was seen as essential. In May 1557, the Worshipful Company of Stationers was granted a Royal Charter. This Fellowship gradually assumed control of the printing and publishing business. In effect they became a special privileged body, holding what approached a monopoly, with a process of self-regulation to protect their own interests.

The number of printers in London was reduced to around twenty, with a total of around fifty presses. The number of apprentices was also controlled. After finishing his seven-year apprenticeship, the young 'freeman' usually accepted a position as a compositor, pressman or book clerk.

In a few fortunate cases however, especially if the young man's family had a little capital, the newly made-up freeman would set up business as a small stationer, starting his career in a shed in Fleet Street, selling second-hand books, paper and writing materials. William Jaggard began as a bookseller, and then over a few years, developed his business as a printer and bookseller.

The Worshipful Company required that all books that were to be printed, must first be licenced, with severe penalties for the printing of *unallowed books*. There was a Master, two Wardens and a 'Court of Assistants', always men of substance, who in cases of doubt or dispute, over who held printing rights, acted as adjudicators.

In 1612, John Jaggard, once described as William's *more reputable brother* was *clothed* and made an Assistant.

The 'Title' of the work, had to be entered into the Hall Book or Register of the Stationers' Company prior to printing/publication. Once legally entered no other stationer might print it, and providing the owner, or his 'assigns' kept re-printing it, the life of the 'copyright' was unlimited. There was though provision for a book becoming 'derelict' after twenty years. Penalties for illegal practice included prison sentences, fines or the 'suppression' of the books, involving seizing or destroying the entire batch of copies.

William Jaggard – "An Unlikely Choice"

WJ and Gerald collected and preserved many of the newspapers and articles celebrating the Tercentenary of the First Folio, a century ago in 1923. One of these appeared in The Times Literary Supplement *22nd March 1923, where R. Crompton Rhodes attempts to untangle one of the mysteries of the First Folio ... the connection of William Jaggard, at whose press in the Barbican it was printed.*

Rhodes describes William Jaggard as an unlikely choice as printer of the First Folio and attempts to describe the route by which he achieved that honour.

Pavier and Jaggard were up before the Court of Assistants on 8th July 1619. Presiding over the court was William Leake. In the case of the piracy of *The Passionate Pilgrim,* he was the man who held the copyright for Shakespeare's *Venus and Adonis* from 1596 to 1617. He would have had good reason to punish with severity any Shakespeare piracy by Pavier or Jaggard.

It seems that Pavier must have been acquitted, for at the next Quarter Court, six days later, he was made an Assistant. This was an important and highly reputable role so William Jaggard, as his partner, can therefore hardly have violated the regulations.

However, sometime later there was evidence of a protest by the King's Players against the Corruption of Plays to the Injury and Disgrace of the Authors.

Rhodes concludes that the penalties for Pavier and Jaggard involved the 'suppression of title pages', the printers being prohibited from reprinting the Pavier Quartos (The False Folio), this potentially very profitable collection of plays.

His theory is that in compensation for this loss, the court made recompense by granting:

1. To Pavier for his agreement to allow Henry V and York and Lancaster (Henry VI–II and III) to be included in the Folio edition, the copyright of the authorised texts.

2. To Jaggard's son and printer for the loss of his printing rights of future impressions, the printing of the First Folio, providing that he also bears a share of the costs.

It may also have been a case of necessity, since Jaggard had a large-capacity print shop and he had demonstrated his ability to print a volume of ten plays. Work on the First Folio began almost certainly in 1621.The copyright of the sixteen unpublished plays was in 1623 entered jointly by Edward Blount and Isaac Jaggard.

Andy Jaggard

Incidentally WJ was a member of the Stationers' Company and was granted the Freedom of the City of London in 1918. He was very proud of this honour which entitled him to wear his ceremonial stationer's costume.

WJ would regularly don this costume for galas and fetes in Stratford, startling the locals.

WJ was proud. He was also boastful, desperate to make his mark and to impress. He would have known all about Professor Alfred Pollard's brilliant bibliographical detective work of the fraud established in 1907 in connection with the False Folio

12. WJ in his stationer's costume – 'Rose Bank', Stratford 1930s.

In March 1914, WJ was on a promotional tour in America and, faced with a naive and fawning American journalist, could not resist claiming his own numerous 'discoveries', including his involvement with the famous 1907 discovery.

CHAPTER 9 CITY LIBRARIAN OR NOTHING

Andy Jaggard

WJ had come to "loathe" Liverpool, despite the success of his two bookshops, but having catalogued several libraries, hankered after becoming a librarian himself "relieved of the necessity of depending upon a fluctuating trade to earn his daily bread". *When the City Librarianship of Liverpool itself was advertised, Gerald described how he* "girded his loins to make the assault" *with an over-the-top* "31-page booklet of testimonials, photographs, letters and press notices ..."

The Life and Death of a Stratford Bookshop *(Unpublished book) c. 1974*

Gerald Jaggard

As the months passed, he was growing increasingly restless and discontented with the Liverpool atmosphere. His trips to Stratford, and occasional holidays in Malvern (a favourite haunt) and the Isle of Man emphasised the drabness of Merseyside. Writing to a friend he gave vent to his feelings:

WJ

It was most kind of you to send me these beautiful roses. To the imprisoned bird, caged up in a grimy city, what must a glimpse of the clean green country be? So it is with all country folk like myself. I too am caged up all the year round in a monotonous, dull and repulsive town, which has stamped its evil features on the inhabitants. The longer I live here the more I loathe the place.

But you know the old adage, 'As you make your bed, so you

must lie on it.' However, I look forward to a not very distant date when I can get away for good to the wholesome pure air and green fields, to the sound of the wild birds' song and the hum of the bees. For one of these I would exchange willingly a dozen of the artificial pleasures of the town.

1909 arrived, with my father still planning and scheming to 'emigrate' to Warwickshire, but still somewhat entrenched in Liverpool. It was a complicated business. His Moorfields shop was threatened with development (as No. 4 Sheep Street was to be) and the lease was near its end. No. 92 Dale Street was too small for his expanding business. He was still talking of 'establishing a little branch' in Stratford but must have known in his own mind that running two businesses 120 miles apart would never work.

Having catalogued libraries at Warwick Castle, Tonbridge School, Woolton and Leamington Spa, he hankered after becoming a librarian himself. How ideal it would be to live among books, relieved of the necessity of depending upon a fluctuating trade to earn his daily bread, feeling secure and free to indulge in all his hobbies. The librarianship of Wallasey, Liverpool's suburb across the river, had fallen vacant, and WJ, with many others, had applied for it. He could not conceive of any man more suitable for the post than himself and was bitterly disappointed when he failed to get it. Then the City Librarianship of Liverpool itself was advertised, and he girded his loins to make the assault. Once again he sought the help and support of patrons, friends, acquaintances, customers, officials - anybody whom he could persuade to favour him.

As the testimonials came in, he incorporated them into a thirty-one-page booklet, illustrated with photographs of the various libraries which he had catalogued and reorganised. Besides forty-five signed letters and twenty press notices, there were sixty names of prominent people who supported his candidature.

Letters came from Sir Edward Russell (life governor of the University of Liverpool and the University of Wales; editor of the *Liverpool Post & Mercury*: past president of the Literary & Philosophical Soc. of Liverpool and the Institute of Journalists); Joseph Wood DD MVO, headmaster of Harrow School; the Right Honourable George Guy Greville, 4th Earl of Warwick; (these commendations both referred to the cataloguing of the Warwick Castle Shakespeareana).

The forty-five letters varied greatly in their contents and wording. Some were formal statements; others had a genuine ring about them:

From **THE RIGHT HONOURABLE GEORGE GUY GREVILLE, 4th EARL OF WARWICK.**
Warwick Castle.
Lord Warwick is much obliged to Mr Jaggard. The catalogue of the library is very satisfactory, for which he thanks him very much.

THE DOWAGER COUNTESS OF AYLESFORD is very pleased with the Catalogue made by Mr Wm Jaggard.

Lower down in the social scale, however, the tributes were much more eloquent.

The Chief Constable (and book collector for many years) said *"impossible to find a gentleman more suitable"*. The Deputy Coroner spoke of *"your deep knowledge of books and your readiness to impart knowledge to others"*.

Edward Rae, the chairman of the Liverpool Stock Exchange, regarded him as a *"deep student, endowed with infinite perseverance, order and method, to say nothing of his hereditary association with English literature"*.

The best tribute of all, however, came from a writer, Dixon Scott (author of *Liverpool* and contributor to the *Liverpool Courier*) who wrote:

> *... it gives me much happiness to confess, more frankly than I have yet had the courage to do, how deeply I admire your immense bibliographical gifts and attainments ...*
>
> *... it has always seemed to me a little tragic, indeed, that the circumstances of your trade make it impossible for the general public to draw similar drafts upon your quite exceptional knowledge ...*
>
> *... in assuring you of the heartiness with which I wish you success in the candidature, I am actuated far less by any desire to be of service to you than by an eagerness to be of service to the readers and writers of Liverpool.*

WJ, armed with this battery of superlatives, was still deploring his lack of influence with the Selection Committee themselves. His only friend on the Library Committee, he said, was an Irishman whose age and poor health handicapped his support in the matter. His witty aphorism - *'while Committees rarely choose the worst man, they invariably reject the best'* - did nothing to raise WJ's spirits.

His opinion of the Library Committee, apart from his Irish friend, was not complimentary. His testimonial booklet, he said, *"ought to create an impression on* the minds of the retired tinkers, bakers, publicans and other 'cultured' gentlemen who so ably mismanage our civic affairs."

In April 1909, the City Council announced their choice; out of eighty-three applications, they had decided upon a Mr Shaw, from the local Athenaeum, Church Street. WJ was not even in the shortlist. He immediately criticised the appointment on the ground that the chosen applicant was a man of fifty; this was too old, he said, for the job, the librarian should be in his forties (WJ was forty-two).

To a friend he described the successful applicant as a *"man of mediocre ability, but possessed of political influence, which weighs far heavier than talent. I am not in the least disappointed. It fulfils my forecast."*

Andy Jaggard
In all of my grandfather's writings there is very little by way of reflection on his own character ... or weaknesses, but writing to a friend, he did reveal a little about his own philosophy and behaviour:

> *It is an unfortunate defect of mine, wanting to put this old awry world straight and all the crooked individuals in it – and I am too impatient to work by circumlocution as the crafty ones do. I like to go straight to the fault or the point. So when I come across a square peg in a round hole (like his Majesty 'Sidney Lee') I am promptly found tilting at a windmill, like Don Quixote.*

Before we leave Liverpool, as it were, let's contrast WJ's ability to go "straight to the fault" with Gerald's more romantic view of the city of his birth (and of the trams).First WJ complaining about those annoying, noisy trams outside his bookshop:

Shakespeare Press

The Life and Death of a Stratford Bookshop *(Unpublished book) c.1974*

Gerald Jaggard

WJ

Dear Sir,

<u>*Tramway repairs*</u>

May I venture to draw your personal attention to a grievance upon which I have twice written in vain to Mr Mallins.

Something like 300 or more cars pass our door daily, the <u>needless</u> noise they cause not merely gives annoyance, it actually interferes with business. Yesterday a customer walked out after endeavouring in vain to shout the title of a book she wanted in a hurry. It was impossible to hear through the tram roar, grind, and screech.

I have discovered two of the chief causes of the excessive noise. Just opposite my Dale Street shop is a rail joint so worn away that there is a hole about ½ inch deep in the steel itself. Every passing car gives a lurch and loud jolt on jumping this hole.

Then again, all the overhead wires at this spot are hung quite <u>two feet too low</u>. They depress all the trolley poles and set up a hideous whistling and screeching. Another potent cause of needless noise is the protecting board round the base (of the trams) near the wheels, which acts as a sound box. If these boards were replaced by a strong wire network, it would allow the sound to escape.

Trusting you will endeavour to get something done,

Yours truly, W. Jaggard

Probably my father would have liked to return to the days of the old horse-drawn tramcars, which had been superseded not many years before this.

For me and my brothers, the trams and the Mersey ferries were the two main delights of Liverpool, and we never failed to patronise both forms of transport when, as schoolboys living in Stratford, we re-visited the city of our birth. To us, there was something friendly and secure about these lumbering creatures. Their paintwork, a deep chocolate, was enticing, and their warm odour had a reassuring tang about it. Their drivers, enveloped in huge overcoats and wearing heavy gauntlets, stood in the open fronts to manipulate the controls. How fascinating it was to watch them turning the twin vertical handles which governed brake and acceleration. How we longed to step into their place and guide the great monster on its gentle and predictable way through the crowded streets. Staying with our aunt in Aigburth Road, the week's stay would always include at least one visit to a theatre in the city centre, and we went by tram. From the safe but lofty seats on the upper deck, we would gaze with fascination at the glittering shops, the seamen's dives and the thronging pedestrians on the pavements. Lascars from the merchant ships, Chinamen, turbaned Indians, Africans - only London itself could rival the cosmopolitan population of this great port.

As for the Mersey ferries, they were a legend in themselves; small wonder that, years later, Gerry and the Pacemakers (themselves a Liverpool product) produced a song about the Mersey ferries.

For us the magic began as we stepped off the express train (Great Western, of course) at Woodside station, Birkenhead, and walked up the gang plank to the Mersey edge to see the twin Liver birds on the Cunard building on the opposite shore. Then the excitement of boarding the first available ferryboat and watching the murky waters churn past as we made our diagonal crossing. Arriving all too quickly, we would cross the great Landing Stage to the tram stations and scan the numbers on their upper decks and the name of Garston on the illuminated sign below, the tram that would convey us right through the city to the long and sloping Aigburth Road, at the end of whose tributary streets we could still glimpse the wide waters of the Mersey. Safely in bed in our aunt's tall house, the rumble of the trams still passing late at night would be, not an annoyance, but a kind of lullaby, assuring that we were well and truly on holiday in a great and fascinating city.

Andy Jaggard

When I read back 'Gerald's Chapter' on Liverpool I was struck by how completely different the two men were in almost every conceivable way.

WJ's feels 'caged up' dreaming of an escape to the country. He makes his extreme comments to his friend on this "monotonous, dull, and repulsive city, which has stamped its evil features on the inhabitants".

Gerald, on his return as a schoolboy to the city of his birth, can only find things to take pleasure in: the Mersey ferries with "the murky water churning past, the glittering shops and the seaman's dives, the deep chocolate trams" *with their comforting interior* "... its warm odour had a reassuring tang". *It's the pure pleasure of these sensory experiences, together with his flights of fancy, longing* "to guide the great monster on its gentle and predictable way through the crowded streets".

In later life, I can think of few people who had as many hobbies and interests as Gerald. Although he had a real talent for some of these – writing, solving fiendish crosswords, wordplay and storytelling come to mind – there were many other activities that he took part in purely for the enjoyment and pleasure they gave, reading, sketching, his watercolours, composing rhyming verse, chess, bridge, tennis, golf, watching snooker, listening to the radio, and even building ramshackle sheds in the garden.

He was naturally introverted, self-contained, he didn't need to be noticed or try to impress, although he could come to life and entertain when in the right company.

WJ in complete contrast had a desperate need to achieve, to be admired, to make his mark. With men in particular he went 'straight for the fault', he was superior, combative, aggressive and often, it would seem, angry.

It was no wonder that Gerald, a quiet and imaginative boy, found his father difficult.

In The Life and Death, *aged seventy Gerald described his boyhood memories of life with WJ at Rose Bank, his Stratford family home.*

CHAPTER 10 LIFE AT HOME WITH WJ AT 'ROSE BANK'

Andy Jaggard

In 1910 WJ and the family, his wife Emma Frances, eldest son Geoffrey, and the twins Gerald and Aubrey, made the long-planned move to Stratford-upon-Avon. The youngest, a daughter, Wendy was born in Stratford in 1912. As Gerald described in Chapter 2, WJ established his misleadingly named 'Shakespeare Press' at No. 4 Sheep Street in the Bard's home town, complete with its fake Tudor facade.

Initially the family had a rented house close to the 'tram-way' on the Shipston Road.

In 1911, one of the first publications of the Shakespeare Press was WJ's massive Shakespeare Bibliography. *It had taken him twenty-two years to compile, working mostly in his 'leisure' time. It didn't make him a fortune but enough to have a large architect-designed house built (in 1913) on the Tiddington Road, close to the River Avon and to Clopton Bridge.*

It was a beautiful house, although I never visited it, or even had it pointed out to me.

Looking back, this was very strange as our family home was only one mile away in Tiddington. We passed the house almost every day on short car journeys to school in Stratford, usually in one of my father's old bangers.

After completing the research for this book, I now understand why Gerald never talked about his boyhood home.

In The Life and Death Gerald describes the house, the joy of punting on the Avon, his elder brother's tempestuous personality, similar to his father, and WJ's many hobbies and obsessions.

The Life and Death of a Stratford Bookshop *(Unpublished book) c. 1974*

Gerald Jaggard

The large rectangular garden at the back of the house was a tangle of fruit trees and vegetable patches. Relaxation was impossible, there was not a square foot of grass. Over the road in front there was the river garden. A place to enjoy the summer sunshine? No. It was completely devoted to that utilitarian vegetable, the potato. We three boys, and such male cousins as happened to be staying with us, knew all about their presence. We formed the 'potato brigade' which, under paternal supervision, did the planting every year. There was not even a boat in which to explore the (then) beautiful stretch of the Avon leading to Alveston.

We got round this by persuading the genial Mr Rose at the nearby boathouse to lend us a punt during the weekdays, for the princely sum of one pound per season. We three boys poled or paddled our way upstream (much more exciting than downstream), up past 'Avoncliffe', the great, white house which literally hung on the riverbank, past Bird's Corner, so shallow on the meadow side, so treacherously deep on the inhabited side. Towards Alveston Mill we would come to the shallows, where the Avon rushed turbulently over pebbles, and it was necessary, or so we persuaded ourselves, to leap overboard and push the boat on into deeper waters. I suppose we took some risks. Not one of us could swim, and in those days the varying depths of the river, its deep holes and clinging riverweed caused many tragedies.

We were always hearing about them, and indeed quite a few happened opposite our river garden. My father, a strong swimmer himself, was called upon quite often to give assistance. Unhappily, the call usually came much too late, and all he could do was to advise the solitary policeman with his grappling hook where to cast it to the best advantage. Father was working on the potato patch when one call came and, having ascertained that there was no hope of the victim being found alive, he went back to the house and carefully changed from old gardening clothes into his bathing-dress before sallying out to the rescue, or rather the recovery of the body.

I never thought of it much at the time, but looking back, I realise that my father, a bookseller all his life, was quite unlike the popular image of a person in this sedentary occupation. In plays and novels, they are so often depicted as frail bespectacled figures, poring over their books, or perched precariously on the top step of their library ladder, searching for a book in the upper shelves. My father was just over six feet high, bespectacled certainly, but immensely strong and fond of many outdoor pursuits. Tennis, cycling, walking, climbing, fishing, photography he indulged in them all. Riding he never took to, probably because of the expense involved, and he never owned or drove a car. 'Rose Bank', his self-designed and treasured residence in the Tiddington Road, had no garage and indeed no space for a car to stand in front of the house during his lifetime. When, after his death, it fell into other hands, they cut down a magnificent magnolia tree to make a drive. This shocked me and my family. It would have driven William Jaggard into a murderous frenzy.

Like the celebrated Forsytes of John Galsworthy's novels, he loved his property, and that included not only bricks and mortar, but all his possessions. Having built up his bank balance the hard way, he was excessively careful in his spending. Yet, by an odd quirk (and he had many of these) he was a gambler. Backing horses or greyhounds he regarded as "a wicked waste" (a favourite phrase), yet he would spend pounds on competition entries in 'Titbits' and 'Answers', fancying his ability to produce a witty phrase that would bring the fabulous reward of £500 cash or 'a Pound a week for Life'. He once purchased a large number of issues of 'Home Notes' to obtain multiple entries for a contest. After spending hours filling in scores of alternative lines, he announced gleefully that he could not possibly fail to win. He failed to win, and I shudder to think of the explosive correspondence he conducted for weeks afterwards with the unfortunate organisers.

On another occasion he entered a contest which involved collecting coupons from 'Black Cat' cigarettes. A non-smoker himself, he saw nothing incongruous in buying dozens of packets just for the coupons. The cigarettes were stored in a large cupboard in the dining room. As usual, alas, no prizes came his way, and the cigarettes remained in the cupboard until we boys discovered them, and my elder brother sampled a few. I think he was sixteen or seventeen at the time, but when the 'crime' was discovered, the row that followed was out of all proportion to the offence. The blazing denunciation was not so much for the actual smoking as for abstracting goods that did not belong to the purloiner. Such incidents did not improve relations between father and eldest son, and as Geoffrey possessed much of his father's tempestuous nature, it ultimately resulted in his departure from 'Rose Bank' to earn his living as a cub reporter. He did well in journalism, enjoying the bohemian life and unconventional hours of the roving reporter.

From a brief spell in murky Wednesbury, Geoffrey went to Leicester, and from there to his birthplace Liverpool, where he settled happily for twelve years with the *Liverpool Post*. At one house where he stayed, he was known as the 'human cyclone' but held his job because he was a good journalist. One assignment, however, that he did not enjoy was to cover the activities of numerous amateur dramatic companies in the city and around. Such groups, in the pre-television days of the 1920s, were thick on the ground. I believe there were 250 of them in Liverpool, Birkenhead and the Wirral peninsula. I think the strain of attending a week of 'first nights' and of summing up performances which ranged from tolerable to positively ghastly, nearly got him down.

Reverting to 'Rose Bank' in those earlier days, I remember how its contents reflected my father's love of music. His days in the choir at Leamington Spa had given him a passion for singing. He had formed a Glee Society in Liverpool (nowadays it would be called a Choral Society) who would meet in various homes and lustily sing part-songs, roundelays of the Elizabethan era. An upright pianoforte with the carved face of Beethoven reposed in the dining room, and one thing I did envy about my father was his ability to sit down and strum a tune at will - he never played from music.

In the hall were two further music machines. They were piano-players which by themselves would not play a note, but when laboriously pushed up against the pianoforte the keys could be operated mechanically. The music roll was inserted, the bellows operated by foot pedal, and the ensuing torrent of music played with 'expression' by manipulation of the right levers. He probably picked them up at an auction sale, but why it was necessary to buy two, both in working order, I never found out.

Late at night, when we children were in bed, my father would demonstrate the player to his friends, a demonstration that we could clearly hear, and we always waited for the inevitable boast "this machine will play chords that no human hand can compass!" Naturally we boys were expressly forbidden to use the piano-player. We were not supposed to have the skill to adjust it or the strength to play the pedals. However, we found weekdays a convenient time to falsify this supposition, when by teamwork we brought player and piano into accurate contact (rather like joining the two parts of a space machine) and played selections from *The Mikado*, *The Gondoliers* and *Patience* to our hearts delight. The selections were not vocal, so we became familiar with the notes of Arthur Sullivan long before we heard the words of W.S. Gilbert.

Of course, a Glee Society was founded in Stratford, meeting at 'Rose Bank' once a week. We boys attended one session only, the trouble being that we were quite unable to contain our mirth when the paternal baritone shook the rafters. We were banished to the kitchen to get on with our schoolwork.

CHAPTER 11 WJ's MISSIONS AND MAKING ENEMIES

" Pox on it – I'll not meddle with him" Twelfth Night Act III Scene 3

Andy Jaggard
Gerald believed that WJ had first set his sights on 'his three great missions', during his apprenticeship at Warwick Castle, cataloguing the collection:

The first to produce a complete bibliography of the poet's works.

The second to trace the family descent back to the famous printer of Shakespeare's plays.

And the third to establish a bookshop in the poet's home town and to become either custodian of the Birthplace or Librarian of the Shakespeare Memorial Theatre.

He was already part way towards achieving mission number three in 1910 having established his bookshop, the 'Shakespeare Press', although as Gerald knew his ambitions did not stop with the bookshop, "he still felt a strong urge to wake up its inhabitants, and to shape or dominate its institutions."

WJ's compulsion to be a man of influence and closely involved in the life of the town began even before he had made the move to Stratford. He was already meddling in the small town's affairs.

Gerald Jaggard – The Life and Death of a Stratford Bookshop (Unpublished book) 1974

The Birthplace Trustees were considering replacing their secretary and custodian Mr Richard Savage. Some leading townsfolk thought him ill-used, among them the authoress Miss Marie Corelli. She had strong views upon the way the town and theatre did their business, and made active use of her money, and pen, to combat injustice. In this she was joined by Mrs Stopes, and WJ wrote to the latter, to put his oar in:

WJ

If, (as you suspect, and confided to me) the Board (of Trustees) mean to get rid of poor Savage I shall most certainly stick up for him. If he retires, he is strongly entitled to a pension, which can be easily arranged if humanity prevails, and I have a voice there.

Am glad to hear Miss Corelli is going to do as you wish over Savage's book. I believe she would do a great deal more if people would but make allowance for her nature and little short-comings. But on the contrary the Stratfordians never give her credit for good motives, and utterly disregard the hard life she has led, the cause, I am convinced, of those little drawbacks in an otherwise able and admirable woman.

This is the first criticism of 'the Stratfordians' that WJ has made, but possibly he was referring to the 'Establishment' – the theatre and council officials rather than the ordinary townsfolk. This letter was written before the move to Stratford, but soon he was to be among them, trying to carry out his own little reforms and meeting with the same lack of appreciation. The little market town of 8,000 people was much too small for the tempestuous personality of the Edwardian authoress, as it was also to be for WJ himself. Small wonder that they were drawn together for a time in mutual indignation at the ingratitude of the town's leaders.

Feuding with Sidney Lee

My father usually got on well with women authors. Even in the sensitive field of Shakespearean studies and research, he not only approved of their work, but frequently gave them help and advice. The reason for this was that they invariably recognised him as a man of intellect and vast Shakespearean knowledge, adding to the lustre of his family name and descent.

With male authors it was a different story. They were inclined to come up with theories with which he disagreed, and, crime of crimes, with criticism of the Tudor Jaggard who had published the First Folio.

For example, WJ's relations with Sidney Lee, Shakespearean scholar and writer (later to be knighted) resembled those of two belligerent captains of warring galleons. Sidney Lee, in a book or literary article, would fire a broadside into the reputation of Shakespeare's printer - WJ would return fire by personal missive or in whatever newspaper or journal was handy. Mutual friends (Charles Edward Flower among them) would try to negotiate a peace, but before very long, the guns would be blazing again. WJ never forgot or forgave an injury, whether against himself or his revered ancestor.

In April 1908, Sidney Lee himself tried to heal the breach by letter, and this was the reply he received:

Dear Sir,

On my return home today, I found your letter awaiting attention, and hasten to say that I am in entire accord with its general sentiment.

There are many points in your writings upon which you and I are at variance, but on the few occasions I have expressed dissatisfaction I have endeavoured to avoid personalities. You occupy such a prominent position compared with those ignorant critics who first assailed the early Jaggards that I confess to no small surprise at your accepting, using and magnifying their statements, without enquiry or caution. For instance, your life of the poet has had a wide sale. It contains many unjust, ungenerous, and highly personal aspersions upon my ancestors, all of which, coming from you, will be accepted by your readers generally as gospel. Indeed, one rarely finds the Jaggards alluded to in your books and articles unaccompanied by abuse. If these accusations could be substantiated, then I could only hang my head in shame – but!

If, as I gather, you rely for your 'facts' upon the forger J P Collier, and others of his period, I fear your reputation as a historian is built on quick sands.

At present I am sure you hardly realise how much credit is due to the Jaggard family for rescuing at least twenty of Shakespeare's plays in the nick of time from oblivion. In fact the history of the Jaggards is more intimately bound up with that of the dramatist than any other publisher. I am glad to hear you nourish no real bias against the Jaggards. Knowing this, your attitude towards them in the past is very difficult to understand. You have condemned them wholesale without trial, without shadow of proof. To say the least, this is very un-English, but let it pass.

WJ continues the lengthy letter by saying that his name had been mooted as suitable for election to the Board of Trustees of Shakespeare's Birthplace, and he wondered whether Mr Lee thought it would be acceptable.

I have (unfortunately) no record of Mr Lee's reply to this naive request, but the existing Trustees must have promptly closed their ranks, for WJ was never elected as a member of their Board.

WJ's tolerance of Sidney Lee had been steadily diminishing and vanished completely when he heard him described as "<u>the</u> authority on Shakespeare, and an expert in the field of Shakespearean bibliography". He promptly sent to the *Stratford Herald* (under a pen name), a list of twenty-five questions on the latter subject, challenging him to answer them from memory. The challenge was not taken up.

Governor of the Shakespeare memorial

Another distinction WJ was very anxious to attain was to become a governor of the 'Shakespeare Memorial' (the Stratford theatre, library and picture gallery). Fortunately for his aspirations, to achieve this, all one had to do in those days, was to contribute £100 to the Memorial funds. WJ therefore informed the Memorial Librarian (his friend Mr Brassington) of his intention to contribute £100 worth of books! Typically, he explained the proposal in an elaborate letter:

> *Dear Mr Brassington,*
> *In conformity with your suggestion, I confirm my verbal offer of One Hundred Pounds worth of books from the original Jaggard Press (being duplicates of my unique collection) to the Memorial Library, in order to qualify as a Governor of that admirable institution and shall be glad if you will kindly lay it before your Council at a convenient time.*
> *My reasons for this step are threefold*
> > *(1)   Because I take the deepest interest in this noble project of Mr & Mrs Charles Flower, and desire to be associated in promoting its welfare.*

(2) Because your Library is a fitting place for examples of a press so intimately connected with the poet.

(3) Because your income has so many demands upon it as to exclude from the range of purchase such valuable books.

Upon hearing the decision of your Council, I will take the earliest opportunity of submitting an inventory in detail of the books I propose to give.

WJ and Marie Corelli – Kindred spirits

Andy Jaggard

Gerald had already made mention of Marie Corelli*. He would only have been an impressionable young man of nineteen by the time of her death in 1924. He seems to have had a fascination with her. In Stratford Mosaic *(1960)* he devoted a chapter to her. She also made good 'copy'; she had a gondola on the Avon but sacked her Italian gondolier after he got drunk one night at Stratford Rowing Club. These days it's doubtful whether most people have even heard of her.

----

*Marie Corelli.

From an article by Nick Birch

In the 1890s, Marie Corelli's novels were eagerly devoured by millions in England, America and the colonies. Her readers ranged from Queen Victoria and Gladstone, to the poorest of shop girls. In all she wrote thirty books, the majority of which were phenomenal bestsellers. Despite the fact that her novels were either ignored or belittled by the critics, at the height of her success she was the bestselling and most highly paid author in England.

In 1899, after a serious illness and sick of the "spite and meanness" in London, she moved to Stratford-upon-Avon with her devoted companion, Bertha Vyver. In Stratford, Marie Corelli took up the cause of protecting Shakespeare's legacy, opened fetes and discovered a gift for public speaking. Unfortunately, the eager enthusiasm with which she got involved in local issues, and an apparent lack of sensitivity did not endear her to many of the town's male-dominated hierarchy. Nevertheless, she bestowed money on many worthy causes, and became one of the first true conservationists, preserving the towns' heritage.

Gerald Jaggard - The Life and Death of a Stratford Bookshop (Unpublished book) 1974

When my father arrived in Stratford, the Edwardian novelist Marie Corelli had moved from Old Town to her established residence 'Mason Croft' with its grounds, paddock and a kitchen garden across the road (Chestnut Walk). There Marie reigned in state, the whole residence exuding her presence and personality. The visitors were left in no doubt as to who occupied the premises, as they were greeted at the front door itself by the author's monogram 'MC' set above the lintel in coloured glass, the same insignia being displayed over the great fireplace in the music room.

Behind the house, at the end of the flower garden and lawns, a somewhat isolated stone archway led towards the gazebo. The latter, modelled after an Elizabethan watchtower, was Marie's den, a place to which she could retreat and do her writing. In the house itself Marie had a 'winter garden' a kind of indoor greenhouse, where, besides the exotic flowers, she had canaries and other feathered songsters to preserve the illusion of eternal summer.

As an accomplished musician herself, she made great use of the spacious music room, and it was a convenient place in which to entertain her gifted friends. As it borders the street, the strains of classical melody could often be shared by appreciative passers-by.

Here too, she entertained other intelligentsia - the artists, poets, and writers whom she admired or wished to impress.

For a year or two at any rate, my father and Marie were kindred spirits. Both felt the same strong urge to reform Shakespeare's town, to wake up its inhabitants, to shape, or dominate its institutions, from the Shakespeare theatre down to the local amateur operatic society. Both had a common weapon - the pen. Neither of them were great orators, but both could frame a biting letter, a pungent article, and a devastating pamphlet to further their views. When the victims of these onslaughts retaliated, both the assailants complained bitterly of insult and ingratitude, Marie also resenting the discrimination against her sex.

My father and my mother, Emma Frances would therefore be invited along to 'Mason Croft' and Marie would engage in long intellectual conversations with WJ, giving an occasional patronising smile to my mother, whom she thought incapable of rising to the standard of conversation in progress.*

At his bookshop, WJ had a small Queen-Anne type occasional chair, which I found there when I took over. All four legs had been shortened by several inches, and this was the chair which Marie occupied when she called in at No. 4 Sheep Street for a chat.

Andy Jaggard.
* This is only the second mention by Gerald of his mother in his unfinished book, why so few? The first about her 'filling in the slips' for WJ's bibliography suggests she was an accepting and willing assistant for this onerous and tedious task. This second comment, with Marie Corelli "giving her an occasional patronising smile, whom she thought incapable of rising to the standard of conversation in progress" demonstrates Gerald's sensitivity to how his mother was being treated. Perhaps Gerald didn't like to make his own comments about his mother's character. Was she quiet and unassuming? They were to spend many years together.

The Bibliography

Gerald in his Stratford Mosaic *(1960) describes how his father's* Shakespeare Bibliography "was already in the printers' hands when, in 1910 he tore up the roots of city life and, with family books and furniture, travelled to Stratford".

In 1911, the Bibliography made its appearance. WJ was rightly proud of the immense feat, and never shy of a little self-promotion, produced a Shakespeare Press Pamphlet with a compilation of over forty independent opinions.

In his speech at Stratford-upon-Avon Town Hall on Shakespeare's birthday, 1911, Frank Benson described the Bibliography as, "A work which only Mr Jaggard would, or could, undertake."

"*The maker of this wonderful book well deserves to be included in the list of great Shakespeare critics, commentators, and editors. Its range is marvellously wide. Students of Shakespeare will welcome this admirably printed volume of the Shakespeare Press. In its combination of valuable information, carefully collected and collated, its wealth of allusion and suggestion. Its concise yet lucid style, and its wonderful comprehensiveness, the work stands out as one of the noblest tributes to Shakespeare that the world has so far produced.*" Manchester Courier

This was Gerald's more reserved description (from Stratford Mosaic*):*

Gerald Jaggard

My father had spared no pains to make it an attractive volume. It is a foolscap quarto, identical in shape with the First Folio and containing over 700 pages. There are more than 36,000 distinct entries. The subject has been analysed, dissected and microscopically examined on all sides. Obscure beginnings and sources have been traced and followed through to remote consequences. Every scrap or shred of Shakespearean information which can shed light on the poet, or his works is duly preserved and indexed.

Andy Jaggard

Without doubt WJ had achieved his first great mission. Unfortunately, as Gerald described, "Like most great works of reference it was received with acclamation, and agreed to be indispensable to all literary workers in the Shakespeare field, but sold extremely slowly."

By 1914, sales of his 'life's work' were still disappointing so WJ had planned a trip to America in March of that year to publicise his immense Bibliography.

As for his second great mission – tracing the family descent, it would seem that some people already accepted that WJ was a direct descendant of the Tudor Printer, William Jaggard ... if you take the words from some of the reviews of the Bibliography at face value.

"Mr Wm Jaggard of to-day is a descendant of the William Jaggard who helped Heminge and Condell to produce the First Folio in 1623 ... " The Athenaeum

"We congratulate and thank Mr Jaggard and note the historic appropriateness that decreed that the accomplishment of such a work by a descendant of the very Jaggard to whom we owe the preservation of an 'unparalleled literary heritage'." Literary World

*"The present-day William Jaggard, **sixth of his line**, has become known the world over in connection with his life work, published last April, on Shakespeare's birthday."* T.P.'s Weekly

This was wonderful publicity and no doubt WJ was delighted that so many commentators were already prepared to describe him as the direct lineal descendant.

We know that by 1914 his research had already occupied innumerable hours of research, travel and correspondence. He had travelled all over the country in his single-minded quest, to London, to Wales, to Lancashire, to Derbyshire and in particular to Cambridgeshire.

Despite the acclaim and the status that he had already achieved, he was now determined to prove his famous lineage beyond any doubt. WJ's Bibliography had been published on 23rd April 1911 – Shakespeare's birthday. WJ planned to publish his Jaggard family tree in time for another significant Shakespearean celebration.

Four years on from his arrival in Stratford, WJ's attempts to dominate the town's institutions and his meddling in the town's affairs had already earned him several enemies.

But world events were about to cast a shadow over these machinations and petty jealousies in the small market town with the outbreak of the 'war-to-end-all-wars', the Great War of 1914 to 1918.

CHAPTER 12 WJ IN THE FIRST WORLD WAR

Andy Jaggard

Gerald was just ten years old, and WJ forty-six in 1914. With his military background (in the Liverpool Volunteers) we wanted to find out about Captain Jaggard's war service, his experiences in the Great War and how he spent his time during these difficult years.

First, just a few months before the outbreak of the war, WJ made a visit to America in March 1914. This was both to publicise his Shakespeare Bibliography *and to give a lecture to a Literary Society in New York. WJ had also spotted an additional business opportunity.*

Despite WJ's failure to sell Henry Folger his First Folio back in 1903, he still clearly had the avid collector of Shakespeareana on his radar. By 1914 the Folger's Shakespearean collection already included a large, although unknown, number of First Folios but Henry and Emily Folger were also in the market for all manner of acquisitions — playbills, books, paintings, furniture and relics. The Folger Institute in Washington had sent me some information confirming the details of a Shakespearean 'relic' that WJ had sold to Henry Folger during his 1914 visit.

Back in 1847, the Shakespeare Birthplace Trust in Stratford raised money to buy the house where Shakespeare was said to be born. (The campaign was successful because Barnum, the American impresario and exhibitor of oddities, had plans to buy the house, dismantle it and ship it to America.) The house was saved from its American fate and during the renovation some oak beams were removed. Someone had the bright idea of making a wooden casket out of one of the spare beams.

WJ contacted Folger and offered him this ancient wooden casket, "made from Shakespeare's House". *Folger was keen on the idea. During his visit to America, WJ met up with Henry Folger who was happy to add the relic to his collection. A description of the wooden casket is kept in their archives* (see appendix).

We know that WJ also gave a lecture to The Macdowell Club of New York City, 108 West 55th Street, *a Literary Society (now defunct). WJ kept the invitation card, amongst his 'treasures' for* Tuesday Evening, 3rd March at half past eight o'clock.

An Illustrated Lecture by MR WILLIAM JAGGARD from Stratford-upon-Avon, England

Mr Jaggard is a direct descendant of the authorised printer of the famous First Folio of Shakespeare's Dramas of 1623.

THE SUBJECT: SHAKESPEARE'S COUNTRY FROM ROMAN DAYS TO NOW

I imagine that WJ's lecture was comprehensive.

We discovered that later during his stay WJ was interviewed by an American journalist for an article, 'Twenty Years with Shakespeare – The Bibliographer-Descendant of Shakespeare's First Publisher'

The journalist's article based on his interview with WJ did not disappoint. It was 'typical WJ'. The American journalist gave 'free rein' to WJ's 'fairy-tale' stories, his unashamed self-promotion and some highly dubious claims.

The article by the apparently star-struck interviewer starts with WJ's romantic tale of Shakespeare, forced from the seclusion of Stratford by his father's financial difficulties, *journeying to London,* making the acquaintance of the printer William Jaggard who, published some of the boy's work in a pamphlet called *The*

Passionate Pilgrim. (No mention was made of the 'piracy'.) Since then, there have been eleven generations of the Jaggard family and today another William Jaggard of Stratford-upon-Avon ...

posed another copy (unbound) of the "unique" 1603 *Hamlet*, this time lacking the title page but possessing the priceless last leaf. Rooney secured the copy for one shilling, reprinted the last leaf, and then sold the volume for seventy pounds to Boone, a London bookseller, from whom J. O. Halliwell bought it for £120 and transferred it to the British Museum at a further advance, where it now rests for aye.

This is only a sample of hundreds of discoveries made by Mr. Jaggard in the course of his work. At one time he proved the fraudulency of a set of volumes purporting to be 1619 quartos by showing, among other things, that the paper on which the books were printed was made at a considerably later date.

Mr. Jaggard's work, resulting in a book which is rapidly becoming indispensable to the greatest scholars of the world, is perhaps most remarkable in that it has been done by a man whose scholastic education extended no further than the grammar school. Circumstances deprived him of university study, and forced him to earn his living at seventeen. Nearly all his education, therefore, has come thru his work with Shake-

Photograph by Paul Thompson
THE PRESENT WILLIAM JAGGARD
The compiler of the only complete bibliography of Shakespeare has devoted twenty-two years to the task

There follows a glowing description of WJ's Bibliography, in every sense a labour of love, done as an avocation in his spare time. *After documenting some of the* little romantic incidents *(book related) from the great Bibliography, there is a sense that WJ is getting a little carried away in his responses to the gullible interviewer's questions.*

This is only a sample of hundreds of discoveries made by Jaggard in the course of his work. At one time he proved the fraudulency of a set of volumes purporting to be 1619 quartos by showing among other things, that the paper on which the books were printed was made at a considerably later date ...

The piracy of the 'False Folio' was described in Chapter 8.

The famous discovery of 1907 was attributed to the painstaking research by Professor Alfred W. Pollard and W.W. Gregg, who as the result of a piece of brilliant detective bibliography, established in 1907 that all the ten plays were printed in that year (1619) and not in the false dates on the title pages. This was proved by the testing of watermarks and the comparison of type.

I have no evidence that WJ had any involvement at all with this discovery. If he had he would certainly have publicised this elsewhere.

There is one other interesting comment. Clearly WJ had been talking about his education. The journalist describes how Jaggard's bibliography was rapidly becoming indispensable to the greatest scholars of the world and that this is perhaps most remarkable in that it has been done by a man whose scholastic education extended no further than the grammar school. Circumstances deprived him of university study, and forced him to earn his living at seventeen.

This is quite ironic, as WJ a few years later, did exactly the same to Gerald, and his twin Aubrey, depriving them of a university education.

WJ GOES TO WAR

A few months after WJ's return to England the Great War began. There is nothing in Gerald's book on the impact of the war. We do know that, because of his military experience in the Liverpool Volunteers, WJ was called up for war service in 1914 as a Recruiting Officer for Warwickshire.

During one of the lockdowns of 2020, I was trying to get hold of a Shakespeare Press publication by Captain Wm Jaggard – Army Records Human and Humorous *(1919) which I hoped would have information on his role and experiences in the war. The Birthplace Trust Archives had a copy, but their archives were closed during the pandemic.*

WJ's war service around the battlegrounds of France during the War (1914–1918) turned out to be both bizarre and comical, although it took many months to discover the strange story.

I did eventually manage to obtain Army Records Human and Humorous. *This was bought from an online rare books dealer for £12. It was published just after the end of the war in 1919. It was not quite what I expected. The publication turned out to be, not even a booklet, but just three sheets extracted from the front of* 'B.A.R.' (Book Auction Records).

Of the three sheets, one page has WJ complaining that he has, for five years, been struggling with adversity in the shape of inability to complete the 'Ten Years Index' to 'B.A.R.' through having been called up to war service. *(Later I was to understand the significance of WJ's obsession with his* 'Ten Years Index' *– a massive reference book compiling all the data from his regular book auction publications.)*

Another page is taken up promoting a list of CAPTAIN WILLIAM JAGGARD'S WRITINGS, *which includes:*

Shakespeare Bibliography, 1911 (greeted with world-wide appreciation)

And now for the humorous section. WJ describes how, "finally in Happier National Circumstances", *he regards this,* as the "Holiday Number, when the season's work was done, and one felt licensed to frivol." *His* "original article would immensely aid the future historian of these times, giving the real human touch, and sidelight."

The humorous quotations were taken from correspondence with the Army Records Office.

WJ apologises that "the language of these fair ladies is not always fit for print, but their unconscious humour often redeems their coarseness."

Here are three samples:

1. Sir, unless I get my husband's pay at once I shall be compelled to lead an immortal life.

2. Sir, My Bill has been put in charge of a Spitoon (platoon). Shall I get more pay?

3. Sir, I have been in bed with the doctor for three days but he does not seem to do me any good. If you don't send at once I shall have to have another one.

That was it, quite funny, but there was nothing on his experiences of the war or of the battlefields of France.

Over a year later, as the result of a search for newspapers and magazines linked to Captain William Jaggard, I found several articles from 1924 all telling the same story of how he had spent most of his time in France during the war.

The Graphic – 19th July 1924 – Utopia in Book land – By James Milne

Captain William Jaggard of the Shakespeare Press, Stratford-upon-Avon, has just issued a volume of Bibliography with a preface that reads like a short story. It is a volume of General Index to Book Auction Records – 1902–1912. In compiling this piece of stupendous industry Captain William Jaggard was mostly single-handed, his assistants having deserted their tasks one by one. It was carted about all over France during the war.

The next extract from The Halifax Courier *is my favourite madcap version of this extraordinary story.*

The Halifax Daily Courier and Guardian – 6th June 1924

COMPILED IN THE TRENCHES

Many Misadventures of Massive Work

Romance and Adventure are revealed in the General Index to Book Auction Records just issued by the Shakespeare Press (500 copies: 65s net)

The Compiler Captain William Jaggard is ten years overdue in his ten years task.

First the commission to do it came three years late. Then after a fair start, five of the seven assistants deserted gradually, dismayed at the drudgery, and the chief, attempting himself to carry on their labour, was threatened with blindness.

Then war came, and with the Royal Warwickshires, the work was humped about over France growing steadily in bulk and weight with the additions of every leisure moment. Total 'Avoir Dupois' Three Hundredweight. The death of the proprietor and his successor, and of the chief 'comp', labour troubles, General Election, and a narrow escape from drowning added to the calamity of breaking faith with subscribers.

But it is here at last, with hundreds of thousands of entries, on 1,150 pages …

Unbelievable.

'THE FRAUDS AND THE CRANKS'

WJ spent a great deal of time during the war years on research, on writing up his notes and penning various essays in preparation for future lectures. Despite some forays into philosophy and the analysis of some eccentric books, his two favourite topics which he returned to time and time again were:

1. *Defending his famous ancestor's reputation.*

2. *Attacking the 'frauds, cranks, and naysayers' who were besmirching William Shakespeare's reputation.*

He knew all their stories.

The Baconians, Lord Strange, Earl of Derby, Ignatius Donnelly who claimed the First Folio was a Great Cryptogram, W.J.J. Looney *(yes, really)*, who insisted that the real author was Edward de Vere, the seventeenth Earl of Oxford *and many more.*

WJ was the self-appointed defender of the reputations of William Jaggard and William Shakespeare.

If this was another lifelong mission, proving his direct descent from William, the printer, was his lifelong obsession.

JAGGARD family jottings through ten centuries

Most significant for our own mission to discover the truth about the direct descent were his hand-written notes from his many research trips around the country

WJ, in his thorough and painstaking manner, recorded the many details on scores of pieces of card and sheets of paper, now faded and yellowing, from well over a hundred years ago. Amongst his essays and lecture notes there were also some pages titled Jaggard family jottings through ten centuries. *When I first browsed through WJ's papers at Christmas 2019 these pages were mixed up with his essays and other notes but eventually I managed to reassemble most of the document. It was written in his neat script with many changes and additions.*

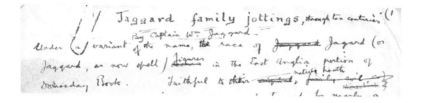

The document makes reference to some books pre 1914 as well as including his notes looking forward to the 1923 Tercentenary of the First Folio.

A SELF-IMPOSED DEADLINE

In this document WJ was complaining about the lack of recognition for his famous ancestor and promising to put that right by the time of the Tercentenary in 1923:

WJ

By a strange accident all the Jaggards were omitted from Ames and Herberts' Typographical Antiquities. This probably accounts for the sparse references to them in 19th-century works of reference such as Watts' Bibliotheca Britannica, ... Anyway, due acknowledgement of William Jaggard's priceless service to literature is made in the Shakespeare Bibliography which is dedicated to him, while fuller justice to his pioneer claims is in preparation for the 1923 celebration.

In all Great Britain we have not yet recognised that he existed ... America shows more intelligence in this matter ... One must journey 4,000 miles to the North Gallery of the lovely Family Library of Congress at Washington. There you may see his name and crest emblazoned in colours among the Great Printers.

Andy Jaggard

So WJ was committed to a self-imposed deadline of the 1923 Tercentenary of the First Folio for the publication of the Jaggard family tree, proving the direct descent.

But had he published anything by 1923? There was one Shakespeare Press publication from 1921 that might provide the answer but during the lockdowns of 2020 was proving very difficult to access.

PROVING THE DIRECT DESCENT

It seemed that these 'jottings', were in effect the write-up from his ongoing research (which he started around 1890), and his hypothesis of the direct descent from "William the First" to the famous bibliographer himself, "the Sixth William".

There were several other lines of enquiry:

My own 'amateur' version of the Jaggard Tree, on Ancestry.co.uk, going back to Tudor times.

I'd also just obtained a copy of the family tree by a Jaggard relative, which had been cited on Wikipedia, as proving the direct descent.

In September 2020 I was going on holiday to Menorca for three weeks. I decided I would take all the digital information and WJ's original paperwork with me (sad I know) to attempt to make sense of all these different sources of evidence.

We would finally establish the truth, one way or another, in time for the 400th anniversary of the First Folio in 2023 ... better late than never.

CHAPTER 13 GERALD – SMITTEN BY SHAKESPEARE

" ... *this is the stuff that dreams are made of* " *The Tempest Act V Scene 1*

Andy Jaggard

Gerald's other book, Stratford Mosaic – The Shakespeare Club and a Medley of Memories, *was written in the late fifties and published in 1960. My sister, Anthea, remembers as a child overhearing Gerald and Diana having several tense late-night discussions with Gerald worried about the cost of having his book published. Eventually Sir Edward Salt, his father-in-law, helped finance the book. They say it still commands a very good price in second-hand bookshops.*

When I re-read it I was interested in the few sections on his father. Gerald was in his mid-fifties when he completed Stratford Mosaic, *WJ had been dead for over ten years, but there are only a few, mostly polite and respectful references to the man, with just a couple of 'veiled' comments. This is very different from* The Life and Death. *What had happened in the intervening years from 1960 to 1974 to cause him to cast aside the 'reserved and correct' Gerald and finally speak his mind and express his very strong feelings?*

I was also looking for any personal, autobiographical sections in Stratford Mosaic *... and fortunately, there are a few.*

In the chapter on THE OLD MEMORIAL THEATRE Gerald describes how he started to visit the theatre in 1912 (when he was eight). It then covers his teenage years (he was ten when the First World War started and fourteen when it ended). In some charming passages he describes his growing love for the theatre.

In 1920, aged sixteen, he was taken out of school by his father, no mention of this, but by 1923, he was working and had been enrolled in commerce classes. With his twin Aubrey he wrote and directed his first production.

Of his father in this chapter there is no mention at all. However, Gerald writes warmly about a man called Archie Flower, a local businessman and 'servant of the town', who it seems was something of a father figure to Gerald and the antithesis of his real father.

And finally of his vivid memories of the dramatic destruction by fire of the Old Memorial Theatre.

Extracts from, Stratford Mosaic 1960 by Gerald Jaggard

The first Shakespeare Memorial Theatre was an odd-looking place! Hans Andersen would have admired it, for it was an enchanting medley of different architectural styles, with towers, spires, half-timbering, patterned brickwork, striped chimneys, and many other fancy touches. But we loved it and woe betide any visitor who made disparaging remarks. In 1912 when I started to visit it, it was just halfway through its eventful life. Nobody, of course, at the time dreamt that in another fourteen years it would be a blackened hulk.

17. The First Shakespeare Memorial Theatre – Stratford-upon-Avon.

As a small boy, I saw my first Shakespeare play. Almost inevitably, it was *The Dream* with Mendelsohn's music and local children to play the fairies. The settings were elaborate, and during the lengthy intervals one could hear sundry knockings and tappings from behind the curtain with an occasional husky curse from the stage manager. I can't say how much I got out of *The Dream*. Possibly Theseus and his lady, and an old Egeus, verged on the tedious, but to an imaginative youngster it was all thrilling, and the thrust-and-parry of the lovers' dialogue struck as deep a chord in me as did the fairy music and the rustics' foolery.

For those with small financial resources yet anxious to haunt the theatre there was only one way – the gods. We stood on a stone staircase for two or three hours until, with a clanging of iron and a rattling of bolts, the great doors were unlocked. Up the stairs we rushed, raced around the gallery passage, then dived down to our wooden pews. Perched in the front row a play-goer could be 'monarch of all he surveyed' for he was literally poised in the centre of the auditorium.

Andy Jaggard
Gerald later described an amateur production of Henry V *at the Old Memorial Theatre the year before the start of the First World War.*

Nobody can say that the youth of Stratford were not given encouragement to prove their talents during the Benson regime. This applied particularly to the boys of the Grammar School. To allow them on stage in May 1913 in an almost entirely amateur production at the height of the Shakespeare Festival seems generous enough and when one learns that it was a play (*Henry V*) that was in the season's repertoire, the limits of astonishment are reached.

I was deemed too young to take part and I was somewhat envious of a slightly older brother who was included in the French Court.

Watching the battle scene, few of us realised that in a little over a year the senior boys would be engaged in a war of hideous reality. Two of them, neighbours of mine, were the Jennings brothers, both of magnificent physique and great promise. H.A. the elder was to fall in action early in the war, H.H. after gallant service as a dispatch rider was killed soon after his eighteenth birthday.

'Supers'

Frank Benson always engaged local men as 'extras' for his crowds and armies. He tried to get men of normal proportions, but this was not always possible. The result was that a file of soldiers crossing the stage and wheeling behind the backcloth to cross again looked impressive until you spotted the tall youth with the helmet over his eyes and the tubby man with the slight limp – on their fourth time around. These stage mercenaries were known as 'supers' and were paid something like 2/6d per performance. When I volunteered with some friends to swell the ranks of the attendant nobles in Mr Bridges-Adams' productions of *Richard II* and other plays, I mentioned the word 'super' to the stage-manager and he firmly pointed out that I was not a 'super' but an 'extra gentleman'.

As a lord in *Richard II* I always remember the night when Randle Ayrton was ill, and the title role was played at short notice by Worrall Thompson. The understudy did splendidly from start to finish and was duly murdered by Piers of Exton and his body brought in a coffin to Bolingbroke. The curtain descended, and Worrall Thompson sat up in his coffin and said, "How did I do?" at which point the curtain went up again, to the applause and laughter of a delighted audience.

18. Andy Jaggard - With more than a touch of Blackadder this picture of the 'Supers' has Captain William Jaggard (back 2nd from right), and twins, Aubrey Jaggard (front, left) and Gerald Jaggard (front, 2nd from right)

Gerald Jaggard

I was still at school when I had the chance to take part in the festival, as an actual, if temporary, member of the company. My own modest connection with the company was flatteringly foreshadowed in the local paper by the announcement that 'Master Jaggard' has been engaged to play the part of Lucius in *Julius Caesar*! The implication that I had been lured from tempting contracts in other theatrical spheres was pleasant, but ill-founded. It was great fun rehearsing with the company. Mr Bridges-Adams, suave and smiling, seemed to get the best out of his company by quiet suggestion rather than more autocratic methods. James Dale, playing Brutus, dispelled my initial nervousness by encouragement and coaching.

The dress rehearsal gave me the opportunity to watch the other parts of the play. Hannam-Clark as Caesar, Basil Rathbone as a lean, handsome and sinister Cassius, Murray Carrington as a truly noble Mark Antony, and the seasoned William Calvert - a notable Casca. From a vantage point in the wings, I watched every performance throughout the season, never failing to feel tense as the moment for Caesar's death arrived. From a few feet away I watched the conspirators daubing their daggers with Caesar's 'blood'.

After this great experience, I was a keener lover of the theatre than ever, and all available shillings went on a seat in the gods. The old theatre had seven years to run, seven years in which a rich variety of plays, Shakespearean and otherwise, were to delight our eyes. It was a never-failing pleasure to come away from a summer evening's performance of *The Dream* or *As You Like It* and walk home by the moonlit river or leave the battlements of Dunsinane and the pageantry of *Richard II* to linger on the Clopton Bridge. How fortunate we were, and are, to have our theatre in a setting that rekindles the imagination, so that the matchless lines live on in our mind long after the curtain has fallen.

Andy Jaggard
Inspired by his early theatrical involvement with The Old Memorial Theatre, Gerald aged nineteen was soon planning his first amateur production, together with his twin Aubrey in 1923:

This year my brother and I made use of the Memorial Theatre Lecture Room to present our first amateur production. The room was a small theatre in itself, but the stage was so small that you could cross it in five paces. There were two tiny dressing rooms, and a scenery bay which fortunately ran the entire length of the lecture room, so that it could be used for properties and as a supplementary dressing place. We were then studying at the Stratford Technical School, which ran evening classes in commercial subjects and elocution.

Andy Jaggard
Gerald and Aubrey had been taken out of the Grammar School by WJ, when they were both sixteen years old and before finishing their education. WJ had insisted they must both start work (in clerical roles) so that they could contribute to the family finances.

Over fifty students volunteered to take part, and in order to provide them all with parts we wrote our show, *Through the Ages* in the form of an historical burlesque in several scenes with songs. Actually, it was a forerunner of *1066 and All That*. When writing it, we little knew what a profitable vogue this type of entertainment was to enjoy a few years later. Our characters ranged from cave dwellers to Henry VIII and Queen Elizabeth, with William the Conqueror landing to be interviewed by pressmen, King Alfred displaying his ignorance of domestic science, and King John using a fountain pen on the Magna Carta.

During final rehearsals, Mr A. D. (Archie) Flower, the chairman of the governors of the Memorial Theatre, sent me encouraging postcards, attended the first performance with his daughter and seemed highly pleased with the whole venture. From two shows we were able to hand £40 to the Shakespeare Memorial association.

Andy Jaggard
Gerald's warm comments about 'Sir Archie' suggest that he represented something of a role model and a 'father figure' for Gerald.

In a later chapter, SIR ARCHIE FLOWER – MAN OF ACTION – AND OF DREAMS, Gerald describes his background, his qualities and values, and his role in the creation of the Royal Shakespeare Theatre after the destruction of the Old Memorial Theatre by fire in March 1926.

Archibald Dennis Flower long held his place in the esteem and affection of the town, and his achievements shine in the civic records. He was fourteen when, in 1879, the first Memorial Theatre opened with a performance of *Much Ado About Nothing*. This was the culmination of his uncle's vision of a Stratford Playhouse.

Archibald Flower, by inheritance came into control of a large business organisation, the family brewery in this town, and that, with the chairmanship of the governing body of the Memorial Theatre, might well have filled his working days. But, Sir Archie (as he later became) showed a characteristic thoroughness in entering all aspects of civil life. He displayed an unruffled serenity and patience that never deserted him in almost 60 years of service to the town.

His skills as a businessman and his gift for administration and leadership were one part of his nature, his dreams for the future were another. Yet such dreams were no impracticable fantasies, they were projects and ideals that could come true, and by patience, diplomacy and perseverance he made them come true.

George Bernard Shaw – "It is a wonder that fire did not descend from the Heaven"

In 1925 the Shakespeare Birthday Celebration Committee made the 'bold' decision to invite Mr Bernard Shaw to propose 'The Immortal Memory'. It gave Shaw a wonderful opportunity to pull the English leg completely out of its socket! Fortunately, Shaw chose to let Shakespeare off lightly, and to concentrate his batteries on the Memorial Theatre – the building itself. Many of his sallies were completely justified. He described it as an admirable building, adapted for every conceivable purpose other than that of a theatre. He would say nothing about the ventilation because one could not speak of things that do not exist! Bad productions of Shakespeare produced another salvo. He could remember a time when *Coriolanus* was compressed into a one hour's performance, and it was described as *a great triumph*. It was a wonder that fire did not descend from heaven and obliterate Stratford-upon-Avon.

After Mr Shaw's condemnation of the Memorial Theatre, the governors may have considered what improvements they could make. I am sure they did not contemplate replacing it with a new one.

Someday a book will be written – perhaps one already exists – on the many hundreds of theatres, from Shakespeare's Globe Playhouse onward, which have ended their days in smoke. Apart from the occasional demolition, it is the inevitable end of theatres. The plywood and paints of the property room invite combustion. The Memorial Theatre fire started on the stage, spread to the property rooms, and quickly worked its way round the fire-proof curtain to the auditorium. Had a performance been in action, the outbreak would almost certainly have been dealt with long before it could take hold.

19. Destruction of the Old Shakespeare Memorial Theatre by fire – March 1926

On that windy March afternoon in 1926, the theatre was empty. That brisk March wind blowing eastwards was the salvation of the Memorial Library and Picture Gallery. Their valuable contents were removed by willing hands as a precaution, but the wind continued to blow steadily away from town. Thus, the fire gave the appearance of being selective. It devoured the playhouse and consumed the hundreds of paperback copies of the Memorial Theatre editions of the plays, stored in the Tower. This, like a factory chimney, belched flames and smoke. And from it the wind carried the blackened pages right across the Avon, as though the dying spirit of the old theatre were making a final effort to spread the poet's message over the countryside.

But nobody watching the valiant but hopeless efforts of the fire brigades to subdue the inferno felt in poetic mood. All fires great and small, are depressing affairs, and the loss of a place that had given us so many years of intimate entertainment held a sadness that would linger.

The bombshell of 1926, the destruction of the first Memorial Theatre by fire, seemed at first to be not only a tragedy for Stratford, but the wreck of all Sir Archie's hopes and dreams.

A man of lesser vision might have been content to build a theatre of similar pattern to that intimate little playhouse that his uncle had brought into being. But as from a chair, Sir Archie watched the thick pall of smoke rising from the stage and auditorium, I have little doubt that even then he was visualising that great structure that was to reward his labours and fulfil his hopes, the real 'university of the spoken word'.

Andy Jaggard
A dramatic end to Gerald's chapter with his witnessing of the destruction of the Old Memorial Theatre that would result a few years later in the birth of the Royal Shakespeare Theatre. The plans for the new theatre involved an architectural competition and a winning modern design that was described, rather dismissively, by some Stratfordians as 'the Jam Factory'.

But I was still thinking about Gerald and his two books, written fifteen years apart, but so completely different in style and intensity. Stratford Mosaic, *written in his mid-fifties with its short, fairly anodyne, biography of Captain Jaggard and his admiration for Archie Flower, with qualities almost exactly the opposite of his father, although Gerald doesn't spell this out.* The Life and Death, *written fifteen years later, intensely personal, honest, emotional, highly critical, and even brutal in his condemnation of his father in the book's Preface.*

But what do the two books have in common?

And then it struck me. It is what is MISSING that is significant.

It's the End of the Story.

I had resorted to Stratford Mosaic *to provide some insights into Gerald's boyhood and teenage years and his early manhood. But this personal material runs out in 1923/24 (if we discount his witnessing of the destruction of The Old Memorial Theatre by fire in March 1926).*

This was at a very similar point to the last event recorded in his unfinished book, The Life and Death *which describes Marie Corelli's funeral in 1924.*

The Life and Death of a Stratford Bookshop *(Unpublished book)* *c. 1974*

Gerald Jaggard

She died, quite suddenly, on Easter Monday 21st April 1924, just two days before the town's greatest annual festival. Reflecting on the funeral ceremony, even the leader in the *Stratford Herald*, reflected the sad fact that after nearly twenty-five years in the town, Marie had made many adversaries.

Naturally, many Stratford societies, clubs and institutions were represented at the funeral. My father, no doubt to his chagrin, could find no society, clubs or institutions on whose behalf he could attend. Marie had fallen out with some of them, he had quarrelled with all of them. He overcame the difficulty by picking a bunch of wildflowers and going on behalf of Warwickshire Folk in London.

Andy Jaggard

And that is the end of Gerald's story of The Life and Death of a Stratford Bookshop. *There is nothing after 1924. After Gerald's account of Marie Corelli's funeral two brief chapters follow. The first on, 'The Art of Dyeing' (as in cloth), the second on 'The Postman who loved Flowers', who was a bit of a character. Neither progresses the story of WJ or of the fortunes of the shop at all. Gerald seems to have been 'treading water' not knowing how to proceed. Then the book ends abruptly.*

I don't think it's a coincidence that the period from the mid 1920s until after WJ's death in 1947 does not feature, in both of his books, as regards any kind of personal information from Gerald himself.

Why didn't Gerald complete the story?

I believe the events in the 1920s and beyond made it too painful and too difficult for him. His style of writing, and his approach to life, was always, one step back, observational, witty, a little detached. When it came down to it, I believe he couldn't, or perhaps didn't feel it right, to tell the full story of which he was so much a part.

With the benefit of what we now know, his decision to abandon the book makes some kind of sense. Not that it was necessarily a conscious decision. He may just have given up on the idea. But he preserved the manuscript.

It's significant that Gerald was writing as a man of seventy recalling his boyhood memories, and his feelings about his father.

What did Gerald mean when he wrote that his father's life "ended in bitter failure"?

This is at heart a family story of two very different men, their difficult relationship and how Gerald dealt with the damaging impact on him and on other family members throughout different phases of his life.

How do we finish Gerald's story? Through other sources, his other articles, the crucial family letters he preserved, searches for archive stories and newspaper and magazine articles of the day and particularly through our own research.

First the events that almost certainly precipitated the break-up of Gerald's family – the scandal of 'the housekeeper'.

CHAPTER 14 THE HOUSEKEEPER'S STORY

Andy Jaggard
This was the most challenging research task. First the physical search for 'the housekeeper' with little progress and mounting frustration over many months. Then a major breakthrough, followed by some wonderful help from an unexpected quarter as we started to piece together the events from over ninety years ago. Some big surprises and then, a very strange and rewarding experience, when I was able to talk with someone who knew the woman at the centre of the scandal who was able to provide me with her memories and personal insights into the housekeeper's character, and her life.

Anthea remembers visiting her grandmother, Emma Frances, at Loxley Road in the early 1950s. 129 Loxley Road was the rather dilapidated semi-detached bungalow, half a mile from Stratford, where Gerald had lived back in his bachelor days. First before, and then during the Second World War, looking after his mother, and then in later years with the addition of his twin brother and younger sister all living together in the small property.

Emma Frances died in 1955 when Anthea was not quite five.

She thinks it was a couple of years later that Gerald sat her down and told her of 'the scandal' involving the housekeeper. Anthea remembers Gerald's words: "my father took the housekeeper on a trip to America with him to sell a First Folio." *Gerald said that Anthea* "ought to know".

WJ died in 1947, over seventy-five years ago, and all we had were these few half-remembered events, although we did have a name

– Edith E. Parkin. *We knew the name was correct as Edith had received a bequest in WJ's will.*

Searches on genealogy websites revealed that there are hundreds of Edith Parkins, and even scores of Edith E. Parkins, especially in Yorkshire. One possibility was Edith E. Parkin, born in Rotherham on 28th August 1883 *but she and many other Parkins were ruled out for various reasons.*

Perhaps we would not be able to find her and learn her story. Researching WJ's visits to America and the sale of his First Folio was another possible route to 'find her' but was also difficult as the Folger Shakespeare Institute was undergoing a major renovation, with all the archive collections in secure storage.

Finding Edith Parkin

Then we made an important breakthrough, a search for passengers leaving by ship for New York *came up with evidence that WJ did visit* America *in 1928, probably in connection with the sale of his* 'John Hay' Copy *of the First Folio. This was the First Folio he had attempted to sell to Folger in 1903. He had kept it for many years, making some* 'improvements' *and it was* 'eventually sold in America in 1928', *but not to Folger.*

WJ left for New York on the Berengaria, *a Cunard steamship, on 24th March 1928 from Southampton. He returned a month later on the 25th of April 1928 on the* Ausonia *into the Port of London. The* Berengaria's *register for the voyage has a record of all the passengers departing from Southampton and closer examination of the passenger records for the* Berengaria *show that* Wm Jaggard (Author) travelled on ticket 15102, and an Edith Parkin (Housekeeper) travelled on ticket 15103.

WJ and the housekeeper gave as their last address, where they had been staying immediately before they sailed for America, as what I thought read <u>Rose Bank Holdershaw Cambridgeshire</u> on the ship's register. I couldn't believe this was a real address, but as a stab in the dark tried googling it. It led to an address in <u>Hildersham</u> in Cambridgeshire. This house in Cambridgeshire was, very surprisingly, called Rose Bank, the same name as WJ's house on the Tiddington Road in Stratford. After months and months of searching this was a rather incredible moment.

Soon I discovered that by the time of the 1939 census, eleven years later, Edith Parkin had still been living there, with two Jaggards, Harry, twenty-seven and Ellen, eighty-three.

This was a dramatic development and mystifying.

The entry for Edith Parkin, the housekeeper, however, was 'cancelled'*. She was recorded for that same 1939 census as living in Stratford-upon-Avon. (*as you can't be in two places for a census return)

There are only two occupants of 7 Tiddington Rd, ('Rose Bank') Stratford-upon-Avon by 1939. WJ records his occupations as Author, Bookseller, Publisher, and Air Raid Warden. Edith E. Parkin now is of Private means. (Edith Parkin had also lost two years in her move from Hildersham to Stratford. Her birthdate was still 28th August but now in 1883 rather than 1881.) The rest of WJ's family had moved out, leaving just WJ and his housekeeper.

dillo			Y.	1.	Jaggard. William		M.	11th June	64	M.	Author Bookseller Publ
				2.	Parkin. Edith E		F.	28th Aug	83	W.	Private means.

So, it appears that WJ *and* Edith Parkin *had been in a relationship since at least* 1928, *probably a good deal earlier. Both houses in* Stratford *and in* Hildersham Cambridgeshire *were called* 'Rose Bank' *and sometime between* 1928 *and* 1939 *the rest of WJ's family had moved out of the family home.*

Geoffrey *the eldest, left to become a provincial journalist several years earlier, but it would appear* WJ's wife, Emma Frances, *the twins* Gerald *and* Aubrey *and the youngest* Wendy *had all moved out, or been asked to leave as a direct result of* WJ's *and* Edith's *relationship and the scandal.*

A big step forward but what else could I find out?

Who was Harry Jaggard?

I couldn't work out the relationship between the three people living in the 'Rose Bank' *in* Hildersham, Cambridgeshire *for the* 1939 census. *They didn't appear to be related to each other. The* 1939 census *gives their year of birth, so I had all their ages. The next-door house to theirs is called* "Next Post Office" *so* 'Rose Bank' *is also the* post office.

Ellen J. Jaggard born in 1856, a woman of eighty-three.

Harry William Jaggard born on 2nd January 1912, aged twenty-seven the Sub Postmaster.

Edith Parkin born on 28th August 1881 aged fifty-eight.

Tracing Ellen J. Jaggard (1856–1949), *on* Ancestry *was fairly straightforward. She was married to a* Henry Jaggard (1854–1927). *Both* Henry *and* Ellen *were born in* Dullingham *and back in* 1911 *they were running the* 'Pear Tree Inn' in Hildersham.

They had several children, William, Albert, Bertie, Edith, Ruth and Lilla.

But who was Harry William Jaggard?

Harry *is often used as a derivative of* Henry. *A further search revealed that a* <u>Henry</u> William Jaggard *was on the Electoral roll (of* Hildersham Parish) *in* 1935. *By* 1945 Henry William *and a* Hilda Jaggard *are recorded living at the* post office *in* Great Abington, *the next village to* Hildersham, *and again in* 1950 *and* 1960 *still at the* post office, *and again in* 1965 *this time at* 11 High Street, Great Abington. *The death of* Henry William Jaggard, *with a birth date of* 2nd January 1912 *is recorded on the* National Register in 1970. *His family tree was not clear.*

So, this was 'Harry' but a week later research on Ancestry.co.uk *had failed to identify* 'Harry'/Henry William Jaggard's *parents. How come?*

However, there was another 'private' family tree on ancestry, with Henry William *born in* Carmarthenshire *on* 1st Jan 1912 *(the birthdate was just one day out). Could this be him?*

I sent a message to the tree owner via Ancestry enquiring if it could be the same Henry William. *I received a message back:*

"Ah, there's a story."

This was very intriguing.

*The person who had sent the message (*Alan Harry*) explained that he must first check with the tree owner that she was prepared to talk to me. Alan, a relation by marriage, had completed the tree for her. Her name was* Helen Greenland.

Edith's Story Unfolds

After further messages, and a nervous couple of days, it was arranged that Helen *would ring me. I was on tenterhooks not knowing what to expect.*

The phone rang at the agreed time, and I lifted the receiver ... "Hello Andy," *she said.*

I made some remarks about how grateful I was that she was prepared to talk to me and a brief introduction to how the book had come about.

From our first call Helen *was great fun and very easy to talk to. She is the daughter of* 'Harry' William Jaggard, *and in* 2020 *was in her late* seventies.

One of the first things she said to me was that although, not a spiritual person, she had a premonition that something was about to happen. She had recently been looking at Captain William's *black hat, in a cupboard with other memorabilia. (At first I thought she meant a top hat but then I remembered* WJ's *black* stationer's *hat. Could it be that?)*

It was a very unusual and rewarding experience talking to Helen *who had known* Edith Parkin *as her* 'Aunt Edie'.

Then Helen *told me that* Harry, *her father, had been brought up in* Pen-y-Bank in Llandybie, Carmarthenshire, "but was orphaned aged four". Harry *told* Helen *that* he "had been sent to live with 'Grannie' in Hildersham" *and couldn't* "speak a word of English when he first arrived, so it was very difficult for him".

She told me that her Aunt Edie *had been married to an* Alfred Parkin. Edith *had lived in* South Africa *where she thought* Alfred Parkin *was a* Captain *in the Army.* Edith *had returned from* South

Africa. Helen *wasn't sure what had happened to* Alfred, *possibly he had died.*

Aunt Edie *never had any children* ... "although she would have made a wonderful mother".

Helen *described how her* Aunt Edie *for some reason, had taken* Harry Jaggard, "under her wing".

That cleared up one mystery. The search for Edith Parkin *had been going on for some time, but now it was clear that* Parkin *was her married name, not her maiden name as I had assumed.*

Later, I spoke to Alan Harry, *who, it turned out, had completed the family tree on* Helen's *behalf in an attempt to discover the parents of* Harry William Jaggard, *an issue for* Harry *during his life, and now still for* Helen. *I described how I was struggling to find* Edith E. Parkin's *details.*

"Well," *Alan said,* "I knew her as Edith Jaggard."

That was a bombshell. A few days earlier I had researched the family tree for Henry *and* Ellen Jaggard *(the eighty-three-year-old woman living at* 'Rose Bank' *in* Hildersham *for the* 1939 *census). I had noticed an* Edith Etta *as one of their children but had not thought much of it.*

Helen Greenland

Since that first conversation at the end of 2020, Helen *and I have had many more long telephone conversations.* Helen *has been very generous in sharing her memories of* Edith Parkin née Jaggard *and of her parents,* Harry and Hilda Jaggard. *In* June 2021, Anthea *and I visited* Helen *in* Cambridge, *she showed us around the beautiful village of* Hildersham, *we tried to find the* old post office, *we had lunch together and when we took* Helen *back to her house she wanted to 'return' some of* WJ's *possessions, including his black* stationer's *hat.*

It was always somewhat sensitive and strange discussing the 'relationship' *between* WJ *and* Edith Parkin, *for us the woman at the centre of the scandal that led to the break-up of* Gerald's *family and for* Helen, *her* 'Aunt Edie', *a woman she clearly admired.* Helen *had even visited* Edith *at* 'Rose Bank' *(the one in* Stratford*) as a child of three or four shortly after the end of the Second World War. She shared many stories of* Edith *who came across as a strong, confident woman, with* "a wicked sense of humour".

THE HOUSEKEEPER'S STORY

With a great deal of help from Helen, *evidence from* Ancestry.co.uk *and many other searches we managed to piece together much, although by no means all, of* Edith Parkin's *life story.* Alan Harry *also provided me with his very detailed work into* Harry Jaggard's *family tree.* Harry Jaggard's *life story is itself fascinating and a little mysterious.* * *See* The Mystery of Harry Jaggard in the Appendix.

(Incidentally, Ellen Jaggard *was not* Harry's *real* 'Grannie', *neither is* Edith, Helen's *real Aunt –* Alan Harry *has a theory of how these close relationships may have come about.)*

Edith Etta Jaggard was Edith E. Parkin, *and* Henry and Ellen J. Jaggard's *daughter. She was born in* 1879 *(not* 1881 or 1883*). And not on* 28th August, *but between October and December* 1879 *in* Dullingham Ley, *a hamlet in rural* Cambridgeshire.

**23. Edith E. Parkin (1879–1967). Photo courtesy of
Helen Greenland and Alan Harry.**

Edith *was the eldest child, with younger sisters,* Ruth *and* Lilla, *and brothers,* Willie, Bertie and Albert.

WJ *and* Edith Etta Jaggard *shared the same great grandfather,* John Jaggard (1791–1843).

So, they were second cousins.

Edith *soon spread her wings and went off to* London *to find work. By* 1901, *aged* twenty-two, *she was listed as a servant, working in* Charlton, London. *She was soon promoted to the role of cook to the family of* George H. Bittlestone, a Major (later Lieutenant Colonel) in the Royal Artillery.

In the early years of the century, she spent a period of time in South Africa. *The pictures show her, dressed very much the part of the Edwardian lady, undoubtedly going up in the world.*

In 1906 *she married* Albert Edward Parkin *in* Bakewell *in* Derbyshire. Albert Parkin *had served in the* Orange River Scouts *during the* Second Boer War *in* South Africa *between* 1899 *and* 1902.

**24. Edith Parkin in South Africa –
Photo courtesy of Helen Greenland and Alan Harry.**

By the time of the 1911 *census,* Edith *was living in* Stretford, Old Trafford, Manchester, *with her husband. Confusingly, for a man who was supposedly a* Captain *in the army,* Albert *by this time was working as a* night watchman *in a* printing works.

Edith *was at home on domestic duties (as the* 1911 *census describes the woman's role).*

Edith and Albert *did not have any children.* Albert Parkin *served in the* labour corps *in* southeast England *during the* First World War.

By the time of the census of June 1921 *he was living in* London *working as a* clerk for a clothier company *on the* Charing Cross Road. Edith *was living with him, occupation,* "Home Duties".

Albert Edward Parkin *died a year later on* 28th June 1922 aged forty-seven. *He had a* military campaign medal from South Africa, *and the rank of* Sergeant *from his* First World War *service.* Edith Parkin *received a widow's pension.*

When we visited Hildersham *in* Cambridgeshire *with* Helen Greenland *in* June 2021, *she took us to* Hildersham Church. *Her father* Harry *had played the organ there on Sundays.*

Helen *showed us* Edith's *gravestone also in memory of her husband* Albert Edward Parkin.

Edith Parkin *died in* 1967, aged ninety *according to the gravestone, although by my calculations as she was born in* 1879, *she would actually have been* eighty-eight. *Still a couple of years out, but this time older, rather than younger.*

25. Albert and Edith Etta Parkin's memorial and headstone, Hildersham Parish Church – June 2021.

The Scandal

So, we know that by 1928 *Edith Parkin was* WJ's 'housekeeper'. *It seems they were also in a relationship.* WJ *had an important business trip to* America *lined up in* March *of that year.* He had the sale of a First Folio *to conclude, probably some lecturing opportunities, and I imagine he intended to enjoy the voyage (and probably bluster his way into the first-class lounge). Who better for his escort than a strong confident woman, not fazed by powerful men, who she would disarm with her* "wicked sense of humour"?

By this time, they were sometimes staying together in a house in the small village of Hildersham, Cambridgeshire, *another* Rose Bank, *as they gave this as their last address before leaving for* New York, *sailing from* Southampton.

All we know for certain is that WJ's First Folio *was sold in* America *in* 1928 *through an intermediary on behalf of* Captain Jaggard *to* "an unidentified owner". Alfred MacArthur *purchased the copy from a* Chicago bookseller *in* 1958 *and it was eventually donated by his daughter to* Brown University *on* Shakespeare's birthday, 23rd April 1971, *in memory of her father who was killed in naval action in 1945.*

Looking back, I think it's significant that Gerald *decided to tell* Anthea *as a very young child,* "My father took the housekeeper on a trip to America with him to sell a First Folio." Gerald *thought* "she ought to know". *Perhaps he thought it would be shameful if she found out later and he hadn't told her.*

It also signifies that this event in Gerald's *mind was the trigger for the damaging break-up of the family and would decide his fate for the next twenty years.*

CHAPTER 15 GERALD'S 'LOST YEARS'

"This web of life is a mingled yarn, good and ill together.." All's well that ends well " Act IV Scene 3

Andy Jaggard
Shakespeare's 'lost years' is something of a Shakespearean cliché. Scholars use the phrase to refer to the period between the baptism of the twins Hamnet and Judith and Shakespeare's first-known appearance in the London theatre scene in 1592. It has spawned countless theories of what Shakespeare was up to during those missing years and WJ was to make his own attempt to account for Shakespeare's 'lost years' with his eccentric lecture, 'Once a Printer and Bookman' *at the Stationers' Hall in London in 1933.*

Gerald's 'lost years' were from around 1928 until his father's death in 1947.

We have discovered many of the facts: the jobs he had, his interests and hobbies, newspaper accounts, but there is virtually nothing from Gerald himself by way of any kind of autobiographical account. It was a period he never wrote about or talked about in any kind of personal way. It seems to me that his life was, in many ways, on hold.

He told funny stories about other people and situations, for example auctioneering at the Stratford livestock market, and his time as an auxiliary fireman during the Second World War, but nothing of himself, his relationships, or his own domestic situation during that twenty-year period.

John Barnes, my younger brother's father-in-law, had a conversation with Gerald a few years before he died and in 2003, he wrote up his brief notes on Gerald's jobs.

John Barnes 2003 – Notes about the life of Gerald Jaggard based on a chat with him several years ago.

During his working life Gerald had five jobs after leaving school at sixteen due to the fact that his father lost his job at the Shakespeare Theatre. This brought to an end a promising scholastic career and the probability that he might have gone on to university.

John describes Gerald's jobs:

1921   **Bank clerk** at Lloyds Bank in Stratford. (*Gerald left after six months when the bank informed him, he was going to be transferred to another branch.*)

1922   **Freight clerk** at Warwick Station for the Great Western Railway Company. (*The move was financially worthwhile as he received four times the salary that Lloyds bank had paid him. Before long the railway company transferred Gerald to Stratford.*)

1926   **Goods clerk** at Stratford Station. (*He stayed with GWR for four years, he was in line for promotion provided he move to Banbury. The thought of lodging in Banbury did not appeal and Gerald handed in his notice.*)

1927   **Clerk (eventually Chief Clerk) for Walker Barnard and Dobson – Estate Agents and Auctioneers.** (*Again the work was clerical involving two days a week at Stratford Livestock Market where he was involved with pigs. He continued working with this firm until his father died.*)

I'm not sure if all this information is entirely accurate. I know nothing of Gerald's involvement with the pigs, but it does provide an outline of Gerald's working life from when he was forced to leave school in 1920 until his father died in 1947. He had a series of clerical roles in, or close to, Stratford and he resisted any moves that would take him away from his home town where he was so immersed in the life of the town. It's also likely that he had concerns for his mother's welfare.

So, by 1927 Gerald was working for Walker Barnard and Dobson, Auctioneers. By a strange twist of fate their offices were in Sheep Street almost opposite, No. 4 Sheep Street, the Shakespeare Press, WJ's place of work. As far as I know Gerald was still living at the family home, 'Rose Bank' in 1928, aged twenty-four.

A short time after gathering the research on the housekeeper we were able to narrow down the time of the break-up of the family. We discovered that by 1930 the only two registered voters, and therefore occupants, of 129 Loxley Road, were Gerald and his mother Emma Frances. This was the small semi-detached bungalow half a mile from the family home, Rose Bank, in Stratford. Aubrey and Wendy had also moved out of Rose Bank.

It seems likely that the family either decided to leave or were asked to leave Rose Bank by WJ during 1928 or 1929.

WJ and his housekeeper Edith Parkin were then the only two occupants of Rose Bank. *In a small parochial town such as Stratford in the 1920s this must have been a shocking and very public scandal. Gerald, I'm sure, felt it was his duty to go with his mother and he was still living with her in 1947 when his father died.*

What did he feel at the time of these damaging events: shame, embarrassment, anger, depression? Did he still speak to his father? They must have seen each other around town and in Sheep Street, where they both worked, almost every day.

Wendy, the youngest, lived in Warwick in a shared house for a few years and later had a job as a receptionist at the Birthplace Trust in Stratford.

Aubrey, after starting work as a clerk for a gas company aged sixteen, eventually took up a role in insurance with the NFU where he remained until he retired – a job for life.

If his stories are anything to go by, Gerald enjoyed his two days a week at the livestock market, sometimes standing in for the chief auctioneer, but I can't imagine that he found his predominantly clerical role very interesting or fulfilling. Instead, he threw himself wholeheartedly into his many interests and hobbies. Perhaps a distraction from the family situation.

He played tennis and some golf, he was a member of the Union Club, *a male-only institution with snooker tables and card schools with a Dickensian atmosphere. It was still much the same in the 1970s when I played snooker there with Gerald.*

Gerald was also a member of Stratford's Shakespeare Club, *the first in the world, founded in 1824. There are now hundreds of such clubs. Gerald joined as a young man, and between 1933 and 1935 he was the Club's Secretary. Gerald was still only twenty-nine when he started his two-year stint, with the responsibility of arranging the yearly programme of talks by scholars and actors and organising social events.*

The Story of the Shakespeare Club of Stratford-upon-Avon by Susan Brock and Sylvia Morris *has several references to my father which quite neatly illustrate the dual and, on the surface, rather contradictory sides of his nature.*

He was a traditionalist. By the late 1940s the Club's connection with the (Shakespeare) Birthday celebrations was somewhat diminished as the civic authorities were increasingly taking over this high-

profile event. "Gerald Jaggard, one of the Club's representatives expressed the familiar anxiety that the Club should take the utmost care to ensure that its historical responsibility for the inception and continuance of the celebrations were recognised by adequate representation on the executive body."

Gerald also had a great sense of fun. In 1948 "an ambitious proposal to hold an Elizabethan Costume Ball in the Town Hall was abandoned *(due to the high cost of hiring costumes).* Instead, Gerald Jaggard offered to organise some entertainment and so set the pattern for a mixture of music and participatory games for several years. *" This was one example:*

The evening concluded with "a brutal and Jaggardly, but successful attack on the company's shyness and self-consciousness, in which each table was required to sing in a competition against the others."

Throughout the 1920s and 1930s, both Gerald and Aubrey were members of the Stratford-upon-Avon Amateur Players, taking part in numerous productions. The twins were also something of a double act in Stratford, entertaining the Grammar School's Old Boys at their annual dinner with their stand-up routine.

I was amused by this account of an open-air production of A Midsummers' Night's Dream *from the 1930s. Gerald was* Snug the Joiner, *and Aubrey was* Bottom the Weaver *– part of the* 'rude mechanicals' *in the play within a play. According to the* Leamington Spa Courier, 'A Great Attraction' … was a vigorous production which more than compensated the audience for the cold and the gnats which appeared to be making a determined assault on the orchestra behind their foliage screen.

By the late 1930s, just before the commencement of the Second World War, Gerald had moved on to more ambitious creative projects.

In August 1938, Gerald and Aubrey had created a village pageant in the local village of Ilmington. Gerald himself wrote the article in the Leamington Spa Courier – 'Ilmington Manor Awaits Her Cue.' The Miniature Pageant will be staged in front of the Manor's time-honoured walls, a pageant that will tell the intimate and stirring points in the Manor's history. The production will start with fact and end as darkness falls with a touch of fancy. At the beginning, faithful to history, a courier from King John will present the deeds of the house to the first Simon de Montford. At the close cloaks and crinoline will invade the courtyard and a Victorian wedding will take place from the house.

A few days later, the theatre critic of the Leamington Spa Courier *gave his verdict. After complaining first of the* 'Disease of Pageantitis' *sweeping the country he admitted,* "the effect at Ilmington is so delightful that it turned the present writer into a second Oliver Twist or melancholy Jacques wanting to cry 'More – I prithee More!'"

Gerald was himself the theatre critic for the Stratford Herald *for a year or two writing under the name of Hotspur. He also wrote the 'Buster' column for many years and was paid 1¼ (old) pence per printed line.*

In May 1939 the Birmingham Daily Gazette's *report* 'Queen of Shakespeare Land', *described that,* "over 2,000 people watched the crowning of Miss Iris Courtney of Tiddington as Rose Queen of Stratford-upon-Avon. A golden crown was placed on her blonde head. Mr Gerald Jaggard who wrote the ceremony in Elizabethan verse and produced it also played the part of the Court Chamberlain."

Six months later Shakespeare Land *was at war.*

Aubrey served in North Africa and gets a mention in Nicholas Fogg's Stratford-Upon-Avon – The Biography:

On 13th November 1942, the bells of Holy Trinity sounded out in a manner reminiscent of the seventeenth century, for the victory at El Alamein, a major turning of the war's tide. In the subsequent advance, the 8th Armoured Division had overrun the supply lines of the retreating Germans. "At the moment," wrote Corporal Aubrey Jaggard, "I am smoking a Jerry cigarette, of which I have several boxes, having just finished a dinner of jerry bread, coffee and jam *(made from beetroot)* The German bread was done up in airtight packages, 3" thick, but it was made of rye and tasted like very stale Hovis."

Gerald stayed in England during the war years. He was a special constable and served in the Auxiliary Fire Service. It could be dangerous and stressful work attending the scene of plane crashes and bombing raids, although the stories that Gerald chose to tell, as I remember, were more along the lines of Dad's Army-*type escapades.*

Another volunteer and neighbour of ours in Tiddington, Fred Wincote, *a lovely man, told this story of the insensitive reception he received after returning to their base after attending a plane crash.*

The Stratford Auxiliary Fire Service, 1943. (Image courtesy of the Shakespeare Birthplace Trust Records Office)

27. Gerald Jaggard is second from the right.

A senior officer upbraided Fred *for not wearing his tunic.*

I said, "Wait a minute you haven't asked me what happened to it." He says, "What happened to it then?" Then I said, "It's in holes. I have been at a plane crash and the petrol tank exploded." And I says, "Look at my eyebrows, no lashes." He said, "I thought your eyes looked a little red."

Birthplace Trust Records Collection

After the war, both Aubrey and Wendy returned to 129 Loxley Road to live with Gerald and his mother Emma Frances. The four of them were all living together in the run-down and very cramped semi-detached bungalow.

WJ and his housekeeper Edith Parkin meanwhile were still living at the family home, Rose Bank, *on the Tiddington Road. They were occasionally visited by Hilda Jaggard from Cambridgeshire, Edith's best friend, (the wife of Harry Jaggard) with her daughter Helen, who was only three or four at the time. Helen shared her memories with me of her visits to Rose Bank just after the war to see her 'Aunt Edie' and 'Uncle'. Although* Uncle *was usually away on business.*

No. 4 Sheep Street, the Shakespeare Press, *was also run down, after the privations and the hardships of a Second World War, that had lasted for six long years.*

On the 27th of April 1947 WJ died. This must have been a seismic moment for the occupants of 129 Loxley Road, his wife Emma Frances, Wendy, Aubrey and Gerald.

What would happen to Rose Bank?

And gazing across Sheep Street from the Auctioneer's offices of Walker Barnard and Dobson no doubt Gerald was also wondering, and perhaps dreaming of what would happen to the bookshop, the Shakespeare Press *now that his father was dead.*

CHAPTER 16 A VOICE FROM THE DEAD

Andy Jaggard
WJ was abrasive, self-righteous, driven, and obsessive, these days he might be categorised on some kind of spectrum. During his tenure at No. 4 Sheep Street, from 1910 until 1947, the Shakespeare Press had to face the difficulties and ravages of two World Wars. In its heyday, though, the shop was naturally a glorious reflection of WJ's eccentric character and run in his own image. You have to admire his boldness, his innovations (the Tudor makeover) and his many achievements.

In the early stages of our research, we came across a famous Shakespearean scholar's story of her encounter with 'Captain Jaggard' in his bookshop in the 1920s.

First Gerald, in this extract from his unfinished book, sets the scene with his description of WJ's 'Information Bureau.'

The Life and Death of a Stratford Bookshop *(Unpublished book) c. 1974*

Gerald Jaggard
My father was well versed in all the local legends, the natural history, the customs and history of the county. Nothing delighted him more than to be asked about them, and on more than one occasion he would shut up shop in order to escort a party of enquiring visitors down to the Avon, or along the High Street to point out some particular beauty spot. He was a mine of information on all local subjects, and indeed became so involved with the service that he erected a large sign over the

door saying 'Information Bureau'. His landlords, the Stratford Corporation, promptly asked him to remove it, pointing out that they already had an official bureau to cater for visitors' demands. WJ responded by removing the sign a little further inside his doorway, so that it was not visible from the street but still an eloquent invitation to visitors.

Andy Jaggard

The notable visitor calling upon WJ's 'Information Bureau' services was the renowned Shakespearean scholar and author, Caroline Spurgeon. When Spurgeon's book was finally published many years later, Shakespeare's Imagery and What it Tells Us, *not only was WJ revered for his Shakespearean knowledge but his status as the direct descendant was powerfully reinforced.*

The Shakespeare Press, Sheep Street, Stratford-upon-Avon – Spurgeon's account

I feel as sure as I can be of anything that these many pictures drawn by Shakespeare of the movement and behaviour of a river in flood are all boyhood memories of the Avon at Stratford. This, I believe, is peculiarly true when he compares the movement of the waters to the emotions and passions of men. I had an interesting confirmation of this belief on one visit to Stratford recently, when I made the acquaintance of Captain William Jaggard, the owner of the old print and bookshop in Sheep Street, and descendant of the William Jaggard, who, in 1599 and 1612, printed and published *The Passionate Pilgrim*, and from whose press, in 1623, the 'First Folio' was issued.

I was telling Captain Jaggard that I was very anxious to see the river in flood, and particularly to stand on old Clopton Bridge and watch the movement of the current, as Shakespeare often referred to it. "Oh yes!" he said, "and you should stand on the eighteenth arch of the bridge (the one nearest the London side), for when the river is in flood, the force of the current under the adjoining arches, combined with the curved shape of the bank on to which it is driven, produces the most curious effect. I have often stood there and watched the current being forced beneath the narrow Tudor arch, on to the right bank at an angle which produces a swirling eddy, so that the water is then forced back through the arch equally swiftly and in an exactly contrary direction to that in which it has just come." "I have," he added, "sometimes hardly been able to believe my eyes when I have seen sticks or straws, which I have just noticed swirled on the flood downward through the arch, being brought back again just as swiftly in the opposite direction and against the flood weight."

Captain Jaggard, as he said this, was at the further end of his shop, searching among its piled-up masses of books and papers for some prints he wanted to show me, and his voice, coming thus somewhat muted from the distance, gave me the most curious thrill and start, as if it were a voice from the dead.

For here was a present-day Stratfordian describing to me in prose, in minute detail, exactly what a Stratford man had thus set down in verse nearly three hundred and fifty years ago.

I at once called out to Captain Jaggard asking him to write down what he had just said, which he kindly did, and I then said, "Can you find me a copy of Shakespeare's Poems?" and he laughingly answered, "I think perhaps I can", and returned to me bringing back a volume along with him. I turned up the above quotation and showed it to him. He had not previously noticed it and was extremely interested.

As through an arch the violent roaring tide
Outruns the eye that doth behold his haste,
Yet in the eddy boundeth in his pride
Back to the strait that forc'd him on so fast,
In rage sent out, recall'd in rage, being past:
Even so his sighs, his sorrows, make a saw,
To push grief on and back the same grief draw.
(The Rape of Lucrece, lines 1667–73)

Later, I went down myself to the riverbank and stood looking under the eighteenth arch. The river that day was perfectly calm and smooth, but, even so, on watching closely, I could easily follow the characteristic movement of the current, even though it was slow and gentle.

There happened to be a big tuft of grass on it which sailed under the arch at an acute angle straight on to the bank, as in the sketch, then swirled round in an eddy, and proceeded to return under the arch in the direction whence it had just come.

There is a sort of little hook or bend in the bank just below where the current strikes it after coming under the arch, which produces the eddy and helps to send the water back again just because, when I saw it, it was quite gentle, this unusual and unnatural movement of the water was perhaps more curious and marked than it would have been in furious flood. But there was no question that here was the very spot where Shakespeare must often have stood as a boy, and this was the very phenomenon he had noticed and described with such meticulous accuracy.

Years ago, before I knew Shakespeare's ways as well as I do now, I had rather carelessly always thought this image probably referred to the current under one of the arches of old London Bridge, which, we read, was very swift, so that at times it was quite a feat to shoot through it in a boat; but closer knowledge of his habits and methods convinced me that Stratford was the place to seek for the original of it, with the result just described.

Andy Jaggard

WJ would have been delighted with Caroline Spurgeon's reverential testimony when her seminal work on Shakespeare's imagery was published in 1934. The famous Shakespearean scholar said it was like "a voice from the dead". *Captain Jaggard had* "described in minute detail" *what Shakespeare had set down in verse 350 years earlier.*

To top it all Spurgeon, in her book, described my grandfather as " the descendant of William Jaggard, from whose press, in 1623, the First Folio was issued."

But had he proved it? And by his promised deadline of the Tercentenary of the First Folio in 1923? There was a Shakespeare Press publication from 1921 called 'Jaggard Jottings from olden days'. *It seemed likely that this publication was based on WJ's own research notes compiled during the years of the First World War.*

During the Covid pandemic of 2020/2021 we were still unable to obtain a copy from various archives due to the restrictions in place.

CHAPTER 17 FORGERY

" O never say that I was false of heart" Sonnet 109

Andy Jaggard
The Tercentenary of 1923 did represent a turning point in WJ's life, but not quite in the way that I had expected.

In July 2021 I was still working on a complete restructure of the book and therefore, as I was unable to start the rewrite, I conducted a search of newspapers and periodicals (1900 to 1949) for Captain William Jaggard.

This unearthed a very rich seam of rather amazing newspaper stories and magazine articles of the day all involving WJ: discoveries, finds, forged relics, court cases, and even a Tudor mural discovered in a Stratford pub. Into the 1920s, and now in his mid-fifties, his life seemed to take an entirely new direction with ever more ambitious and outlandish projects to pursue.

One of the court cases, involving WJ as the plaintiff, mentioned the Ireland Forgeries. I googled the Ireland Forgeries and, of course, there were many accounts, including this rather romanticised version.

William Henry Ireland (1775–1835) grew up starved of his father's affection. Samuel Ireland was a man who loved his collections of books, pictures and curios far more than his family. But what he loved beyond all else was William Shakespeare. One day, in 1794, the nineteen-year-old William Henry sneaked into his father's study and started looking through his Shakespeare books. He then took a sheet of paper and traced a facsimile of Shakespeare's signature from a book. With this harmless little act, William Henry Ireland commenced his career of fabricating a series of deceptions.

In 1795, Ireland presented his father with a gift: a parchment deed signed by William Shakespeare. He told his father that a friend, whom he called "Mr H", had found an old trunk filled with Renaissance manuscripts and documents, many signed by Shakespeare. Ireland continued to bring home letters Shakespeare had apparently written to famous figures of the Elizabethan and Jacobean ages; love letters written to his wife, Anne Hathaway, as well as locks of Anne's hair …

The story goes on in this vein describing how Ireland, encouraged by his success, eventually wrote two full length plays which he claimed were newly discovered Shakespeare manuscripts.

Then, just before Christmas 2022, I remembered a Shakespeare Press Publication from 1912, written by WJ. It was called Shakespearean Frauds: the story of some famous Literary and Pictorial Frauds. *I had heard of this publication before but had assumed that this book would focus mainly on the frauds, cranks and naysayers, as WJ had called them, (who argued the plays were not written by Shakespeare). As I had read much of this material before in his research notes I hadn't thought it necessary to study this book. This turned out to be a big mistake.*

My purpose was to make sense of WJ's strange and decidedly suspicious behaviour in the courtroom and also, if I could, to understand his mindset in relation to forgery. Fortunately, the University of Michigan had digitised the Fulcroft Library Edition 1974 – in online books and so I was able to dig into WJ's book straight away. It is fifteen pages, nicely illustrated with pictures of famous forgers of Shakespeare – Lewis Theobald, George Steevens, Samuel Ireland, William Henry Ireland and John Payne Collier.

WJ's writing style is a strange mix of grandiose sentences, of his critical and judgemental opinions, together with some authentic inside stories from his deep knowledge of Shakespearean history (a year earlier, after twenty-two years of labour, he had just completed his massive Shakespeare bibliography).

These extracts, it seems to me, reveal something about his attitudes to forgery, his thought processes and perhaps his future plans?

WJ
"The subject of Shakespearean Fraud appears to be one that largely escaped attention, due to the natural modesty attached to victors and vanquished in the delicate field of imposture."

WJ speculated on the forger's reason for entering the field: "Probably it arose from vanity, from a desire to make a name, as hanger-on, in connection with the greatest of literary names."

"Now let us pass to the impudent Ireland …"

WJ describes some of the methods and resources for successful forgery.

The son whose full name was Samuel Wm Henry Ireland was a lawyer's clerk in New Inn London, where he had access to certain Elizabethan documents and was thus enabled to copy and imitate legal or court handwriting of the period. He acquired his paper from the flyleaves of early printed books and found ample copies at the lawyer's office for his calligraphy.

And how Ireland had overreached himself.

Becoming more ambitious with success Ireland actually wrote two plays entitled *Vortigern and Rowena* and *King Henry II* and palmed them off as genuine and newly discovered manuscripts. Such colossal impudence was bound to meet its deserts sooner or later.

In competing with the most transcendent genius in all the world's literature there could only be one result.

While he kept to transcripts of known plays his forgeries had only to run the gauntlet as paper and handwriting.

Later WJ revealed that as a young man at Warwick Castle, (he had catalogued the Earl's Shakespearean Library in 1890) he had studied the fine collection of forged Ireland manuscripts and he had found this note written by Wm Ireland himself … "Upon my confession, the sale of the Folio was stopped by my father … I committed to the flames the complete impression of the reprint."

Hanging had been the fate of convicted forgers a few years earlier but WJ concluded,

"Ireland didn't hang but escaped Scot-free and lived to make money out of his exposure – as he did out of the fabrications." In 1796 he wrote and published his *Authentic Account of the Shakespeare Manuscripts*, explaining how he had embarked on his career of crime. Having achieved a reputation for authorship in an unorthodox way, Wm Ireland gained a living for some years writing for London publishers.

Andy Jaggard
What does WJ's book on famous frauds tell us about his suitability for a career in literary forgery?

1. *He had a deep knowledge of the history of Shakespearean forgery.*

2. *He knew that to be successful he would need access to the calligraphy and paper for 'authentic fakes' (or to the work of Henry Ireland).*

3. He should stick to known plays or books, *not attempt anything as risky as writing an entire play.*

4. But why would he want to attempt it? WJ in his book had speculated on the motivation for forgery: "Probably it arose from vanity, from a desire to make a name, as hanger-on, in connection with the greatest of literary names."

WJ's first 'find' was not that remarkable. He shared the news of his happy 'find' *just a couple of months before the start of the Tercentenary year.*

"Mr William Jaggard of Stratford-upon-Avon, whose ancestors printed the First Folio, has made a discovery which he believes will prove of considerable interest to Shakespeareans the world over.

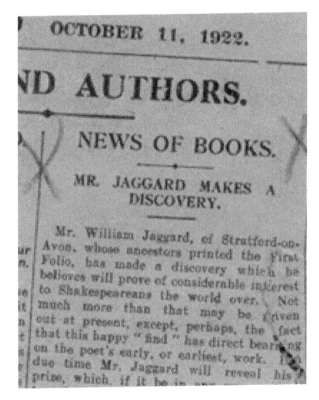

"This happy 'find' has a direct bearing on the poet's early or earliest work.

"In due time Mr Jaggard will reveal his prize."

By the mid 1920s, WJ was involved in a much more ambitious project.

In 1927 he was in court on two occasions, in March and again in November. These court appearances concerned some forged Shakespearean relics that WJ had bought from a man called Hunter Charles Rogers in 1925.

The Article in the Daily Mirror *on 22nd March 1927 reporting on the first court case included Rogers own story of his 1925 discovery:*

"IN LEAD COFFERS"

Letter Clue to Treasure

Story of Digging by Candlelight

(At times during this chapter it might seem like we have slipped into a work of fiction as some of the events involving WJ and some shadowy characters are rather unbelievable. They are all drawn from magazine and newspaper articles of the day, and as far as I know are all 'true', although clearly I can't vouch for the veracity of this Boy's Own *story told by Rogers, a part-time gardener from Slough.)*

It was in 1925 that Mr Hunter Charles Rogers told of how as the result of a letter which came into his possession, he dug up Shakespearean Treasures in Compton Wynyates on the Warwickshire Estate of the Marquis of Northampton.

"By the flickering light of a candle at the dead of night I dug up two lead coffers containing 140 genuine Shakespeare manuscripts," he declared. "Fearing that the MSS might be claimed," Mr Rogers told the *Daily Mirror* representative, "I boldly took the matter into my own hands and accompanied by an American whose name I cannot divulge and a Slough man who shall also be nameless, we started to dig in a place indicated by some trees planted to form a certain pattern."

Mr Rogers was unable to show any of the documents, as he said he sent them all to America to a town the name of which he would not disclose. He declared however that four plays had been sold for £20,000.

The article in the Daily Mirror *continued describing the court proceedings in March 1927.*

TREASURE DUG UP AT NIGHT

Judge Baffled by way Expert was Deceived

The Civil Action was brought by Captain William Jaggard alleging Fraudulent Misrepresentation of Pretended Shakespeare Relics.

*WJ had negotiated, back in 1925, t*he purchase of a collection of ninety-one manuscripts for which he paid £800, included in the purchase were a bible of 1577 and several documents bearing what Rogers claimed were Shakespeare signatures certified by experts. There was also a manuscript book, *An Apology by the Earl of Essex*, represented to be in the handwriting of Shakespeare.

Rogers did not appear.

Captain Jaggard in the witness box said, "These signatures are not genuine and the majority of the papers included in the purchase have not been delivered."

Mr Justice Rigby Swift awarded £800 with costs to Captain Jaggard. *He also declared that he* could not understand how Rogers had managed to impose on a gentleman of the obvious intelligence and experience of Captain Jaggard.

It certainly did not seem credible that WJ had been fooled by Rogers. I assume that WJ negotiated the purchase of these documents knowing they were forged. Then he saw the opportunity to get his money back for the documents that had not been delivered.

This would mean that WJ had, or was intending to make use of these forged documents for some purpose. Over the next few years, WJ made several business trips to America.

The second court case was to take place six months later, in November 1927.

But first, incredibly, in July 1927, just a couple of months after the first court case, there was yet another find in Stratford-upon-Avon ... and WJ was involved.

Birmingham *Gazette* 22nd July 1927

TUDOR FINDS AT STRATFORD

One of the finest pieces of work of the Tudor Period still existing in Stratford-upon-Avon came to light this week during alterations at an old Inn now known as The White Swan Hotel but which was previously called the King's Head.

Removing some old oak panelling, workmen discovered mural paintings in very fine condition and only slightly coated with dust. The existence of the paintings was entirely unsuspected and for some time no clue to their date or meaning could be found.

Fortunately an eminent archaeologist inspected the new treasures and as the result of further research an authoritative opinion on them is now possible.

(The centre of the mural had been unwittingly destroyed by the creation of a serving hatch but it seems sufficient remained to envisage the original which measured fourteen feet wide by six feet high. There followed a very detailed description of the mural and its origins. These are just a few extracts from the article in the Birmingham Gazette.*)*

The work of some monks of the Middle-Ages depict scenes from the Book of Tobit in the Apocrypha ... It tells of a huge fish which sprang out of the water endeavouring to swallow Tobias ... Raphael, an angel, forbade Tobias to remove the fish from the Tigris which they roasted, having first saved the heart, liver and gall wherewith to make a decoction to cure his father's blindness ... this picture was done about 1460 to 1480 at the actual time that Caxton was setting up his first printing machine.

This discovery has excited the liveliest interest in Stratford and every precaution is being taken to preserve such a unique link with the past.

As far as I know the discovery of the mural in the White Swan in 1927 was genuine. (Sylvia Morris, an official of the Shakespeare Club, has the story on her Shakespeare blog.)

I must admit that I had a few misgivings about the story based on the identity of the eminent archaeologist who gave his authoritative opinion having inspected the mural – Captain William Jaggard. I have no other information on WJ's career or expertise as an archaeologist.

In November 1927 WJ was back in court for the hearing, this time with the man who had sold him the forged relics. The exchanges between Rogers and WJ in court were intriguing.

Shakespeare Press

The Scotsman 27th November 1927

Alleged Forgeries

Man Sent For Trial

After a hearing lasting two days Hunter Charles Rogers (47) was last night committed from Slough Police Court charged with Forgery and False Pretences in reference to Alleged Relics of Penn, Milton, and Shakespeare.

The charges included obtaining two sums of £800 each by false pretences from Captain William Jaggard, author of the Bibliography of the Shakespeares of Stratford-upon-Avon.

The supposed Relics were produced in court.

Captain William Jaggard deposed to buying two collections from Rogers, who guaranteed that all things were genuine. He found that they were not and when he asked for the return of his money Rogers told him "to go to blazes".

Mr Williams, the magistrate, asked how many signatures of Shakespeare are there?

Captain Jaggard – Only six genuine ones, about that there can be no doubt. *Jaggard claimed that he* saw at once that a number of things he was buying could not be genuine, but there was a chance that one document might be true and authentic.

After being questioned about why he had parted with his money WJ maintained that the First collection was stowed away because he wanted to see different experts to make sure everything was right or wrong. And then before he could get help on the First collection he offered me the Second collection and I thought I might as well take the whole lot.

At this point Rogers challenged WJ.

Rogers: You said in court at Birmingham that they were old forgeries.

Captain Jaggard: What I said was that I believed that some of the forgeries were old ones.

Rogers: Did you not offer Dr Tannenbaum of New York one of the documents for £10,000?

Captain Jaggard: No this is the first time I have heard of it. I have never offered Dr Tannenbaum any document in my life.

Rogers: You knew that Dr Tannenbaum had seen me at a hotel in New York.

Captain Jaggard: I did not know.

Rogers: If it was worth £10,000 you have not paid me the right price for the collection.

Captain Jaggard: I have never offered it to Dr Tannenbaum. It is very unfortunate that you do not produce the letter with the offer.

Rogers: You knew that the greater number of these things were Henry Ireland Forgeries.*

Captain Jaggard: I did not know that.

Rogers: Did I not inform you?

Captain Jaggard: You did not.

Andy Jaggard

WJ's explanations are implausible. "I might as well take the lot" *when offered the second collection, despite the fact he had not yet verified the first collection with* "different experts".

The entire exchange about Dr Tannenbaum is highly suspicious.

*Given his very detailed knowledge of the Ireland Forgeries, his response that he "did not know" *that they were Henry Ireland forgeries is not credible . He must have planned to sell, or use, these forgeries in some way. A few years later he was involved in a* 'Great Find' *that may have a connection to these suspicious dealings.*

Given Roger's inept performance in court it's hardly surprising that he was committed for trial on the offences, the magistrate no doubt believing the testimony of a famous bibliographer of Shakespeare rather than that of a part-time gardener.

The next year in March 1928 WJ, accompanied by Edith Parkin, took his First Folio on his trip to America where it was sold to an unidentified buyer. Who knows what other items he was also offering for sale to some American customers on that trip.

CHAPTER 18 A GREAT FIND

Shakespeare's 'Lost Years' – 'Once a Printer and a Bookman'

Andy Jaggard
There have been countless theories about Shakespeare's Lost years between his ill-considered marriage in 1582 and his first play in 1591/2. WJ had formed his own hypothesis about Shakespeare's profession during these lost years.

In typical WJ fashion, it involved some very laborious and detailed research to support his hypothesis. He was immensely proud of his status as a Freeman of the Worshipful Company Of Stationers. Now he had the opportunity to give his lecture at the Stationers' Hall in London.

In his book, Selling Shakespeare, Biography, Bibliography and the Book Trade, *Adam Hooks, sets the scene:*

On the twentieth of October 1933, at Stationers' Hall in London, Shakespeare Biography and Bibliography came together as never before. That evening, Captain William Jaggard, proprietor of the Shakespeare Press in Sheep Street in Stratford-upon-Avon, delivered a lecture on the Printing Trade in which he told an 'Unwritten Chapter' in the biography of Shakespeare.

The lecture and the subsequent publication, Once a Printer and Bookman *(1934) may have been prompted by a book by William Blades claiming that Shakespeare was, at one time, a printer.*

In the magnificent Stationers' Hall, WJ started that night by saying that he had developed, "a reasonable hypothesis … that those ten years between Shakespeare's ill-considered marriage in 1582, and the appearance of his earliest play in 1591/92 provide the keynote to his subsequent career and fame … I propose to go a step further than Blades and say that our Poet was for several years both Printer and Bookman."

WJ's account of the start of the story proceeded swiftly:

"Richard Field, a friend of Will Shakespeare had left Stratford in 1579 to become a prosperous printer in London … the penniless Will, unable to afford a horse for the journey, faced four days of weary tramping to reach London, but once there, he was assured of food and shelter, with his friend, Dick Field, until work could be found."

WJ reassured his audience, "Thus far we are on sure ground. The rest is deduction-based upon ample circumstantial evidence."

In brief, this was WJ's deduction: books were essential, but expensive; Will needed them to acquire the mountain of knowledge, and his vocabulary of 16,000 words; Will Shakespeare he claimed, had become a proofreader in Henry Denham's printing office (where he would also be-friend Denham's young apprentice, William Jaggard); this had given him the access to books he needed, including the new edition of *Holinshed's Chronicles** whilst in his spare time he would get some practical experience into the art and mystery of printing.

*The famous source book for Shakespeare's plays.

And then to support his hypothesis that Shakespeare was a printer, WJ provides the evidence of 500 quotations from Shakespeare's plays all of which demonstrate, he says, an intimate knowledge of the printing trade

Here are just three examples of how he sets out the evidence with the printing/publishing terms, the quotes, and his notes:

BROADSIDES
Pistol – "Fear we Broadsides? No! Let the fiend give fire" – 2 KING Henry IV, ii 42

Note: As no newspapers existed until long after, the usual way to expose an abuse, attack a foe, or right a wrong, was to print a single sheet or 'broadside'. These passed from hand to hand until worn out. They were often libellous, or rudely personal; hence the point of Pistol's remark.

COIGN
Gower – "By the four opposing coigns
       Which the world together joins" – Pericles. iii, I

Note: Here Shakespeare accurately pictures the iron or steel frame called a chase, holding say two pages of type, making ready for press. Small and hard wooden edges, termed coigns or quoins are filled in, are forced in around the type, with a mallet to make the chase tight and safe, etc.

DEVIL
Rosalind – "Tis not your inky brows" – As You Like It iii, 5

Falstaff – "And learning, a mere hoard of gold, kept by a devil" – 2 King Henry IV, iv, 3

Macbeth – "The devil damn thee black, thou cream-faced loon" – Macbeth, v, 3

Othello – "For here's a young and sweating devil here
       That commonly rebels. Tis a good hand" – Othello, iii, 4

Note: The fitting connection of 'Devil' and 'Hand' is apparent to any printer. The apprentice or youngest hand of any printing staff is the 'Jack-of-all-jobs', who fills odd time by picking up dropped type, cleansing utensils, conveying proofs, etc. Because he manages to convey daily much ink to his hands and face, he has been dubbed for centuries the printer's devil, etc.

There are pages and pages of these terms, the quotes, and then his notes. The mind boggles at the hours and hours that must have been involved in selecting these 500 quotations, cross-referencing them with the printing and publishing terms, and writing the detailed notes.

These three examples may demonstrate, an intimate knowledge of the printing trade, but many of the terms WJ cited could have different associations, terms such as, LETTERS, PAGE, OVER-READ, PAPER, RHYMES, SCRIBE, SONNET, TITLE, WORM-HOLES.

After WJ's lecture, the chairman opened by saying he didn't quite understand, because surely the various terms could equally apply to scholars, rather than printers. *Others talked about them* demonstrating a knowledge of the classics, and the links to bookselling. *WJ seized on these comments.* The references did indeed demonstrate Shakespeare's knowledge of at least eighteen of the thirty 'Classics', and yes, my aim was to show that Shakespeare was more than a printer, indeed it is my conviction that Shakespeare was also a Bookman.

Adam Hooks in his critique, comments:

"Captain Jaggard's foray into the field of Shakespearean biography, that evening, was a thoroughly researched argument, and may also have been a self-reflexive act of wish fulfilment. But his eccentric exercise differs only in degree, rather than in kind, from the methods of mainstream biographical and bibliographical scholarship."

Hooks goes on to say, "my objective is not to condemn the Captain, who seems to be aware of the more speculative elements in his argument ... but to illustrate both the possibilities and problems of merging biography and bibliography. Captain Jaggard told a story in which printers and booksellers made Shakespeare, a story about how books and the book trade shaped his life. He is the descendant who begets both his forefathers and his objects of study in the image of his own profession."

Just as a footnote. At the end of his lecture, WJ put forward an idea,

"perhaps apropos to the occasion … Since William the Norman Conqueror of Britain, several other all yclept *(called)* William have done a little conquering …"

WJ proposed that, it might be well to briefly record their names, dates and doings on 'A Scroll of Fame', printed on vellum, and glazed, to hang in Stationers' Hall.

His tentative list of the seven famous stationer WILLIAMS were: Messrs

Caxton, Tyndale, Shakespeare, Jaggard, Lowndes, Blades and Hazlitt

William No. 4 was of course his famous ancestor, not WJ himself.

I wonder now whether WJ's eccentric lecture was intended as a forerunner to what WJ had planned as his crowning achievement. A GREAT FIND.

WJ had argued that William Shakespeare had been a printer and a bookman. Shakespeare had worked in Henry Denham's office where he had befriended the young William Jaggard. As a result, Will Shakespeare had access to a copy of Holinshed's Chronicles.

You may remember the enquiry from the American researcher that had been the trigger for our research and for completing my

father's book. He knew that Captain Jaggard had owned a copy of Holinshed's Chronicles *in the 1930s and wanted to know whether it was still in the family. Now I know the reason for his inquiry. We had come full circle.*

Wouldn't it be amazing if one day the very copy that Shakespeare had used in Henry Denham's office were to turn up, perhaps even with evidence of a link to the Bard himself.

Who knows it did in February 1936

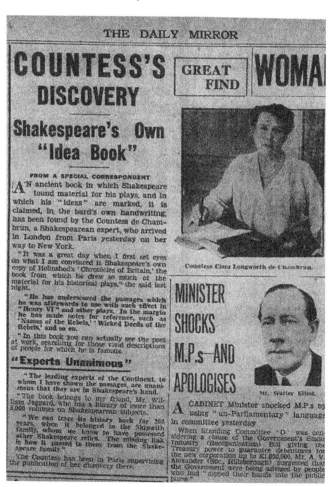

The Great Find was made by Countess Clara Longworth de Chambrun "a Shakespearean expert". *

Her claims were straight-forward for the book she had 'found'.

It was, she said:

The ancient book in which Shakespeare's 'ideas' for his plays had been marked in the Bard's own handwriting.

He has underscored the passages he was later to use with such great effect in *Henry VI* and other plays. In the margins he had made notes for reference such as 'Names of the Rebels', 'Wicked Deeds of the Rebels' and so on.

The leading experts of the Continent to whom I have shown the passages are unanimous that they are in Shakespeare's hand.

The book belongs to my friend Mr William Jaggard who has a library of 5,000 volumes on Shakespearean subjects.

We can trace its history back for 200 years to the Skipwith family whom we know to have possessed other Shakespeare relics.

The missing link is how it passed to them from the Shakespeare family.

*Countess Clara Eleanor Longworth de Chambrun, was an American patron of the arts and scholar of Shakespeare. Her father was an Ohio State Supreme Court judge, and her brother, Nicholas, was a congressman from Ohio, eventually becoming Speaker of the United States House of Representatives from 1925–31. He married Alice Roosevelt, daughter of President Theodore Roosevelt, in 1906. She was married in Cincinnati on 19th February 1901 to Aldebert, Comte de Chambrun, a direct descendant of the Marquis de Lafayette.

Her 1938 book Shakespeare Re-discovered *was prefaced by Professor G.B. Harrison, in words notable for their mental reservations about the Countess:*

He set forth her qualifications for research into Shakespeare's life. She loved Shakespeare from the age of six until over sixty ... and when she was a child in Cincinnati her grandfather told her tales from Shakespeare.

She has published various other scholarly books and articles which read somewhat like fiction and several works of fiction that abound in the paraphernalia of scholarship.

Clara and WJ's 'Great Find' generated a great deal of interest and controversy in 1936.

In America, the Boston Herald *had interviewed WJ about the discovery.*

5th November 1936 – Boston Herald – *A Shakespeare Discovery*

Capt. William Jaggard is, as he says, of 'the old Jaggard race' who founded in 1590 in Fleet Street, the original Shakespeare Press ... Furthermore, he has made more than one Shakespeare Discovery, although the reported finding of the *Holinshed's Chronicles*, with the poet's own annotations will be, if verified, the most important of all.

In England the discovery had first been announced in The Sphere *on 4th April 1936.*

A follow-up article in the week of the Birthday celebrations of 23rd April 1936, gave WJ the opportunity to respond to several letters sent to the magazine with **sceptical comments:**

"It is pure assumption that the marginal notes on the copy of *Holinshed's Chronicles* are in his handwriting."

"How can Captain Jaggard be justified in speaking of having recognised the familiar writing of Shakespeare."

"The only authentic specimens we possess are signatures to legal documents and even these are not above suspicion."

The unknown author of The Sphere *article seemed to be remarkably supportive of Jaggard's claims,* "Captain Jaggard makes a very clear reply to these letters stating his case in terms that appear to leave no possible room for doubt."

After which we have WJ's reply, a typical mix of bluster, outraged defence and withering attack.

"It is possible for writing to be familiar with fewer than eleven characters."

After which he delivered a mini lecture on, "the fourteen distinct majuscules and minuscules in the six legal autographs to wit – a, B, e, h, I, k, l, m, p, r, S, s, W, y. If your reader's opinion equals his arithmetic we may pass him by and say "We are amused".

"What can be meant by the bare-faced assertion that those six autographs are not above suspicion. The documents themselves are backed by centuries of public custody that place them entirely outside carping mistrust."

And so on.

The sequence of events of WJ's exploits captured in these newspaper stories and magazine articles are extraordinary, from buying forged relics, to his eccentric lecture about Shakespeare's early career as a printer and bookman, to his amazing discovery, together with the Countess of Chambrun, of Shakespeare's 'Ideas book'.

Why would WJ, a successful businessman, take the risk of getting involved in these illicit, possibly criminal activities involving forgery and fraudulent dealings?

Possibly for financial reward, the sums of money cited for the sale of Shakespearean literary items, whether genuine or historical forgeries, were considerable. Perhaps for the excitement of pulling off the deception, the opportunities to live the high life, and to impress 'the ladies'.

'Vanity' and 'Overconfidence' are the words that Gerald used to describe his father.

In his 1912 book, WJ had speculated on the motivation of the Shakespearean frauds: "Probably it arose from vanity, from a desire to make a name, as hanger-on, in connection with the greatest of literary names."

WJ's acrimonious relationship with the man he called ''His Majesty Sidney Lee', may have been rooted in his jealousy of his arch rival's 'AMAZING FIND' of the Vincent First Folio in 1899?

Perhaps in his own mind WJ had now topped that with his own 'GREAT FIND' – Shakespeare's own copy of Holinshed's Chronicles complete with his research notes, in his own hand, in the margins.

If it does still exist in some collection ... well ... we'd like it returned to the rightful owners.

CHAPTER 19 HE WALKED ALONE

"Reputation is an idle and most false imposition, oft got without merit and lost without deserving " Othello Act II Scene 3

Andy Jaggard

Helen Greenland, Harry Jaggard's daughter, had shared her memories with me of Rose Bank, the one in Stratford, shortly after the end of the Second World War. Helen, a child of three or four at the time, had been taken to Stratford by her mother, Hilda, to visit Edith Parkin. Her 'Aunt Edie' and 'Uncle', as Helen knew him, were still the only two occupants of the family home. Helen told me that Aunt Edie had the run of the place when 'Uncle' was away on business. Helen recalled what a beautiful house it was, with a lychgate, a portcullis window, an orchard and rose garden, and a "half moon landing on the first floor", with all the bedrooms going off.

On one occasion, Aunt Edie gave Helen some pots and pans to play with in the garden. She used to wheel Helen around in a little wicker shopping basket, taking her across Clopton Bridge and up Sheep Street to the Shakespeare Press bookshop, letting herself in with her own key.

Edith and Hilda were great friends and on another visit to Stratford they took the four-year-old Helen to see Quo Vadis *at Stratford Picture House.* "Not a suitable film" *for Helen, a serious* child, who was "extremely embarrassed by Aunt Edie and her mother's exaggerated stage whispers throughout the performance".

WJ died on 27th April 1947. Probate wasn't granted until February 1949. His estate was worth just over £23,000 (around £700,000 in today's terms). The money was left to Edith Parkin and Joseph Storer, a coal merchant from Lancashire. (We know nothing of Storer's connection with WJ.)

Edith returned to Cambridgeshire and bought a house in Cambridge city where she lived from 1952 until her death in 1967.

She and Hilda went to Switzerland each year, skiing and staying in the best hotels. Helen also joined them for some of these trips. When Edith died in 1967 her house was left to Harry, and her money was shared between her sisters, Ruth and Lilla.

32. Edith Parkin by the lychgate, Rose Bank, Stratford 1940s.
Photo courtesy of Helen Greenland and Alan Harry.

One story from Helen about her Aunt Edie has really stayed with me. Helen had shared some confidential information with her and Edith had responded, *Helen, my dear, you need to know that I am completely unshockable.*

The Times – *30th April 1947* – Capt. William Jaggard Bibliographer of Shakespeare.

The passing of William Jaggard will be deeply felt by his many friends in this country and the United States of America, and especially by his fellow townsmen of Stratford-upon-Avon where he was a notable public figure. Throughout his long and active life William Jaggard was a fervent Shakespearean in the best sense, and twenty-two years of it was devoted to the preparation of his monumental 'Shakespeare Bibliography', which he published in 1911. Educated at Leamington and Cambridge, Jaggard was later trained as a printer and bookseller to follow the same vocation as his illustrious namesake, from whom he was a direct lineal descendant.

WJ had been proud of his long association with the Stationers' Company. This is their resolution of sympathy, together with his Obituary in The Times on 30th April 1947.

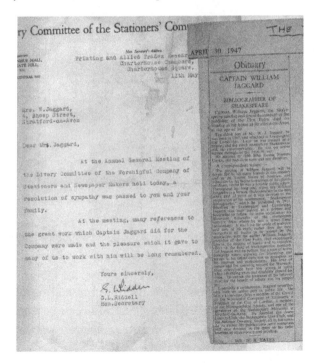

*Another obituary entitled **'Eminent Stratford Bibliographer –
Death of Captain William Jaggard'** didn't pull any punches with
this more accurate assessment of WJ's character:*

On the morning of Shakespeare Sunday Captain William Jaggard
died. He would have felt the appropriateness of ending his earthly
existence on a day of Shakespearean Celebration, for his life was
devoted to our National Poet and his deepest pleasure was to discuss
with others the influence that Stratford's greatest son continues to
exercise. He was known best and to most through his remarkable
bookshop in Sheep Street. Thither came many in search of literary
treasures and there the learned found their knowledge and perhaps
their faith strengthened. Baconian or Oxonian who ventured within
the precincts found their heterodoxy overwhelmed, for William
Jaggard was a man of deep erudition. He countered theory with fact
so effectively that argument became one-sided declamation.

WALKED ALONE

William Jaggard walked alone – the fate of many men who have
experiences beyond those of the common man. This troubled
him not at all, for he was largely self-sufficient. Fools he did not
suffer gladly, and both his pen and his tongue could flay those who
offended. Such contributions did not add to the gaiety of nations,
but complaints left him unmoved.

During the stormy winter Mr Jaggard was confined to his home at
Rose Bank, Tiddington Road: when the weather improved he felt
no inclination to resume his usual avocations. He has passed on,
full of years and some of us will miss his strange figure passing
through the town to his literary home ... Most notable of all was
his *Shakespeare Bibliography* published in 1911 after twenty-two
years of preparation.

Captain William Jaggard – Courtesy of Helen Greenland and Alan Harry.

Writing in **Stratford Mosaic**, *Gerald, after recounting WJ's early life, reflected that:*

The Bibliography would occupy his spare moments for over twenty years. Recreation, holidays, even sleep were all sacrificed to the supreme object. My brothers and I, born a few years before the book was published, could make no practical contribution to the labour involved, although one of our games was an assiduous imitation of extracting details from catalogues which formed part of the work.

Andy Jaggard

It must have been an emotional and difficult time for the family, and the contents of his will may have come as an unwelcome surprise?

After the war WJ had built his 'Poet's Arbour' further down Sheep Street and here he concentrated his large collection of the finest and most valuable rare books and prints.

No. 4 Sheep Street, the Shakespeare Press, was left "a run-down mouldering treasury of unsorted volumes".

A family conference was called to decide the fate of the bookshop.

CHAPTER 20 GERALD'S 'SHAKESPEARE PRESS' – 1947–1960

36. Line drawing by Gerald (GQJ) from Stratford Mosaic 1960.

" *What is past is Prologue* " *The Tempest Act II Scene 1*

Andy Jaggard
Sadly, Gerald never did write his chapter on the bookshop for The Life and Death. *There are just some comments about his 17 years' occupancy from his chapter about the founding of the Shakespeare Press in 1910 (Chapter 2 of this book).*

Fortunately we have plenty of other sources: his article about Sheep Street in 1972 looking back at his time at No. 4; memories from customers, newspaper articles, family stories, and our own fond and vivid childhood memories of the old bookshop.

After school, Anthea and I often met up there, so we soon became familiar with the long narrow building, dark, damp, cold and incredibly dusty, crammed full of bookshelves with thousands of old books. Gerald had a small 'office' at the front of the shop, created by more bookshelves with his antique desk and chair. There was a battered filing cabinet in one corner, an ancient till on top. The small inadequate paraffin heater in the centre of the 'office' had little impact on the ambient temperature which Gerald described as "the largest refrigerator in town" or more poetically, "as cold as Juliet's tomb". A selection of old prints adorned the plate glass window.

When our younger brother, Patrick, was born in 1961, with childcare still a problem, he spent two years outside the shop in his pram (not continuously). Passers-by spent a good deal of time retrieving toys thrown out of the pram, sometimes resulting in new clientele, if they took a moment to gaze in the shop window.

April 1947 must have been a strange and in some ways exhilarating time for Gerald. His father was dead and he was freed at last from his overpowering presence. He had spent the last twenty years living with his mother at 129 Loxley Road. Gerald, aged forty-three, was, it would seem, a confirmed bachelor. His twin Aubrey and sister Wendy were also unmarried and had joined Gerald and Emma Frances after the end of the war in 1945. They were all living together in the cramped semi-detached bungalow.

Not long after WJ died, there was a family conference. Wendy, Aubrey and Gerald would have been joined by elder brother Geoffrey, who had been a Major during the war. Geoffrey was another dominant character with some of his father's tempestuous personality.

In an article for the Birmingham Sketch on Sheep Street in 1972, Gerald ended the section looking back on his time at No. 4 with this:

When my father died in 1947 he had transferred to his Tudor-gate, and No. 4 was a mouldering treasury of unsorted volumes. When family differences had been sorted out, I crossed the road from the Auctioneers office and tackled the Augean stables.

Andy Jaggard
Gerald was the master of understatement but surpassed himself here with just these seven words. *When family differences had been sorted out.* We don't know what the differences were. Perhaps they argued over what should happen to the bookshop. Geoffrey had returned to his work as a senior journalist, Aubrey had a good job in the NFU, Wendy was a receptionist at the Birthplace Trust.

So Gerald, despite his twenty years working for Walker Barnard and Dobson, now as cashier and chief clerk, made the decision to *cross the street* from the auctioneers office and muck out *the Augean stables at* No. 4 Sheep Street. He may have convinced himself that he was only going in temporarily but very soon he had given up his safe job and committed himself to the bookshop.

Gerald was always cautious, not a risk-taker in any way. He had acted completely out of character. It was an impulsive decision and perhaps he had a romanticised vision of what his life would be like as an antiquarian bookseller. He was drawn to the bookshop like a moth to the flame because it aligned so well with his interests and his desires – books, literature and the theatre.

Again in 1972, in his article about Sheep Street, he looked back on those early days at the shop:

The war had not long ended, hard-cover books were scarce, and if the bookshop was to be kept going, now was the time. Going in

*as a temporary expedient I fell victim to the challenge and charm
of the place, and ran it for seventeen years. Knowing little about
antiquarian literature, and less about salesmanship, I look back
and wonder how it all happened. I realise now the advice of literary
friends, the innate kindness of book-lovers, and complete inversion
in the business itself helped me to keep going.*

Andy Jaggard

He had no experience as a salesman, or of the antiquarian bookshop
trade, or of running a business. In addition, he had little or no
capital to invest in the ailing and run-down business, after the
ravages of two world wars and WJ's neglect as he pursued his more
exciting Shakespearean *ventures* in his final years. WJ had removed
a very large number of the most valuable books and prints to his
storage facility further down Sheep Street. His fine collection was
auctioned off in 1949 and the money went into his estate.

Within months of making his first bold decision, Gerald was soon
contemplating a second. Shortly after *crossing the road from the
Auctioneers* and taking on the challenge of making a go of the
bookshop, Gerald met a young woman called Diana Salt. Perhaps
a weight had lifted off Gerald's shoulders and he was ready to start
life afresh.

The family story of how they met may well have been embellished
over the years, but it goes something like this.

No. 4 Sheep Street had no kitchen or washing facilities, only an
ancient outside toilet in a backyard right at the rear of the building.
Gerald was therefore in the habit of closing the shop, and going for
coffee, just down the street, at some charming old tearooms called
The Cobweb. On one occasion the tearooms were very busy, and
Gerald asked the young woman if he might join her at her table.
They soon struck up a conversation. This developed into more
regular meetings for coffee, with Diana agonising over various
boyfriends and Gerald in the role of 'counsellor' (or at least doing

most of the listening). As there was a twenty-year age gap between them this was perhaps to be expected.

Diana confided in Gerald that there was one, eminently respectable, but decidedly boring 'suitor' (as they were termed in those days) who she had tried to 'loosen up', by taking the man country dancing, as well as daring him to hang from a tree over the river. Unfortunately, for the suitor, he also frequented the Union Club in Stratford and was playing a game of snooker against Gerald, who, innocently asked him:

"How's the country dancing? I hear you've been ... hanging around with Miss Salt."

Whether the man did miscue on the black is open for debate.

37. Diana Salt and Gerald Jaggard, shortly after they met in 1947.

When Gerald and Diana met again for coffee at The Cobweb, Gerald, perhaps calling on his dramatic skills, announced:

"I'm sorry, Diana, but I won't be coming any more."

I imagine Diana's face fell. "Ohh ... why?"

"The summer season is coming and I can't afford to be away from the Shakespeare Press."

Diana smiled. "I'll bring a flask of coffee."

The romance blossomed quickly, and just over a year later, in August 1948 Gerald went to see Diana's father, Sir Edward Salt, at Avonhurst, his country house in Tiddington, to ask for her hand in marriage. (My *other* grandfather was a successful and very respectable businessman in Birmingham, a former MP for Yardley and knighted for his civil work during the Second World War.) The engagement was sealed and Gerald confirmed the alliance, shortly before Diana left for a two-week family holiday at The Waterhead Hotel, Ambleside, in the Lake District.

Tuesday 1st September 1948

My Dear Diana,

I enjoyed the flashing lights as I left Avonhurst – they gave me a friendly send off. It was <u>very</u> late before I finally dropped off to sleep, but I don't blame the English Liqueur, which was delicious, especially when made by a certain Popsy.

The family have been duly advised of the proposed alliance and are <u>very</u> pleased. I have completed the application form for the lodge …

Over the next two weeks, Diana wrote twelve letters to Gerald from The Waterhead Hotel in Ambleside.

They were married in April 1949. With no money to buy their own house they lived initially in the lodge at Sir Edward's country house, Avonhurst, in Tiddington, on the banks of the River Avon

Anthea was born there in July 1950.

38. Anthea, Diana and Gerald – Avonhurst, December 1950.

A couple of years later the plans for a gardener's cottage in the grounds of Avonhurst were altered to create 'Greensleeves', a detached house, and Sir Edward very generously gifted Gerald and Diana the land.

This is where I was born on 27th April 1952, also the date of WJ's death exactly five years earlier. Five years on Gerald's life had changed dramatically, with a wife and two young children to support, whilst trying to build a business out of the bookshop.

Although we lived in a detached house on a large plot, we had very little money. Diana was a teacher in a private preparatory school in Stratford, a notoriously poorly paid profession in those days. Gerald had only the meagre amount of money he could afford to pay himself from the income from the bookshop.

The dual challenge of attempting to make a living from the bookshop and starting a family transformed his life. It was very tough for him in many ways though. He was still deeply affected by memories of his father although this manifested itself to us as young children through his 'funny stories'.

Steve Newman writing in the *Trinity Times* – 2017

I remember the bookshop well as a dark place which felt like something out of a Dickens' novel, and there were plenty of those around, including small leather bound first editions that reeked of the past.

Jaggard was a very quiet man who acknowledged your presence with a nod, allowing you to meander around the two floors of his shop, all the while keeping a discreet eye on you. Back in the late 1950s and early '60s most of his books were out of my price range, although I recall buying a copy of R.L. Stevenson's Travels with a Donkey in the Cevennes!

Gerald Jaggard was born in Liverpool in 1904, with a family steeped in Shakespearean folklore, not least that of being related to William and Isaac Jaggard, the father and son printers of Shakespeare's First Folio of 1623, which isn't a bad link for a Stratford bookseller.

Andy Jaggard - We got used to hearing of the struggle to make a living wage from the shop. Gerald, according to Diana, "didn't earn much ... could only afford to pay himself £7 a week." He was, "good at buying [from book auctions], but not much good at selling." He "didn't like to sell the valuable books ... the summer season could be busy, but the winters were very quiet."

The total family income was very limited. Diana's speciality was exploiting free offers, vouchers and scores of sample products as ways of feeding the family. To this day I can't face a Blue Riband chocolate bar or an Angel Delight.

Looking back, Diana's criticisms of Gerald, whilst they had some truth in them, were more than a little harsh. The first twenty years of his working life had mostly been in clerical roles, and then for many years, working in the auctioneers office again in a predominantly administrative role, although he did do a little stand-in auctioneering. He had to learn how to run a business.

Back in the 1940s and 1950s you couldn't take a course in how to be an antiquarian bookseller. It wasn't a profession, there were no entry requirements, no qualifications and no code of practice.

It's doubtful if there was much, or indeed anything, in the way of business support and advice at that time. And whilst there was a lot of stock – around 18,000 books – the vast majority were not particularly valuable.

Just because a book is old, or an antique, doesn't mean it has significant value. The factors that may create value may include whether it is a first edition, its scarcity, if it has an author's signature, special binding, artwork, and its overall condition. John Baxter, the book dealer and biographer of Graham Greene, describes how the famous author was a "committed bibliophile" and so "Greene deliberately signed obscure copies of his works in far-off locations, in the certain knowledge that these would become sought-after rarities."

39. The Shakespeare Press, first floor, built c.1490 (a WJ postcard).

A more recent, book collector turned book dealer, Rick Gekoski, in his article, *'How to get ahead – or at least stay afloat in the rare book trade' (July 2014)*, neatly describes some of the challenges and perils of trying to turn a 'hobby' into a viable business. As a collector he had built up an impressive catalogue of books by famous authors, Conrad, Joyce, Eliot, Forster, Waugh, the typescript of Virginia Woolf's *Freshwater* and many more.

When he set himself up as a book dealer, and sent out his catalogue of 179 items, it was easy to spot which of them came from his personal collection, and which were *additions and fillers (priced between £10 and £50)*. He issued his catalogue, total retail value £38,663, to around a thousand potential customers. Within three months half the items were sold ... *most of the better ones,* and he had some working capital, which he re-invested in new inventory.

Analysing, in retrospect what had happened ... which he didn't at the time:

I had recovered what I had invested in the books, plus a few thousand pounds over. I had thus made a profit and – I hadn't thought about this either – tax was going to be due on that. When my accountant told me we had made some £10,000 in my first year, my wife was both pleased and surprised, and enquired if she could buy a new winter coat.

Looking at our bank balance, I said glumly, *'There's nothing there.'*

'So what happened to the profit?'

I pointed to my modest inventory, sitting on the shelves.

'That's it: all of them are paid for. The profit consists of the books I can't sell.'

Rick quickly concluded: "It was becoming clear I had no idea – economically speaking – what I was doing," and goes on to describe the many things he learnt in order to run a successful book-dealing business.

Gerald was faced with a number of, mostly financial, problems. He might only realise a modest profit on the majority of the stock. It's unclear how many of the more valuable books were passed down to the bookshop. There were some valuable books, but you could only realise the value from each one, once, with the lingering fear that you were letting it go for less than its true value. He had very limited working capital to invest in new stock. In addition, he had all the overheads to take into account, rent, banking, accountancy, business equipment, light and heating (although there was precious little of that). He was, indeed, running the business on a shoestring.

Some of this is conjecture. We don't have a profit and loss account for the business. It's fair to say, though, that Gerald was probably not a natural businessman. He was risk averse and cautious by nature. But he had many other qualities that he brought to the challenge.

**40. Gerald Jaggard in the Shakespeare Press, 1960 –
(from Stratford Mosaic).**

If you asked someone for their archetypal antiquarian bookseller – tall, white hair, spectacles, quiet, genial, reflective – he fitted the bill. He dressed the part, as well, with his buttoned-down collar, smart tie and double-breasted blazer. He naturally allowed customers to browse without too much interference, but when asked he could share his considerable knowledge of all things Shakespeare, and his love of the written and spoken word. Despite his generally introverted manner, when encouraged, he was relaxed and charming in conversation and he was an entertaining raconteur, drawing on a rich fund of anecdotes and stories.

Stratford was very far from the all-year-round tourist destination it is today. The shop was over reliant on the summer season, and it must have been soul destroying sitting in the small office over the paraffin heater, in the long winter months, with little trade or income. No doubt he would have spent many hours thinking of ways to create other sources of income, than was possible from just book sales, some old prints, postcards and a few brasses.

A bonus was that through his many years in the Auctioneers Company he must have been very familiar with, and confident in the tactics to buy at auction in order to get a real bargain. Keep a poker face and time your moment to make your bid.

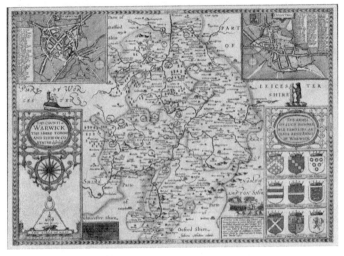

41. Speed County Map of Warwickshire.

An early success was when Gerald bought a job lot of 'Speed' Maps of English Counties at auction. He was delighted with the purchase and spent countless evenings at home, transforming the black and white maps with delicate watercolours.

They made a handsome profit.

He could also call on his experience as a part-time journalist for the *Stratford Herald*, as a theatre critic, and then for several years writing the Buster column. He was a fine writer.

How could he use his skills to increase the shop's turnover and profits?

Amongst WJ's, and now his own collections of treasures and memorabilia there was this pamphlet from 23rd April 1900 commemorating *the 336th Anniversary of our great National Poet's Birthday* with a performance of Pericles.

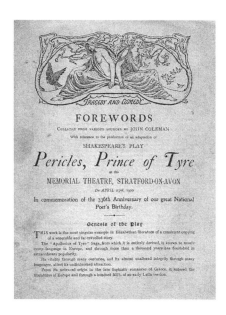

The Pamphlet COLLATED from VARIOUS SOURCES BY JOHN COLEMAN has a single fold creating a four-sided pamphlet with sections on: Shakespeare's Part in the Play; Stage History; and the Genesis of the Play.

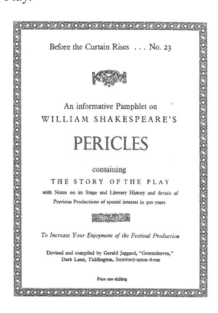

The pamphlet was clearly also the 'genesis' of an idea for some Shakespearean pamphlets of his own. Devised and compiled by Gerald Jaggard, the four-sided pamphlet had sections – *Notes on Pericles – Actors and Performances – The Story of the Play*.

It took him several years, but Gerald eventually produced pamphlets for all of the thirty-eight Shakespeare plays.

It must have been a mammoth job, both the research and writing of the pamphlets.

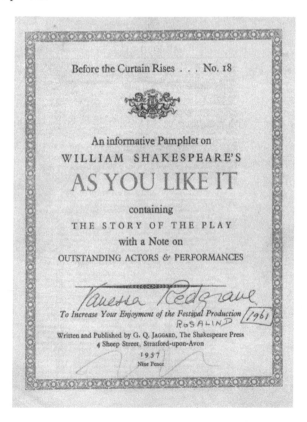

In November 2020, a pristine copy of one of the pamphlets originally priced at nine old pence was on sale on Abe Books for £17.

Vanessa Redgrave as Rosalind 1961.

Famous Actors

The pamphlets were produced in the early fifties. The plays from each year's summer season were naturally the most popular. Thousands were sold over the years, mostly from No. 4 Sheep Street, which was in a perfect location a few hundred yards from the Royal Shakespeare Theatre. Starting at nine old pence in 1955, and then a bold move to one shilling in 1960. By the seventies they were selling for twenty, forty and even fifty new pence. The shop was a magnet for many famous actors, taking a stroll from the theatre along Waterside and up Sheep Street into town. Gerald met most of them over the years, Redgrave, Gielgud and many others who were pleased to be asked to autograph the relevant pamphlet.

Gerald used to tell this story about a customer who wanted to buy his pamphlet for the 'Scottish Play' in the 1950s:

The Shakespeare Press, Sheep Street, July 1955

A middle-aged man and his wife had come into the bookshop, it was a hot day, the man had a sun hat shading his face and was wearing sunglasses.

Gerald asked how he could help and the man, in an American drawl, had said something to the effect that he'd heard that Gerald was descended from Shakespeare.

Gerald had corrected him, "No, not quite, just his printer, William Jaggard, I'm afraid."

The American and his wife had laughed then the man had said, "Heh, Mr Jaggarrrd, that'll do. Vivee and I are going to see some of your Shakespeare. They say it's the Scottish Play but its real title is *Macbeth*, weird. We wanted to get the story straight before we have to sit through it."

Gerald picked up his pamphlet and handed it to the man. "Of course, 'Before the Curtain Rises, No 13, the Story of the Play', some people find it helpful to understand the gist before ... "

The American looked confused. "What's the gist?"

Gerald apologised, "Sorry ... the er ... general idea of the story. People can find Shakespeare a little difficult to fathom at first."

Then the American had said, "Hey Mr Jaggaarrd, could you read us some – in your cute English accent?"

(Whenever Gerald told this story he played both himself and the American.)

Gerald had agreed, of course, although first he'd scanned the story of the play for a suitably dramatic section. Then moving into performance mode he declaimed,

"Macbeth, torn between his own great ambition and the horror of the method of gaining it, leaves the supper-room to wrestle with his conscience. Lady Macbeth, fully alive to the vacillating nature of her partner, comes to quell his forebodings, and outlines the plan she has devised. When Duncan is asleep, she will drug with wine the two soldiers keeping watch at the door; the King can then be killed, with the almost certain result that the two guards will be suspected. Macbeth at length agrees to this plot."

At this point, the American had removed his sun hat and sunglasses and said, "May I, Mr Jaggard?" in a perfect English accent. He had taken the pamphlet from Gerald, who was open-mouthed. Sir Laurence Olivier then continued the story in his clipped tones. "The appointed hour arrives, and the sleeping King is slain by Macbeth. But, in his haste and confusion, he returns to his wife still carrying the blood-stained dagger. [He mimed holding the dagger.] He refuses point-blank to return to the bedchamber, and it is Lady Macbeth who takes them, and places them in the hands of the sleeping attendants. There comes a knocking at the outer gate, and while Macbeth hurries away to change his garments, a Scottish lord named Macduff is admitted to the castle. He has come at the bidding of Duncan, and going up to the King's apartment, he discovers the crime. All is horror and confusion ..."

Olivier's intense stare slowly dissolved into a broad smile.

Gerald always maintained that at this point he'd instinctively dropped his head in a bow and mumbled, "Sir Laurence, I'm honoured ... um ... you've passed the audition. Excuse me, I'm sorry ... but what should I call you?"

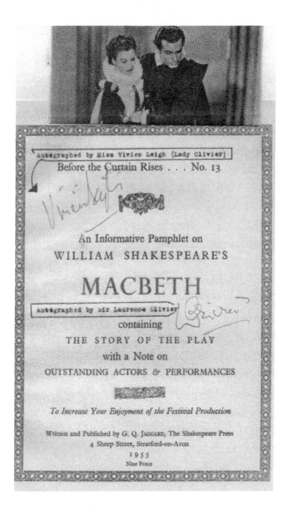

Olivier laughing apologised for *his little charade* ... then said, "If you call me Larry, and I call you Gerald it would be much better. I very much enjoyed your marvellous pamphlet, 'Before the Curtain Rises'."

After which Sir Larry and Miss Vivien Leigh kindly agreed to signing Gerald's Macbeth pamphlet.

There was one rather awkward moment before the famous pair left.

Kenneth Tynan, the respected (and still very young) theatre critic, had given Olivier a glowing review for the RSC performance but slated Vivien Leigh's performance.

Gerald had politely said how much he had enjoyed her performance.

And Vivien Leigh had replied, "You are very kind, Gerald, but as your Mr Kenneth Tynan wrote in his review of this American movie actress, 'Sir Laurence shook hands with greatness ... Vivien Leigh's Lady Macbeth is more niminy-piminy than thundery-blundery, more viper than anaconda, but still quite competent in its small way'."

Gerald still a little tongue-tied could only say, "The world can be very unkind, Miss Leigh ..."

Gerald writing in his 1972 article on Sheep Street reflected on his time running the Shakespeare Press:

American, Dominion, German, French, Italian, Finnish, Japanese, they all came along. There was a Korean professor who wanted to know the most suitable play to translate into his language; an Eastern prince who wanted a play synopsis. J.B. Priestley bought a novel and lamented the lack of a real tobacco shop in Stratford.

The winters were grim, but the long festival season brought its stream of international visitors. I could well have put the time-honoured notice in the window 'Fourteen Languages Spoken Here'. Happily for me, they all spoke English too.

By 1960 Gerald had been running the Shakespeare Press for thirteen years. The pamphlets were a great success. The summer season with the draw of a much-expanded RSC programme was a busy and exciting time for the bookshop. The old-fashioned, chaotic, but charming character of Gerald's bookshop was immensely popular both with local book enthusiasts and particularly with those overseas visitors. The quiet winter months were still a drain on the bookshop's profits, but Gerald had built a viable business.

The Stratford Corporation, responsible for the commercial operation of No. 4 Sheep Street, had other ideas.

CHAPTER 21 GERALD'S 'SHAKESPEARE PRESS' – 1960–1964

Andy Jaggard

In 1960 the Stratford Corporation who were responsible for No. 4 Sheep Street started talking about re-developing the property. The original plan was to demolish both No. 4 and No. 5 (a cottage) Sheep Street and build a row of new shops. It was a large and valuable retail space, which if redeveloped, would command a higher rental yield. This was the start of a four-year battle with the Stratford Corporation.

The *Birmingham Post* on 1st March 1962 reported on the *Fight to Save 15th-Century Stratford Bookshop. The Council claimed the support of expert advice for its opinion that the condition of the building whose frame dates from 1490 is such that it can not be allowed to remain.* The town clerk at the time stated, *Neither from an historical or an architectural point of view does it warrant the expenditure to put it into a fit state.*

Gerald had started a petition to save No. 4 from demolition and already had over 750 signatories including, *A New Zealand farmer namesake, a Texan customer who had never visited the shop, a Japanese girl who wrote her name in her own language, a Frenchman who called in, and a group who travelled specially from Manchester to add their signatures.*

He also had this photo call pointing to the original bark on the old beams in the *Old Curiosity Shop*.

On *4th May 1962* the *Birmingham Post* reported the *1,000 Protests over Stratford Demolition*

Not only had Gerald's petition hit this landmark but there was an offer by a Mr and Mrs Wassing who owned an antique shop in Meer Street for *an Ideal Solution*.

They were prepared to pay to preserve both No. 4 and No. 5 Sheep Street. There would be a new lease both for the bookshop tenancy and a retail space.

Stratford-on-Avon Borough Council however were *being urged to reject this private offer in favour of demolishing them and redeveloping the site at a cost of £15,000.*

On 9th May 1962 the Birmingham Post reported New Hope for Two Old Buildings in Stratford:

A step forward in saving old buildings from demolition when by a majority of twenty votes to four the Town Council 'referred back' the decision for demolition ... Councillor P.M. Ray said, "The buildings included a genuine Tudor bookshop which formed an essential part of the character of Stratford. If demolished it would render an irrevocable disservice to our priceless heritage."

It seemed that Gerald had saved the building, No. 4 Sheep Street, through the publicity surrounding his petition in 1962. Shamed by the outcry, the Corporation had reversed their decision for demolition.

However, by 1963 the outcome was still far from clear.

The ***Birmingham Post, 6th September 1963, Scheme to Restore Old Bookshop.***

The article started by reporting again on Gerald's petition with over a thousand signatures. It seemed like good news as *the Land and Building Committee was urging the Council to proceed with the restoration of the building.*

It also reported that *the Borough Surveyor had come up with a modified scheme ... but the cost of the scheme would not be borne by the Council.*

A Letter from Geoffrey

1964 was to be a very significant year for Stratford-upon-Avon, the 400th anniversary of Shakespeare's birth in the town.

Gerald was in the habit of preserving some important family letters, either copy letters or as in this case, the original. This letter was from Geoffrey, Gerald's elder brother, written on New Year's Day 1964.

It said quite a lot about his plans for the 1964 Shakespeare celebrations, about Gerald's future in the event of *the destruction of the bookshop,* and of most interest to me, about Geoffrey's character.

Gerald received his letter from his elder brother Geoffrey on 3rd January 1964. There were also some brief notes of Gerald's under *The Human Cyclone* (one of the first newspapers Geoffrey worked for had given him this nickname). Gerald had also made a list of the books Geoffrey had requested for the 1964 London Shakespeare Exhibition and a sketch of a new window display Gerald was planning in January 1964.

Greensleeves, 3rd January 1964

Gerald opened Geoffrey's letter. It was on impressive headed paper, ***Gore Hotel, Queens Gate, SW7* ... KNIGHTSBRIDGE 4222 – 10 LINES.**

Gerald read the opening line:

New Year's Day 1964 – Dear Gerald, An auspicious day on which to wish you, and all of yours, a happy and successful New Year with plenty of interesting problems and all of them solved by next Christmas!

Gerald glanced at a long section of family news, then decided he would take the letter with him to the shop to find out what Geoffrey was after. There would be precious little business to be had today, but that would give him an opportunity to work on the new display he had in mind.

On the short drive to Stratford he was reflecting on the irony that in this, perhaps the biggest Shakespeare celebration year ever, the 400th anniversary of the Bard's birth, there was also the depressing prospect that the Stratford Corporation would throw him out of the Shakespeare Press, resulting in the demise of the bookshop, steeped in Shakespeareana, that WJ had founded.

Gerald smiled to himself; WJ may have created his *fake* Tudor façade for the shop in 1910. The organising committee of the 400th celebration was planning an entire maze of *fake* Tudor streets – The Shakespeare Exhibition – in a massive temporary exhibition hall, on the banks of the Avon opposite the theatre. Actually it could be good fun, and very good for business.

It was freezing in *Juliet's tomb*. Sheep Street was deserted with a few flakes of snow starting to fall. Gerald immediately got the paraffin heater going in 'the office', then busied himself with the new display. At least climbing the stairs to the second floor and carrying piles of books around warmed him up somewhat. After a couple of hours, he was quite pleased with the display. Looking round he still felt the charm of the place and was proud of what he had achieved. The shop certainly hadn't made him a fortune but it provoked so many memories.

He had almost forgotten about Geoffrey's letter when he settled down close to the paraffin heater for coffee. *I'll bring a flask,* he thought. When was that, when he and Diana had first shared a flask in the shop, was it forty-seven or forty-eight?

Oh well, here goes, let's see what the cyclone wants this time. After his family news Geoffrey said, *the real occasion for writing was that he'd been trying to find the odd moment to say a word about the illustrations for the booklet Aubrey and I are preparing.*

Gerald had a good idea what was coming next. The *Companion to Stratford – Shakespeare's Town as He Knew It* by Geoffrey Jaggard was a tourist guide Geoffrey was planning for the big year. He'd roped in Aubrey, Gerald's twin to write some verses on Stratford streets and sought Gerald's ideas on some illustrations. Gerald, whilst suggesting some tasteful line drawings, had suspected this publication was really just a money spinner for his elder brother. Yes, here it was:

It was kind of you to let me see your sketches and for some time we dithered round the idea of line drawings ... But finally decided that photos were by far the best answer ... I do hope you will understand and not feel hurt and I'm sure you will not.

Pictures of hotels and pubs would be far more profitable. Gerald noted that Geoffrey didn't require a second party in order to complete a conversation. Next Geoffrey was talking about his lucrative book deal:

Inevitably everything happened at once. My own publishers (MacDonalds) sent me a contract ten days ago for signature detailing the book on SH. London which they want from me by MARCH if you please with thirty-two original illustrations which I have to collect from which they choose sixteen. They want 80,000 words, I never did like the sound of that, for the very good reason that I know with certainty that, on this subject, I have 50,000 words in me and not one more.

He went on to say he was going to ask them to tear up the contract and their royalties cheque and think again:

I have a much better idea for a book that would be really worthy of the Jaggard name in this particular year. The chapter on the printing of the First Folio is already written and makes 5,600 words. The BBC have already recorded my talk on the First Folio.

Geoffrey's enthusiasm was now bubbling over:

I'm involved, as you've probably already heard, in this London SH. Exhibition opening in April ... Intensely interesting ... coming up three days a week with my co-director ... A long series of visits to the Top People at places like Westminster Abbey, Barts Hospital, Kensington Palace, London Museum, British Museum, V & A, Public Records Office, Stationers' Hall, Southwark Cathedral and so on ...

... for the second time in my life, last week, I had the thrill of holding the beautifully balanced sword that King Harry carried at Agincourt ... the Abbey keep it backstage and don't show it to visitors.

Gerald, in a strange way, was enjoying this ... would the word *boastful* be a little harsh? A picture had formed in his mind of *King Geoffrey* lustily swinging his *beautifully balanced sword* as he advanced on Agincourt surrounded by all the *Top People.*

What would be next?

Disappointingly there followed a very long list of First, Second, Third and Fourth Folios, Quartos and other famous Elizabethan and Early Jacobean books that Geoffrey and his co-director would be exhibiting at the London Shakespeare Exhibition.

All of these are locked in a small Treasure Room, beneath the one I'm writing this in. It is criss-crossed with invisible rays connected to half the police stations in London

... One thing we are short of it seems to me, is an Editor's set of Shakespeare. Would you care to loan or hire us one. I think you used to have the Capell, that would do nicely ... Don't know what the state of the Exchequer is?

Gerald of course would oblige. He had a funny feeling though that the honour of exhibiting might be his sole reward and the *state of the Exchequer* would turn out to be quite limited.

And finally Geoffrey talked about *a possible opportunity* for Gerald:

If you might be inclined to be interested ... but I can say no more really at the moment ... not knowing what your own thoughts, or plans, may be for the future, in the event of the destruction of 4 Sheep Street.

Well that was a surprise ... *an opportunity* ... and Geoffrey's first mention of the impending fate of the precious bookshop, *in the event of the destruction of 4 Sheep Street.* Geoffrey knew how to couch things in a reassuring manner. Gerald was trying to envisage working *with*, or *for* Geoffrey.

Diana's private preparatory school had talked about offering Gerald some part-time teaching in the event of the sad demise of the bookshop.

Gerald thought he might prefer that.

47. No. 4 Sheep Street, the Shakespeare Press, 1964.

The Death of a Stratford Bookshop

A few months later in 1964, Gerald was given notice to quit with his eviction order timed for Christmas day of that year.

The Birmingham Post, *Monday 21st December 1964 – Shakespeare Shop to Close*

One of Stratford-upon-Avon's oldest bookshops, the Shakespeare Press is to close on Christmas Eve. For four years the proprietor, Mr Gerald Jaggard has been fighting to keep the shop open. "There is nothing else I can do," Mr Jaggard said, "I have been pressed to leave for years."

Mr Jaggard will be keeping 5,000 of his most valuable books, but the majority of the stock, more than 10,000 books will be sold to a salvage firm for £10.

Despite various schemes (a smaller bookshop combined with another business) nothing had been agreed. He was forced to close. Gerald did not have the money or the boldness to make a large investment in the property. No. 4 Sheep Street stood empty and derelict for seven years.

This letter which Gerald wrote to the local paper, during his four-year battle with the Council, can serve as the bookshop's epitaph:

Gerald Jaggard

That the bookshop they visit is run by direct descendants of the First Folio printer and publisher gives them an added pleasure. But the visitors do not come only to browse - they come to talk and ask questions. They love to hear of old customs, legends and the folklore of the neighbourhood, and to discuss the plays. Playgoers, professors, collectors, students, children - all come to wander round and sometimes to buy.

Fifty years ago, Miss Marie Corelli made it a regular port of call to rest in her special chair and to discuss with my father the latest literary topics.

I remember the late Sir Donald Storrs walking in because he had seen one of his early books in the window; Robert Donat lovingly handling a large volume of the Sonnets; Sir John Gielgud with his mother; Sir Barry Jackson; Dame Peggy Ashcroft; J.B. Priestley. Students from all countries, some as far off as Chile and Finland, love to browse through the textbooks, and to absorb the atmosphere of a place where time stands still.

Some time ago an envelope simply addressed to 'The Old Shop - Stratford - England' was unhesitatingly delivered to these premises. It is sad to think that in the near future, not only will such a missive be undelivered, but the very building to which it was consigned will have vanished. In Victorian days it was thought proper to cover half-timbered walls with a thick coating of plaster, but we are going a stage further – we are pulling them down.

Are we wise? Yours etc. Gerald Jaggard.

Writing in 1972, Gerald explained:

Today No. 4 Sheep Street is empty. The Corporation who owned it, took it for development in 1964. To be fair, they offered me a lease if

I would put the place in order to their design. This was impossible: old bookshops are not goldmines. They had wanted to pull it down, but without effort my petition for survival carried 1,000 signatures and No. 4 was reprieved.

Andy Jaggard

Eventually the property was completely and sympathetically renovated. The building still stands today, now The Vintner restaurant. (The story of the renovation is in the appendix.) WJ's mock Tudor façade remains largely intact and inside it's possible to imagine what the bookshop was like.

CHAPTER 22 THE GAME IS NEARLY UP

Andy Jaggard
After the closure of the bookshop in 1964, Gerald still carried on with some book-dealing with a small collection of the more valuable books kept at Mason's Croft, sadly not including the copy of Holinshed's Chronicles *with some notes in the margins in the poet's own hand.*

He also took up some part-time teaching at the Croft Preparatory School, coaching cricket, running the chess club and accompanying Diana on many outward-bound trips with her 'Young Explorers' to Wales and the Lake District. Diana led the hikes over the high mountains while Gerald led the lowland routes with some decent breaks in town for coffee.

In 1972, almost eight years after the closure of the Shakespeare Press, Gerald was writing to his 'uncle', Eric Jaggard, who lived in Vancouver, Canada.

Eric, born in 1889, was WJ's youngest brother (twenty-two years younger than WJ) and only fifteen years older than Gerald. I found out later that Eric had visited England in 1949 – he stayed at Rose Bank in Stratford, almost certainly in connection with probate, which took place that year, almost two years after WJ's death.

Gerald's letter to Eric was significant because 'the Jaggard Papers', which had been missing for twenty-two years, had finally turned up.

Greensleeves, Dark Lane, Tiddington, Stratford-upon-Avon, 10th March 1972

Gerald was in his study typing a letter, his concentration occasionally broken by shouts, manic laughter and the occasional high-pitched scream from downstairs.

Gerald Jaggard
My Dear (Uncle) Eric,

I seize this opportunity to write to you while my younger boy Patrick is holding his eleventh birthday party in another room. He wanted to have some football on the back lawn, but there is a bitterly cold wind, and there has been some snow.

It was no wonder that Gerald had seized the opportunity to escape from the madness that would be kicking off downstairs. Greensleeves was on a half-acre plot thanks to Sir Edward's generosity in gifting Diana and Gerald the land when they married. The large back lawn was the scene of almost daily five-a-side games, such that many residents of Dark Lane thought it was the village football pitch. Unfortunately it was too cold and snowy for even these football-mad eleven-year-olds to venture outside today.

Gerald was replying to a long letter from Eric. In one amusing section, Eric describes his visit to Liverpool in 1904. Eric was left in sole charge of the twins, Gerald and Aubrey, in their pram. They were both screaming continuously and Eric, aged fourteen, decided he'd have a go at changing both their nappies, and was very proud of himself when he completed the job, if a little roughly.

This is the same letter to Eric cited at the beginning of this book, where Gerald described his article on Sheep Street for the Birmingham Sketch *and how this had given him the idea for* The Life and Death.

After the reference to his proposed book, Gerald goes on to say:

The line of descent you have so kindly let me have will be tremendously useful, although I cannot attempt a detailed and scholarly treatment. Not that this is required; it is journalism which today must be succinct and entertaining.

Gerald's next words suggests he and Eric had an open and trusting relationship:

Also, I feel it should tell the truth, and I cannot pretend that relations between WJ and his family were roses all the way; as you know this was far from the case. The best of us are a mixture of good and bad, and I have always believed that much of the trouble stemmed from the fact that my father was determined to mould his family (and many others) into his own particular pattern, and would not tolerate advice or interference. Geoffrey unhappily inherited this trait, with the results that we are only too familiar with. However all that is in the past, and much of it is forgotten.

After some more news about a holiday in August to Austria, Gerald ends with:

Once again, I must thank you for the most interesting family papers you have been kind enough to pass on to me. They will certainly be treasured.

Andy Jaggard

Gerald had described elsewhere how WJ had always promised to publish the Jaggard family tree as the result of over thirty years research. However, when he died in 1947, the papers could not be found.

So it was Eric Jaggard who had been in possession of the so-called Jaggard Papers from after WJ's death until early 1972 when he bundled up the whole collection and posted it to Gerald.

One brown envelope titled 'The descent to 1730" contained all of WJ's research notes and his Jaggard family jottings through ten centuries.

Gerald had carried out his own research into the family tree and the direct descent in the 1950s and 1960s when we were children, but there was always a gap he could not bridge. He would have been intensely interested in the contents of the papers and WJ's jottings. He had a year and a half to make sense of WJ's 'line of descent'.

The 350th celebration of the publishing of the First Folio was due in November 1973. The Shakespeare Club were planning a big celebration for that milestone, with a First Folio on display, and it came as no surprise that they would invite a former Honourable Secretary and a direct descendant of William Jaggard, the printer, to give the speech.

I imagine that Gerald would have given a great deal of thought to how he constructed his speech and to exactly what he would say.

"DIRECT DESCENDANT OF THE FIRST FOLIO PRINTER TALKS ABOUT HIS ANCESTORS

STRATFORD'S FIRST FOLIO DISPLAYED AT SHAKESPEARE CLUB MEETING"

Gerald said it was one of his proudest moments addressing the Shakespeare Club that night.

Gerald Jaggard
In 350 years of the existence of Shakespeare's First Folio, the concentrated efforts of the Baconians, the

cranks, the disbelievers, the action committees, and the monument movers had been unable to displace or discredit one word of the Title Page.

So said Mr Gerald Jaggard, addressing the opening meeting of the Shakespeare Club's 150th session. There was a packed audience of members and guests in the Stratford Room of the Shakespeare Centre on Tuesday last week. My Ray Allen, introducing Mr Jaggard to the meeting, said that as a former Hon. Sec. of the Club and a vice-president of long standing, he was well known to most of them, but that evening he was speaking as a descendant of William Jaggard who, with his son Isaac, was responsible for publishing and printing the precious First Folio.

Also if time permitted, he would tell them something of his own father, Captain William Jaggard, Shakespearean scholar, bibliographer and bookseller. There was added interest in the fact that an original First Folio (kindly lent by the Birthplace Trust) was on view that evening, also a number of books published by the Tudor Jaggard, and also a collection of books, papers and photographs relating to Captain Jaggard, brought along by his son.

49. Stratford-upon-Avon Herald, November 1973.

Mr Jaggard said how honoured and privileged he felt to be standing in that splendid room, and taking part in the 350th celebration of the publication of the First Folio. At that moment, he felt closer to his ancestor, William Jaggard, than he had ever done before. That feeling was intensified by the fact that he had only recently received the papers dealing with his ancestry and compiled over thirty years of work by his father. After twenty-five years, these papers had been sent to him by the youngest brother of Captain Jaggard, from his home in Vancouver, British Columbia.

Describing the actual printing of the First Folio in November 1623, the lecturer said that although Isaac's name appeared on the title page with that of Edward Blount, the book was published at the charges of his father, William, and others. In 1906, Sir Sidney Lee made a Census of the known copies of the First Folio in this country, and found that only a small proportion of those had gone abroad. However, he forecast that the position would be reversed in twenty years or so, and was not far wrong.

Referring to the collection of First and other Folios held by the Folger Institute in Washington DC, USA, Mr Jaggard said that their most treasured Folio was the one given to Augustine Vincent, the herald, who was a close friend of Jaggard. When the First Folio was published, William Jaggard was dead, but Vincent, on receiving the copy, wrote in it 'Ex Dono Willi. Jaggard'.

From Sibthorp, in Lincolnshire, it went to Mr Henry Clay Folger. Mr Folger, who died in 1930, enlisted Captain Jaggard in his search for the Folios, and indeed, on one occasion, instructed Captain Jaggard to bring a precious volume over the Atlantic personally, all expenses paid.

To those who wondered why so many Folios are collected and stored in one place, the lecturer supplied the answer. Mr Folger's ambition was to make from these volumes a facsimile First Folio that would be as near perfect as possible, unlike the volumes in 1623, all of which had imperfections, and the mistakes in type, known as 'literals'.

Of the Droeshout portrait which adorns the title page, Captain Jaggard always held that William Jaggard, unable to take the helm, Isaac Jaggard lacked the judgement to employ a competent artist, hence the oddness of the coat and the eyes on the portrait drawn by young Dutch artists.

Mr Gerald Jaggard described how his father had determined early in life, to compile two great works. The first a Shakespearean bibliography that would record the writings of the poet and all published comment thereon, up to the end of 1910. This massive and monumental task took him twenty-two years and contained 36,000 entries. It was published in 1911 and attracted world tributes. The other enterprise was to trace his ancestry to the William Jaggard who published the First Folio, to whom he had dedicated the bibliography.

With the infinite patience and industry, which characterised his labours in the world of books, he pored over the records of Stationers' Hall, church registers, parish registers, he advertised, corresponded with members of the family, and studied back files of newspapers.

Eventually, after tracing a final link in Wales, he felt that the line of descent was complete, and aimed to bring out a book on the family tree in 1923. The book never appeared, and at his death in 1947 the papers could not be found.

Andy Jaggard
(Gerald may have paused briefly at this point leaving the audience to draw their own conclusions about what this means.)

Gerald Jaggard
Then, twenty-five years afterwards, they came into the lecturer's possession through the generosity of Mr Eric Jaggard, last of the family, who in his middle eighties still lives a vigorous and useful life in Vancouver.

William was described by his biographer, Edwin Willoughby, as undoubtedly a man of high courage and indomitable will, qualities which attracted enemies as well as friends. It would seem that these traits came down through the centuries to Captain Jaggard, who always termed himself 'the sixth William'. He fought many battles, verbal and written, and refused to compromise or take advice. It landed him in many bitter and disastrous situations.

Perhaps his greatest moment was when he was admitted to Stationers' Hall, being elected to their Inner Court, and remained in close touch with them right up to his death.

Andy Jaggard
To end, Gerald wheeled out the Samuel Pepys story.

Gerald Jaggard
A later Jaggard, Abraham, is mentioned several times by the inquisitive Samuel Pepys who dined at his home … Mrs Jaggard, a plain woman with pretty children being entreated by Pepys after supper to play on the Vyall.

Andy Jaggard
WJ had done the same.

The local paper's subheading read 'Known by Pepys' associating the Jaggard line with that well-known diarist.

I wonder how Gerald felt at the end of that high-profile evening? Was he pleased with how he had handled the big occasion? Or relieved? Was it 'his proudest moment?' This was November 1973 and it seems likely that he started writing his book, The Life and Death *a few months later in 1974.*

Maybe his thoughts had turned to the direct descent.

WJ spent a large part of thirty years of his life on that Mission. Other Jaggards have also spent many hundreds of hours in pursuit of their own truth.

The question is very simple. Is there a direct lineal descent from William Jaggard (1568–1623) or from his son Isaac Jaggard, to WJ, to Gerald, and to our family.

Yes, or No?

CHAPTER 23 THE DIRECT DESCENT

" To be, or not to be, that is the question?" Hamlet Act III Scene 1

Andy Jaggard
I had started looking at the Jaggard Papers during the Christmas holidays in 2019. By September 2020, after we had decided to pursue the book project, I had gathered a great deal of information on the direct descent.

It was, after all, one of our prime reasons for setting out to complete the family story.

We had WJ's confident claims throughout his lifetime, often supported by others of the day, who described him as the direct descendant of Shakespeare's printer.

There were other Jaggard family trees with solid evidence for the most recent ancestors, (the first four or five generations) and my own amateur attempt on an ancestry website to extend the tree right back to Tudor times.

Then there was the Jaggard Family Tree, completed by a Jaggard relative, which had already proved the direct descent. This had been cited on Wikipedia and we had finally managed to access a copy of this tree. I needed to study that.

Eric Jaggard had been in possession of the Jaggard Papers from after WJ's death until 1972, when, in his eighties, he had decided to bundle them up and post them to Gerald in England. It turned out that Eric had also made his own attempt to identify the line of descent. And there was evidence that Eric's work had also been used by others.

Gerald had worked extensively on the Jaggard family tree during the 1950s and 1960s but had not, as far as I know, attempted his own analysis after 1972 when he received the Jaggard Papers. His comments to Eric in his 1972 letter were quite pointed ("It's important to tell the truth") while his speech to the Shakespeare Club in 1973 was ... suitably ambiguous.

Most fascinating of all were WJ's original and extensive research notes from his thirty-year search, and his hypothesis for the direct descent, Jaggard family jottings through ten centuries. These jottings were the foundation for everything else that followed.

As I mentioned in an earlier chapter, I took all the historic papers and the digital information on holiday with me to Spain in September 2020. I spent several quiet afternoons in our favourite restaurant, mainly for the Wi-Fi signal, occasionally with the addition of a cool beer. I was poring over WJ's notes and searching genealogy websites. I had to explain what I was doing, and the background to the planned book, to Pere, the restaurant owner, a charming man, and some of the other staff who were intrigued by my brief outline of my grandfather's story, and of what I was up to.

Menorca, Spain September 2020

"It has been proved on Wikipedia."

I started with the Jaggard tree completed by a Jaggard relative. It soon became clear that this tree had connected our ancestors to John Jaggard of Tudor times who was William Jaggard the printer's brother. He was also a printer, but for Bacon, not for Shakespeare. He was not involved in the printing of the First Folio so, in the language of professional genealogists, this would be a collateral descent not a direct descent ... if the tree was trustworthy.

The evidence for the recent ancestors, the first four or five generations was sound and very detailed. However there were some worrying signs for the more distant ancestors, the references identifying each individual in the tree were predominantly from our Jaggard relative himself, not from other sources, and there was a lack of reliable evidence (i.e. original sources such as christening, marriage, and burial data).

After a thorough investigation it seemed to me the tree had been 'constructed' and at a crucial point diverged from our evidenced Jaggard tree at William Jaggard (1758–1828), substituting him with another William Jaggard (1753–1831) with these slightly different dates.

This led to a different father and mother for the second William Jaggard and from there to a different line leading eventually to the printer John.

Amazingly, the two different Williams, with different parents, shared the same wife, Elizabeth Clayton and the same wedding day. It must have been a crowded wedding ceremony with two grooms and the two sets of parents. Not only that but the two Williams had also fathered the same first child, Susanna born in 1783, and another child, Elijah, christened on 2nd March 1788.

One of the William Jaggards was clearly an imposter, and, I thought, an amalgam with data from different William Jaggards (of which there are many in Cambridgeshire). The 'manipulation of the data' was fraudulent. All of this took hours and hours to uncover and was both time-consuming and frustrating. The tree is not credible and if published would not stand up to scrutiny.

But that still did not give us a definitive answer on other Jaggard family trees.

WJ's research and his hypothesis for the Direct Descent

I decided I needed to go back to WJ's original source materials. There are over twenty sheets of paper and card that are the product of hundreds of hours of research by WJ over many years, often travelling to different parts of the country, over 120 years ago. These provide detailed information on hundreds of Jaggards from London, Derbyshire, Lancashire, Wales, Suffolk and, of course, Cambridgeshire.

His *Jaggard family jottings through ten centuries* consists of six pages (although there is an additional page 5a), which seems to have been added at a later date. Page 7 is missing, and page 8 refers to some books published between 1907 and 1914. In these jottings he also refers to his ambition to establish, *fuller justice to his* (the Tudor William Jaggard) *pioneer claims, for the 1923 celebration.*

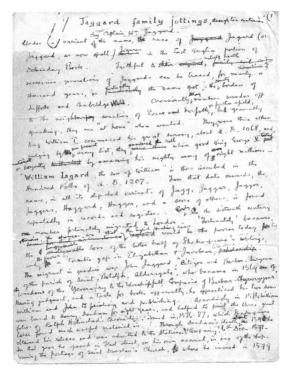

So it looks like these jottings, which are WJ's attempt to establish the direct line, were written between 1914 and 1923. They are in his distinctive script, with many changes, and revisions.

What is the purpose of these jottings? Are they 'work in progress' – an ongoing write-up, possibly over several years based on his many years of research OR his latest, or even his last attempt to describe the direct descent?

There are many 'diversions' throughout from the line of descent, with several 'flowery' stories, and with WJ's views on the recognition that William Jaggard, the printer, deserved. The notes do become increasingly confused. In particular, the additional sheet 5a, which was inserted later, appears to go back to the beginning – "The brothers William and John had several sons and daughters."

I had read WJ's handwritten script/hypothesis many times and was struggling to make sense of it. My head was spinning.

Eventually I decided I should strip out nearly all of the superfluous detail to see if I could discern his proposed line of descent. It looked like this:

WILLIAM JAGGARD died 1623, his son **ISAAC JAGGARD** died 1627.

JANE, William Jaggard's widow died in 1625 – she left many charitable legacies and much property … including a bequest to her younger son, **THOMAS**, now studying at Cambridge University for an MA in 1628–29.

Line of descent starts again on page 5a

The two brothers **WILLIAM** and **JOHN** had several other sons and daughters.

One named **RICHARD** attended St Paul's School.

Another son, **HUMPHREY** studied Law. His daughter married the **Earl of Umfreville**. The line is now extinct.

Humphrey's son **THOMAS** attended Cambridge University.

Another son **ABRAHAM** became a wealthy city grocer (Story: Pepys diary: Mistress Jaggard playing on the Vyall etc.).

ABRAHAM junior who attended Cambridge University.

And his son, **JOHN**, who entered Holy Orders, became the Rector of St Nicholas Church in Kings Lynn, Norfolk. He died in 1702 and is buried in the Chancery.

His son, **JOHN** of Steeple Bumpstead was possessed of a considerable estate in Cambridgeshire and Essex. He managed to dissipate the fruit of generations.

At this point on page 6 the notes are decidedly vague:

The line of Jaggard continues through his son **WILLIAM of Dullingham*** *(1758–1828).*

* (This is the first person I recognise from our Jaggard family tree. But according to our family tree William's father was not John of Steeple Bumpstead, but Thomas Jaggard 1724–1797.)

And the next Generation, **WILLIAM** of Stetchworth.

<u>But surely this was wrong!</u> **(i.e. William of Dullingham and then William of Stetchworth.) According to our Jaggard family tree (and several other 'correlating' Jaggard trees) William of Dullingham's son was John Jaggard (1791–1842/3).**

After this, the line is correct:

JESSE JAGGARD (1820–1898). Migrated about the middle of the 19th century from Cambridge to Winterbourne wood, Berks.

In turn, his eldest son, **WILLIAM JESSE JAGGARD** moved from there to Theale, Berks.

His eldest son, **CAPTAIN WILLIAM JAGGARD (1867–1947)** … **is the writer of these notes.**

This was all very confusing. I decided to simplify it even further with WJ's 'proposed' line of descent. This is it:

WILLIAM and JOHN the Printers

     ABRAHAM plus several other sons THOMAS, RICHARD, HUMPHREY

     ABRAHAM

     JOHN

     JOHN

     WILLIAM

     WILLIAM

     JESSE

     WILLIAM JESSE

     CAPTAIN WILLIAM JAGGARD

The next day, with a headache, and still befuddled by WJ's jottings, I decided to go back to his original research. I laid out the twenty-plus sheets of paper and cards that are the product of hundreds of hours of research on the floor. There was one, yellowing and very faded sheet, which I hadn't noticed before. I took a picture of it on my phone, blew it up, and managed to decipher almost all of the words.

It was WJ's research notes on *John Jaggard (1791–1842/3) as the result of his own visit to Dullingham in Cambridgeshire during the first few years of the 20th century. <u>This was the John Jaggard that was missing from WJ's line of descent. WHY?</u>

1791 married Mary Briggs ***Jaggard (John) Yeoman at Dullingham** **Bapt. Aug 18th 1791** (Mary Briggs sister m. Geo. Piper who rented Widgham Green Farm near Dullingham for forty years) Issue	He died **about 1842**, and on the night of his death wrote some verses on the fly-leaf in the bible including these lines referring to his approaching end:

	Born	Died	
Mahalah	8 Dec 1812		*"I feel this mud wall cottage shake*
Eliza	22 Dec 1814		
Enoch	28 Oct 1817	1870	*and long to see it falls"*
*Jesse	**10 May 1820**	**1898**	
Jack	30 Nov 1822	1837	More than sixty years after his death he is remembered in the district as a clever musician and bell ringer of a most lovable and genial temperament.
John	31 Mar 1825	1899?	
Zephaniah	5 Jan 1828	1870?	
			Mrs Price's son of xxxxx St. had this Bible.

1820 Jaggard (Jesse) – Yeoman 20th March 1844 at Stetchworth
Born 10th May 1820 died 29th Sept 1898 married **Mary Ann Jobson**
Buried at Boxford – Berks She died 27th Nov 1905
Issue
*William Jesse 3rd **Oct 1845**
Charles Jobson 13th Oct 1847
Joseph 1849
Jesse 1857d.
Eliza 1853?
John Feb 25 1855
Letitia 1857?d. Robert George 27th Dec 1870

All the details of Captain William's great grandfather **John Jaggard (yeoman) his grandfather Jesse (yeoman and poacher/ gamekeeper), and his father William Jesse (railway porter) are correct and tally with the Ancestry family trees.*see all their details, which I have highlighted in bold, on WJ's notes.**

WJ had visited Dullingham, he had seen the Bible John Jaggard wrote his verse in, shortly before his death in 1842/3. He had visited Widgham Green Farm close to the hamlet of Dullingham Ley where John and Mary lived, and spoken with local people, *"More than sixty years after his death he is remembered in the district as a clever musician and bell ringer of a most lovable and genial temperament."* If WJ made this visit "more than sixty years after John's death" that would put his visit sometime between 1903 and 1905.

And yet in his jottings he excludes John entirely from the line of descent? He would hardly have forgotten such a memorable visit, even if this had been ten years earlier.

Was this deliberate on WJ's part, excluding John from the line of descent? Or was he just confused or disheartened trying to make the line down from the Tudor William connect to his more recent ancestors. It didn't make any sense.

That night, Moira and I were having dinner at Sa Lluna, the restaurant where I had been working during the day investigating WJ's jottings.

Pere, the owner, asked how the work on the book was going and then took our order.

When Pere had gone Moira said, "He seemed very interested in the book ... you know he's been explaining to a few customers that you're descended from William Shakespeare?"

I laughed, "That's good because I'm not descended from William Jaggard the Printer

... There is no direct descent ... and there never was."

"How do you know?"

I explained about WJ's visit to Dullingham between 1903 and 1905, all the information he had on his great-grandfather, John Jaggard.

"First, it makes no sense because WJ excludes John Jaggard from the line of descent, despite the fact that knew a great deal about his great-grandfather from his own memorable research visit to Dullingham"

"And second I think his proposed line breaks down at the point between John (of Steeple Bumpstead) – supposedly descended from the line down from John – Tudor William's brother 'and William of Dullingham, as WJ called him, our William Jaggard (1758–1828).

Then on a piece of paper I listed, in black, the correct five generations to my grandfather, and then with an X, where I believe WJ's line of descent breaks down.

Abraham?
John?
John (of Steeple Bumpstead) X
William (1758–1828)
John Jaggard (1791–1843)
Jesse
William Jesse
Captain William Jaggard (WJ)

"I'm fairly sure that the father of William Jaggard of Dullingham (1758–1828) was not John of Steeple Bumpstead, but Thomas Jaggard."

Moira said, "That's disappointing?"

I had to think about that. "Not really, knowing my grandfather as I do now, I'd have been amazed if it was true ... he was ... a rogue."

After reaching my conclusion on WJ's hypothesis, I discovered another single page document, with some notes about the two Tudor brothers and printers, William and John.

Someone else had clearly wanted to establish WJ's line of descent, much as I had done.

This sheet has signs of more than one hand, the notes in large capitals were added more recently. They belong to our Jaggard relative who used WJ's line of descent as the template for his own fictitious tree.

The original notes, though were almost certainly the work of Eric Jaggard. We have copies of his letters to Gerald. Eric's normal spidery handwriting is difficult to decipher, perhaps the reason for using the small capitals, while the sentence in the circle, in script, looks like an excellent match for his handwriting. If he had the Jaggard Papers from 1947–1972, it's understandable that he would have wanted to prove the direct descent.

Eric had made notes about the two printer brothers, William and John. Then he had proposed the line of descent under John's name.

Suffice to say it mirrors exactly WJ's proposed line of descent. Eric's conclusion, that is circled, is significant.

"This is as close as I can come to the descent." he says.

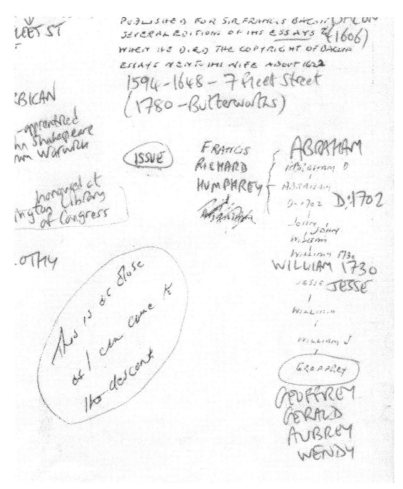

ABRAHAM, ABRAHAM, JOHN, JOHN, WILLIAM, WILLIAM 1730, JESSE, WILLIAM, WILLIAM (WJ) then his children

I completed this analysis in September 2020 a few months before we 'found' the housekeeper in 2021 and had the benefit of Helen's testimony and Alan Harry's detailed Jaggard family trees. Edith Etta Jaggard/Parkin and WJ have the same great-grandfather – guess who? John Jaggard (1791–1843), Edith and WJ were second cousins and yet their shared great-grandfather is the man excluded from WJ's line of descent. I can only speculate on why WJ excluded his and Edith's great-grandfather?

There was one last throw of the dice.

In the early months of 2021, I finally got hold of a copy of Captain Wm Jaggard's 'Jaggard Jottings from olden days'. Like the 'Humorous Army Records', we obtained this from an online rare books dealer at some expense. And again, it turned out to be just three sheets, the frontispiece of another edition of WJ's B.A.R. (Book Auction Records). It was published in 1921, two years before WJ's self-imposed deadline for sharing the Jaggard family tree and proving the direct descent.

Jaggard Jottings from olden days

By CAPTAIN W. JAGGARD.

(Author of " Shakespeare Bibliography *" and other works)*

> " What's in a name ? "   -   -   *Shakespeare, Romeo* . . . *1597.*
> " I believe there is some secret power and virtue in a name." } *Burton, Anatomy* . . . *1624.*

LITERARY genealogy carries its own curious interest for bookmen. The rare surname of Jaggard is derived from :—
    JAG : cut, or ornamented,   GARD : jerkin or doublet,

You can imagine that I was very keen to see what WJ had to say about the direct descent. It consists of three sides, clearly derived from his 'Jaggard Jottings through ten centuries'. After explaining the derivation of Jag and Gard, WJ writes, "Confusion often arises over the Elizabethan brothers William and John Jaggard." Most of the first two sides cover all the material we are already familiar with about the lives of the two printers.

Towards the end of side two, WJ finally comes to the descent. Here it is in full:

"The brothers, William and John Jaggard, left several sons and daughters. One son Thomas graduated at St Catherine's College, Cambridge. Another, Richard, was a fellow pupil with John Milton at St Paul's school, proceeding to Magdalen College, Oxford from whence he obtained the living of Penshurst, Kent, of fragrant

literary memory, as the home of the Sidneys. Milton later became a neighbour of the Jaggards in St Botulph's parish. A third son, Humphrey, studied law, as did his son in turn, Thomas (vide 'Middle Temple Records). Another son, Abraham, became a wealthy city grocer, Freeman of the Grocers Company, and esteemed friend of our unique Samuel Pepys, to whom he was related by marriage. Pepys' father was a Fleet Street tailor. After the great 1666 fire, Abraham largely rebuilt Upper Thames Street (which runs east from Blackfriars Bridge), and caused Pepys to pay him, his wife, and children tribute in some entertaining passages, in his 'Diary', especially after Pepys had dined with him. One daughter became Lady Umfreville, marrying a descendant of the old Norman Earls of Umfreville, a race now extinct."

As you can see the first part is a mix of the names of various sons and their tenuous links to famous characters. He ends, bizarrely, with Lady Umfreville from his own rambling Jaggard Jottings … *the line became extinct.*

The material in the Jaggard Jottings from olden days is no more than a half-hearted token gesture to publish something on the descent by his self-imposed deadline.

And that is it. There is no more about the direct descent. He concludes with:

"The 1623 Shakespeare has given William Jaggard enduring fame, but apart from that, his claim rests upon ample foundation, in his earlier and stupendous labours."

Despite his obsession to prove the direct descent, WJ did not publish a complete family tree during his lifetime. WJ must have realised that his case was hopeless, but he continued to refer to himself as the direct descendant, trading off the connection. He would have had more to lose than to gain by going public with his proposed line of descent.

I was certain there was no direct descent but thought we should see this through. In 2022 we employed the services of a well-respected professional genealogist, Patric Dickinson, who researched our Jaggard family tree. His full report is in the appendix but here are some extracts and his professional view.

<u>ANCESTRY OF JOHN JAGGARD (1791–1843)</u>

There can be no doubt that the ancestral line is fully established back to John Jaggard and his wife Mary Briggs.

John must have thus been aged between forty-five and forty-nine in June 1841 and therefore born after June 1791. Since he was fifty-two when he died in October 1843, it seems safe to identify him as John, son of William and Elizabeth Jaggard, baptised at Dullingham 18 Sep 1791.

*William and Elizabeth Jaggard were having children baptised at Dullingham from August 1783 and it therefore seems safe to identify them with the William Jaggard and Elizabeth Clayton who were married there in May of the same year. Amongst the burials at Dullingham in the 18th century there is more than one William who might be him but **the most likely contestant is William Jaggard, a widower of Burrough Green, who was buried 26th April 1828 aged seventy-one. We know that John and Mary Jaggard were living at Burrough Green between 1820 and 1828, so it seems at least plausible that William (a) joined them there when his wife died and (b) was brought back to Dullingham to be buried.** There can be little doubt that Elizabeth was the Elizabeth Jaggard, wife of William of Dullingham Ley, who was buried at Dullingham 3rd March 1819 aged sixty.*

William Jaggard's age at death does not fit perfectly with the baptism of William, son of Thomas and Sarah Jaggard, on 11th October 1758 but up till the mid-19th century it was nothing less than unusual for correct ages to be given at death, the generality being that the age of the deceased was often exaggerated. Often the next birthday was anticipated, a person of seventy being thought of as in the seventy-first year of his age and the age sometimes recorded as seventy-one. William would in fact have been in the seventieth year of his age in April 1828 but a discrepancy of this order is entirely normal. I would therefore be inclined to accept that he was the William baptised in 1758.

Patric Dickinson presents the evidence and is circumspect in his judgements but he reached this conclusion on the direct descent:

The fact that there are Jaggard entries in the registers of Dullingham and surrounding parishes back to the 1550s strongly suggests that your forebears lived in those parts from at least the early 16th century.

The printer William Jaggard, on the other hand, was born in London and it seems that his father, born in the 1540s or earlier, was also a Londoner.

It therefore seems highly improbable that the Dullingham Jaggards could have been descended from the printer.

If there was any connection at all between the families (and there is no particular reason to suppose that there was), then it must have been several generations further back. *Jaggard (together with its several variants, most notably Jagger) is by no means an uncommon name and* **it is just as likely that there was no connection at all between the printer and the Dullingham Jaggards.**

WJ had not been able to prove the direct descent in his lifetime despite thirty years of research.

Patric Dickinson believes the direct descent is *highly improbable.*

Does it matter? Yes.

Is it important?

It's important to tell the truth and that is what we have done to the best of our ability, exposing my grandfather's long-held lie.

POSTSCRIPT – Reflections on the direct descent

" No Legacy is as rich as Honesty " All's Well That Ends Well Act III Scene 5

Andy Jaggard

For over a hundred years our Jaggard family have traded off the connection to the Tudor William Jaggard, who printed Shakespeare's First Folio. WJ and Geoffrey did, and perhaps others from the Jaggard family may still choose to do the same. It's nice to have a 'claim to fame'.

Our own conclusion, as evidenced in the last chapter is that our Jaggard family are not directly descended from the Tudor Jaggards, printers of the First Folio.

The clues were in WJ's lack of action, masked perhaps by the inferred associations with well-known historical figures, Milton, Pepys et al, and by his flamboyant assertions. His deeply flawed hypothesis together with the evidenced opinion of a professional genealogist leaves little room for doubt. There never was a direct descent.

For WJ, it was *the second great work of his life*, and he had a great deal invested in that claim. If he was not directly related, he certainly *adopted* William Jaggard as his tenth great-grandfather, promoted his importance, and fiercely defended his reputation … so he did him some kind of service.

Many people were happy to cite WJ as the direct descendant, and reinforce his connection to William Jaggard, printer of the First Folio. He would have had more to lose than to gain, by claiming the direct lineage and publishing the evidence, for others to dissect. As far as we know 'Jaggard Jottings from olden days' were his final words, in print, on the subject.

Our father, Gerald, was also imbued with the same family legend. He pursued his own detailed research in the fifties and sixties, which proved inconclusive. There was always *a gap*.

My father was an honest, dependable and respectful man. If he had a fault it was that he was too trusting and accepting of the views of others. That was particularly true in relation to his father.

In the opening chapter of *The Life and Death of a Stratford Bookshop*, Gerald wrote this of his father:

I never thought of it much at the time, but looking back, I realise that my father, a bookseller all his life, was quite unlike the popular image of a person in this sedentary occupation.

What the family search has revealed is that most of our ancestors, stretching back several centuries, originated from a small rural area in southeast Cambridgeshire, around the villages of Dullingham, Dullingham Ley, Borough Green and Six Mile Bottom, Stetchworth, West Wratting, Linton, Hildersham, and Abington, and they worked in the countryside, as woodsmen, as farmers, and farm labourers, and later as labourers and builders and bricklayers, and more recently, as a gamekeeper, a railway porter and a very famous bibliographer.

But as Gerald said, WJ always needed to have the last word: *"Captain Wm Jaggard of Stratford-upon-Avon, who is leaving no uncertain mason's mark upon the temple of English bibliography and of drama, as did his famous ancestor, three centuries since."*

Shakespeare Press

This was the final line from WJ's jottings but in a rare moment of modesty WJ crossed out the comment about *leaving no uncertain mark upon the temple of English bibliography*, substituting,

> *Captain Wm Jaggard of Stratford-upon-Avon, ... is the writer of these notes.*

CHAPTER 24 LOOSE ENDS

" This above all, to thine own self be true " Hamlet Act I Scene 3

Andy Jaggard
Not quite the last word.

In many ways this story is about factual and personal truth. My grandfather's outrageous claims and his lies led to prestige and material gain during his lifetime, but the legacy is his damaged reputation.

My father for many years suppressed the truth about the damaging impact that WJ's domineering personality and callous behaviour had on the family. He buried his own feelings by choosing not to talk about the long and very difficult period of his adult life caring for his abandoned mother. Even many years after his father's death he kept up a pretence of respect for his father's 'stupendous industry' and his 'crowning achievements'.

With the benefit of our research, and with hindsight it's possible to understand now the sequence of events that caused Gerald to start work on *The Life and Death of a Stratford Bookshop*.

In early 1972 he was excited to, at last, receive the Jaggard Papers from Eric Jaggard, twenty-five years after WJ's death in 1947. Given his own detailed research into the Jaggard family tree in the 1950s and 1960s, Gerald must have quickly realised that WJ's hypothesis did not make much sense. Writing to his uncle in March 1972, thanking Eric, Gerald said, The line of descent you have so kindly let me have will be tremendously useful, although I cannot attempt a detailed and scholarly treatment. The implication is clear, he no longer believed in the direct descent.

Gerald had been invited to give the lecture to the Shakespeare Club, eighteen months later, in November 1973 to celebrate the 350th Anniversary of the Printing of the First Folio. Gerald was to give the 'lecture' on *his famous ancestor from whom he was a direct lineal descendant.* This was now a very public and tricky event for Gerald to negotiate. He would have given his speech and his choice of words some serious thought.

His style was always indirect, subtle, allowing the audience to 'read between the lines'. First he made some inferences about the connection of our Jaggard family to the famous Jaggard printer, in order to honour the occasion, *It was his proudest moment ... he felt closer than he had ever done before to his famous ancestor.* He compared the printer's *indomitable spirit* to his father's own character traits and how they both *attracted friends as well as enemies.*

Then he gave a factual account of WJ's lifelong search:

With the infinite patience and industry which characterised his labours in the world of books, he pored over the records of Stationers' Hall, church registers, parish registers, he advertised, corresponded with members of the family, studied back files of newspapers. Eventually, after tracing a final link in Wales, he felt that the line of descent was complete, and aimed to bring out a book on the family tree in 1923. The book never appeared, and at his death in 1947 the papers could not be found.

Having overcome that particular hurdle I imagine that Gerald would have been relieved.

Then he would have reflected on William the Sixth's actions and behaviour throughout all those long years when he made his outrageous claims.

I imagine that Gerald felt angry and cheated. In early 1974 Gerald started work on his book, perhaps in order to express his very strong feelings about his father and because he had decided that he finally needed to tell the truth.

And that is what Gerald did, honestly, emotionally and powerfully.

Preface – **The Life and Death of a Stratford Bookshop** *– Gerald Jaggard – 1974*

Although No. 4 Sheep Street is gaunt and empty, it has a story to tell. It is a tale covering almost a century, when my father set his sights on Stratford and resolved to conquer it. By incredible industry and strength of purpose he achieved many of his targets; by vanity, overconfidence, and a complete lack of tact he made so many enemies on the way that his life ended in bitter failure.

Is WJ's *bitter failure* a reference to the direct descent? Or to the break-up of the family?

When Gerald started his story the floodgates opened, first with his description of his years running the bookshop but then most powerfully with his heartfelt boyhood memories.

Reliving his early years must have been cathartic for Gerald, his arrival in Stratford as a five-year-old boy, clutching the kettle to provide a cup of tea *when we arrived in paradise,* the founding of the Shakespeare Press *complete with its fake Tudor facade,* recalling life at Rose Bank, punting on the Avon, WJ's love of his possessions, the *blazing denunciation of Geoffrey…*

I can't recall a time when my father was ever truly angry. He could be cross for a brief period – when he lost his queen during a game of chess, for example *(oh .. damn!)*– but I never saw sustained anger.

The Life and Death is like that. His Preface suggests that Gerald was angry and intended to brutally expose the truth but his analysis and critique of his father's character soon changes into something more observational, witty, detached, and sad.

He was a one-man consumer organisation but carried his complaints to such lengths that at times we didn't know where to look.

WJ had a horror of putting money into lawyers' pockets, as he was so to speak, a law unto himself.

That endless patience necessary for indexing trade journals and preparing a bibliography was real enough in his bookshop but vanished before he got home.

Perhaps Gerald had convinced himself that his book could be just about the bookshop but he must have realised that he was finally letting go of his deeply buried feelings about his father and the family.

He described Marie Corelli's death and her funeral in April 1924 but now he was approaching the really difficult period in his life, his father's affair with Edith Parkin and the abandonment of his mother.

This was not something that he could describe in his somewhat detached, observational and witty style.

He must have realised that he could never complete or publish his book and that's when he stopped. Perhaps it had already served its purpose but he saved the manuscript and the significant family letters.

Not long after, in the late 1970s, he bundled up all of the Jaggard Papers and gave them to my sister, Anthea.

A symbolic gesture that he was letting go of the 'direct descent' and his anguish over his father's actions? No longer 'haunted by his father' he had exorcised the ghost of WJ.

Perhaps though ...in a final twist and against all the odds, we will discover the missing Jaggard link that connects to the line down from William and Isaac?

One member of our Jaggard clan holds on to the fable from our childhood believing it just needed to be proved – whatever that involved. Another clings to the idea that the descent from our famous ancestor "is still possible", despite the judgement of the professional genealogist that it is "highly improbable".

For me it was never about proving the direct descent - only about resolving the issue and providing the evidence.

The last three years has been a challenging but immensely rewarding journey of discovery: delving into the Printing of the First Folio, the 'Shakespeare Industry', the Folgers, Piracy and Forgery, not for academic study, but as the fascinating backdrop against which my grandfather and my father played out their lives; gaining a deeper understanding of the events of our childhood and of the lives of our ancestors; enduring long periods of frustration with little progress, memorably broken by some amazing discoveries – WJ's letters to Folger offering him his First folio - *"never been out of the family since printed in the Barbican"*, making new connections with living relatives in Cambridgeshire and through Alan Harry's family tree research in Cambridgeshire getting to know Helen and her stories of the life and character of 'the housekeeper', *her* "Aunt Edie".

Most important of all, we now have a far deeper understanding of the course of my father's life, and of how the difficult events and the challenge of the Shakespeare Press helped to shape his character.

Gerald suffered at times during his life, but he was stoical, he endured, and many people loved him for his modest demeanour, his witty and laconic style, and his ability, even through all the tough times he encountered, to put things into perspective.

Diana and Gerald's relationship mellowed as they aged together at Greensleeves, Diana in her seventies, Gerald in his nineties. Diana still cycling to Stratford every day on her bike, returning for mid-morning coffee and cake with Gerald. They played croquet against each other on the back lawn, games of chess with no quarter given. On summer nights they turned the television round so they could sit on the patio watching their programmes through the open French windows as the light faded.

Amongst his many creative hobbies, Gerald wrote rhyming verse (or doggerel as we called it) to celebrate his annual trips accompanying Diana's 'Young Explorers' to the Lake District. In 1999, Gerald and Diana celebrated their Golden Wedding. That morning when Gerald came down to breakfast he exclaimed, "*Ahh … made it.*" At the evening celebration they helped us to recreate their first meeting in 1947 at The Cobweb tearooms just down Sheep Street from his bookshop. I had written some rhyming verse/'doggerel', in Gerald's style.

Gerald was in his bookshop … I took this story on trust

It's not that he was on the shelf, though perhaps he was gathering dust …

The shop was run in his own understated, quiet way. He achieved a great deal, not in a monetary sense, but through his creative endeavours, through his battle with the council to save the Tudor building from demolition, in his reputation in the town, and from his memories of famous actors and his myriad customers during the seventeen years of running the Shakespeare Press.

Sitting in his armchair in 2002 he must have reflected on those two life-changing decisions he made in 1947 when he fought back after his twenty lost years.

When family differences had been sorted out, I tackled the Augean stables ...

I'm sorry Diana I won't be coming anymore ... Ohh why? ...

The summer season is coming and I can't afford to be away from the Bookshop ...

I'll bring a flask of coffee ...

That day's half-finished crossword lay on the table next to his armchair.

APPENDIX – CONTENTS

The Shakespearean Relic/Wooden Casket (Chapter 12)........... 276

The Mystery of Harry Jaggard – Alan Harry (Chapter 14)....... 277

The Ireland Forgeries –
"Vortigern and Rowena" (Chapter 17)...................................... 280

Gerald and Diana – Letters after their engagement – September
1948 (Chapter 20) 282

The Renovation of No. 4 (and No. 5) Sheep Street – Bob
Chambers (Chapter 21)... 283

Geoffrey Jaggard's Tourist Publication for the big celebration in
1964 (Chapter 21) 291

Shop Memories – May 2021 (Chapter 21) 292

WJ's Hypothesis for the Direct Descent (Chapter 23).............. 294

The Jaggard Report – Patric Dickinson (Chapter 23)............... 295

CHAPTER 12 *WJ in the First World War*

The Shakespearean Relic/Wooden Casket (sold by WJ to Folger in March 1914)

Box carved from wood of Shakespeare's house

1 box: oak tree wood; 5 1/2 in. high, 9 5/8 in. wide, and 6 7/8 in. deep

England: s.n., [ca. **1847**?]

Certification: Box came with certification, now catalogued as Y.C.1466, which reads, "This casket was made from oak which was once part of Shakespeare's birthplace discarded at the restoration in the year 1847. The carving upon the lid is the work of ... 'Kendall' of Warwick, being the arms of Shakespeare surrounded by the emblem of immortality. Certified by Alfred Rose, Custodian of Shakespeare's birthplace." Document is not dated.

Provenance: Mr Folger bought the box from Mary Rose, **through William Jaggard, Shakespeare Press, March 10, 1914,** for L25/-/-. See HCF's file, Booksellers: Bills and Receipts (Folger Archives)

Design: Kendall's design for the lid is recessed into an ellipse broken by 4 triangles. It consists of a carved relief of Shakespeare's coat of arms with his crest which is backed by a ribbon having his birth and death dates. On either side of the arms are Shakespeare's initials through which a snake with its tail in its mouth is entwined in the shape of a circle. The contrasting texture of the background may have been made by a rocker or die with fine teeth. The lid, which overhangs the box and the sides and the back and slightly at the front, has been attached to the box with 2 brass hinges, each having been secured with 2 brass screws. The box has dovetail joints and is set on projecting torus molding to which the 4 feet have been glued. The front and back panels have 3 rosettes set into a single interlacement band. The shorter side panels have 1/2 of a rosette at each end. There is a keyhole but no escutcheon. A tray with 2 sections has been set into the top of the box of 4 vertical supports.

Extracts from description of Wooden Casket in Folger Institute Archives

CHAPTER 14 – *The Housekeeper's Story*

The Mystery of Harry Jaggard

This information on Harry is based on several conversations with Helen Greenland, Harry's eldest daughter now in her late seventies, together with conversations with and research on Ancestry.co.uk by Alan Harry (father-in-law of Helen's daughter).

When I first spoke to Helen she described her father as *"an orphan, brought up in South Wales, who returned to Cambridgeshire aged four, only able to speak Welsh ... that made it very difficult for him"*.

According to Alan Harry's family tree, Harry's mother was Edith Morris who was brought up in the local pub in Llandybie, Carmarthenshire – the Golden Lion. She married a John Jaggard in 1907, he was from Cambridgeshire (a hamlet called Dullingham Ley). The only real proof of Edith and John living together is from the 1911 census when they were at an address in Llandybie; he was a Surface Colliery Worker. There is no other evidence on John Jaggard after 1911.

Harry William Jaggard was born to Edith Morris on 1st January 1912. A second child, William E. Jaggard, was born in October 1913 but died aged four months in January 1914. Then Edith Morris herself died in April 1915. Harry would have been just over three by then.

Another mystifying aspect is that if John Jaggard was the father, and was there whilst Harry was growing up, you would have expected Harry to have been able to speak some English? For the 1911 census, John's language is English while Edith speaks both English and Welsh.

When Harry (an orphan) returned to Cambridgeshire he was taken in by Edith Etta Jaggard's family, her mother Ellen is called *'Grannie'* by Harry. (*see Alan Harry's theory about how these apparent family relationships may have come about.) There's a picture of a young Harry with *'Aunt Lilla'*, Edith's younger sister who would have been around twenty-one when he returned. It's not clear what happened to John Jaggard, Harry's father.

By the time of the 1921 census, Harry aged nine years and five months is living in Hildersham with Henry and Ellen Jaggard and their youngest daughter Lilla. Harry is described as their *"grandson"* with *"Both parents dead"*.

Harry studied music in London, but gave it up, *"one step short of his gown and badge"* to start his own dance band.

Harry Jaggard – 1930's aged 23 or 24 at rear of "Rose Bank", Hildersham

Then we know that by the time of the 1939 census, Harry, *'Grannie'* (Ellen Jaggard), and Edith Parkin are listed as living at Rose Bank, Hildersham, the Old Post Office, and Harry aged twenty-seven is a sub-postmaster. Harry met his future wife, Hilda, shortly after this; she had moved to the area from Sheffield. They married in 1941. Helen was born in 1942. Harry and Hilda, with some financial help from *'Aunt Edie'*, bought the Post Office in Great Abington, the nearest village. It needed a lot of work and they built the business to include a small shop. It was the hub of the community through the fifties and sixties.

*A Theory about John Jaggard
Alan Harry

Jesse Jaggard (WJ's grandfather) lived in Widgham Green, close to Dullingham Ley. There were only seven houses in Widgham Green in 1861.

John Jaggard (who went to Llandybie to work in the colliery) was born in Dullingham Ley to Enoch Jaggard and Mary Ada Cook in 1883. A few months after John's birth, Mary Ada Cook died. Only eight households away (from the 1881 census) are Henry Jaggard and Ellen Briggs with Edith E. Jaggard (Parkin) and Willie (who also worked in South Wales – in Port Talbot).

Sometime before 1885 (another son Bertie was born in 1885 in Linton), the Henry Jaggard and Ellen Briggs family moved to Linton. John Jaggard, for the 1911 census, gave his birthplace as Linton. *That would be explained if John was taken in by Henry and Ellen and he went with them to Linton. If he was indeed taken in by them, baby John would have joined the family with Edith aged four and Willie aged one. So they would have been brought up together virtually as siblings.* That would explain the use of *'Aunt'*, *'Grannie'*, etc. and perhaps why *'Aunt Edie'*, when she returned to Hildersham, took Harry *'under her wing'*.

CHAPTER 17 *Forgery*

"Vortigern and Rowena" – First and Last Performance – Captain Wm Jaggard

Edmund Malone, one of the best scholars of the day, was convinced the Irelands were rogues, and pursued them relentlessly. Some three months before the performance of *Vortigern* the Irelands published their precious Shakespeare salvage in a folio volume entitled:

"Miscellaneous papers and legal instruments under the hand and seal of William Shakespeare, including the tragedy of 'King Lear' and a small fragment of 'Hamlet', from the original manuscripts in the possession of Samuel Ireland, Norfolk-street 1796."

Malone set to work to examine the Ireland's credentials. The further he delved, the more suspicious he became, and eventually he wrote and published a rejoinder. The publication of Malone's exposure acted as a thunderbolt.

A Real Fake – The Huntington Library, Art Museum and Botanical Gardens.

William Henry Ireland had written an entire five-act play, emulating his father's beloved Bard. Just like Shakespeare, he drew inspiration from the 1577 *Holinshed's Chronicles* which recounts the history of Anglo Saxon and early Norman rulers. Vortigern was a brutal, usurping, 5th-century King of the Britons.

In the spring of 1795, the playwright Richard Brinsley Sheridan decided he wanted to stage *Vortigern* at his theatre in Drury Lane, and he hired John Philip Kemble, the renowned actor, to star in the title role. Sheridan and Kemble constantly expressed doubts about the play's authenticity, but neither could bear to have the opportunity slip by if there was even a slight chance the play was real.

The play was originally set to open on April 1st 1796 (April Fool's Day), but Sheridan thought that was a little too *'on the nose'* and decided to move the opening performance to the following evening. He left Shakespeare's name off the playbill, but everyone in London knew the controversy surrounding the play. A total of 3,500 tickets were sold, packing the house to full capacity.

Throughout the evening, Kemble delivered his lines in an increasingly over-the-top style, poking fun at the entire thing. At the end of the performance, he returned to the stage to announce that the play would not be performed again. Fist fights broke out in the audience between those who believed the play was by Shakespeare and those who did not. Many people must have also been simply furious at the thought that they had been duped by Ireland and by the theatre.

Ireland realised his deception could not be sustained, and a few months later, he confessed to everything.

CHAPTER 20 *Gerald's "Shakespeare Press" – 1947–1960*

Gerald and Diana – Letters after their engagement – September 1948

Wednesday September 1st 1948

My Dear Diana,

I enjoyed the flashing lights as I left Avonhurst – they gave me a friendly send-off. It was <u>very</u> late before I finally dropped off to sleep, but I don't blame the English Liqueur, which was delicious, especially when made by a certain Popsy.

The family have been duly advised of the proposed alliance and are <u>very</u> pleased. I have completed the application form for the lodge.

Over the next two weeks, Diana wrote twelve letters to Gerald from the Waterhead Hotel in Ambleside.

Letter no 3 – September 4th 1948

Dearest Gerald,

Thank you for telling me how to spell Popsy. Have you thought about the wording for our engagement announcement in the Herald yet. Do you think you will be strong enough to be labelled GERALD THE MARRIED MAN.

Your ever tragic and lipsy, Popsy

Letter no 7 – September 8th 1948

A wonderful walk. Up and up I went, and as I got higher the sun shone through the spencer trees onto the moss and lichen below. The trees were mainly mountain ash and silver birch, their slender trunks covered with grey lichen, it was magical. The rocky path calling me on ... I came to the top of a crag, and sat down panting in the mossy knoll – heather grew among the moss, and this is some I enclose to you.

Suddenly, I came to the edge, and there far below me lay Derwent water – deep, shimmering with dark shadows – and far away the other lake and mountains. It was wonderful, and needed but one thing to bewitch me – you can guess what? Prince Charming – but I thought of you – and that was all I could do."

By the way, 16 or 17 miles the other day, including Helvellyn – not bad for a Popsy.

Tuesday September 13th – very early

My Dearest Diana.

Three of your letters arrived this morning in a bunch. Many thanks for them. You really are a magnificent correspondent, with whom I cannot hope to compete ...

You seem to be having some lovely steamer trips. The energy of Ted is stupendous, but if he teases you too much, just ask him (from a safe place) if he prefers pink or blue satin for his page's dress next spring.

CHAPTER 21 – *Gerald's "Shakespeare Press" – 1960 - 1964*

The Renovation of No. 4 (and No. 5) Sheep Street, Stratford upon Avon – Bob Chambers

Gerald's petition in 1962 had undoubtedly saved No. 4 Sheep Street from demolition but the building stood empty and derelict for many years after he had been evicted from No. 4. on Christmas Eve 1964.

Many years later my sister, Anthea, was catching up with some old college friends. As her friends lived all over the UK, they typically met up in Stratford most years as this was a central location. They always enjoyed 'long chatty lunches' and often chose 'The Vintner' with its nostalgic associations with her dad's old bookshop for their reunions. Gerald's name came up in conversation, that day, and suddenly at Anthea's side was a gentleman from the next table

"Excuse me but did you mention Gerald Jaggard?"

Anthea, of course, proudly confirmed that Gerald was her father and he had indeed run the old bookshop for many years.

Bob Chambers introduced himself and his wife Diana and then told Anthea and her friends the amazing story of how they and their three young children, Lisa, Fraser and Tania, had moved to Stratford, bought the lease, and then restored the building so sympathetically.

It was in 1977 that Bob and Diana had decided that a complete lifestyle change for the family would be a sensible move:

We lived in Maidenhead where I ran a medium-sized engineering company, and Diana traded antiques from a stall on the Portobello Road. So we started to look for a property which could be restored and where Diana could expand her business ... as for me, frankly I had no idea what I would be doing!

We always loved Stratford so we visited, and on our very first trip we came across a run-down property on Sheep Street.

It stood out like a sore thumb ... it had obviously been unoccupied for a number of years, which was a shame as it definitely had character and a presence.

We called in at Peter Clarke and Co ... an estate agent who was then located in Sheep Street. This was a stroke of luck as Peter was able to tell us that the property was owned by Stratford District Council and they had been looking for a tenant who would be prepared to take on the restoration.

Up to this point in time they had been unsuccessful with this and were seriously considering demolishing both properties and making an extra car park for the Shakespeare Hotel. This was our chance, so we asked Peter to negotiate on our behalf. He agreed and within a week or so he got approval from the council. Peter refused to charge us for his involvement ... an act of generosity which we will never forget. We signed a long-term lease on 22nd December 1977.

We managed to sell our Maidenhead house quickly and bought a small two-bedroomed cottage in Stratford Old Town ... Broad

Street ... right opposite the primary school. The children had at the most a thirty-yard walk to school! The school was absolutely delightful, and the children flourished and went on to do very well at the local secondary schools.

Anthea and her friends were engrossed in Bob's story and both intrigued and amazed when he told them that the initial demolition work involved the whole family

We decided that we would carry out any demolition at Sheep Street ourselves as we needed to save money, and more importantly we wanted to preserve any architectural features and rebuild them into the restored building.

So one cold Saturday morning the whole family went to the property armed with wrecking bars, hammers and chisels and started on removing an outbuilding and a lean-to shed at the back of the property. It was a family endeavour ... Diana and I loosened the bricks and tiles and the children removed any loose mortar and neatly stacked them for future cleaning.

By the evening we had completely demolished these two buildings … they were not part of our plans, and in any case they were so rotten that it would have been impossible to save them.

The bricks turned out to be a complete delight … handmade with gorgeous colouring, much shallower than modern bricks, and there was still evidence of the original brick makers' … thumb prints and stacking marks where they were placed in the kilns prior to firing. Likewise the tiles were also handmade and most were in a good enough condition to re-use.

*I'm sure that Bob described some of the story of the restoration on that first meeting with Anthea. However they kept in touch over the years and in May 2022 Bob came along to our event for the Shakespeare Club – '**Walked Alone**' – and at the end of the evening had the opportunity to give a more detailed talk providing some fascinating insights into the challenges of preserving and renovating No. 4 (and 5) Sheep Street.*

Although we were able to save most of the bricks and the tiles, much of the timber was a disappointment … many of the rafters and joists to the rear of the building were made either from softwood or elm. Elm is always subjected to woodworm attack and just turns to powder as soon as its disturbed.

Over the next few weeks, we proceeded with the demolition and we were relieved to find the structure near the front was constructed of oak and was largely free of worm.

The occasional joist was rotted beyond repair, so I contacted a woodyard near Hereford, and they became very interested in the project and cut me 'green oak' to the exact dimensions I needed.

All I had to do was the replicate the stop chamfers and drop them into the slots left by the removal of the rotted joists. The use of unseasoned green oak was commonplace in the past … it twists and cracks a little during drying out and this is exactly what happened to my replacement joists. Once stained it was impossible to tell which the replacements were.

Diana plodded on with cleaning the old mortar from the bricks and we were delighted to discover that we had in the region of 20,000 ... enough to rebuild its internal walls in each property. Meanwhile I lifted all the old quarry tiles from the floor (just over 1,000), took them back to Broad Street and soaked them twenty-five at a time in dustbins full of acid. This cleaned them very well and they are all back in No. 4 where they came from. The same treatment was given to the limestone slabs in No. 5.

While we were demolishing, we looked for a sympathetic builder to take on the rebuilding work and we were very fortunate to locate a young enthusiastic builder and, as we thought we were finished with the demolition, we arranged a start date.

At this point we hit snag! We had a visit from the building inspector and he very nicely said that he expected us to remove all the remaining roof tiles from the front and back and re-fix them on new battens with copper nails. Old handmade tiles have no holes, they are held in place with dabs of mortar. So each one had to be removed and drilled with a single hole to allow for the copper nail. This turned out to be quite a job as there were around 11,000 tiles that needed a hole. Nothing for it but to get on with it, and two weeks and eight drills later, the job was done and they were re-fixed to the roof.

The building work went very smoothly and all was well until the building inspector condemned the staircase in No. 4, and asked for new stairs at the back of the property. Diana refused point blank to comply, and after a short stand-off the problem just disappeared, and the old stairs remain to this day. They are very steep but authentic and certainly add character. The building work went without a hitch and after rewiring and plumbing we were ready to decorate ... Diana coped with this, and just over a year since work started, we were ready to open.

This was the finished result! We were very proud of our achievement and we felt justified in putting in the extra effort to save what we could of the structure and fittings, especially in No. 4 with its rich history and importance to Stratford.

We were also honoured to receive an award from the Society of Architects for our sympathetic restoration.

(No. 4 was at first an antique arcade and the refurbished old cottage, at No. 5, became a wine bar. The antique arcade closed in 1993 and the wine bar was expanded into No. 4 – the removal of two sections of wall opened the whole area up.)

The Vintner has prospered over the years. It has a huge customer base and is busy all year round. Much of this is due to the cosy, beamed construction and the warm colours of the exposed brickwork. Everyone appears quite relaxed once settled down at their tables! I believe that Mr Jaggard and his ancestors would be pleased with the outcome.

Bob Chambers – January 2023

Bob – Thanks so much for this.

On March 1st 1962 the **Birmingham Post's** article **Fight to Save 15th Century Stratford Bookshop** *quoted these words from the town clerk of the day talking about No. 4 Sheep Street:*

"Neither from an historical or an architectural point of view does it warrant the expenditure to put it into a fit state."

We could have had a soulless row of 1960's shops, instead we have the charming and character-full building that is the Vintner.

Gerald was also delighted that No. 4 Sheep Street was saved and so carefully and beautifully restored by you and your family. Stepping inside No. 4 today it's possible to be transported back in time and recall the memories of the Shakespeare Press ... and of its two, very different owners.

Geoffrey Jaggard's Tourist Publication for the big celebration in 1964

Companion to Stratford is an odd booklet/magazine, with numerous local adverts, some densely packed text and some dark photos. The choice of photos rather than the line drawings would no doubt have provided more opportunities for advertising revenue, with additional pictures of pubs and hotels.

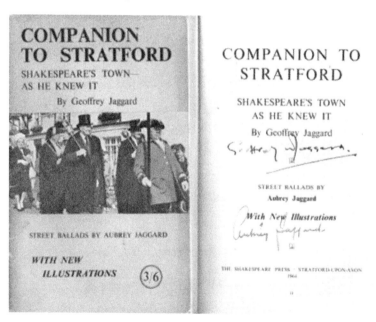

Incidentally an eleven-year-old grammar school boy was press-ganged to feature in a photo standing outside Shakespeare's Grammar School:

"*With his satchel and his shining morning face ... crept unwillingly to school.*"

"*... a bag of sweets wouldn't have gone amiss.*"

"*I was taught a little Latin ... but it was all Greek to me.*"

Shop Memories – May 2021

I had long forgotten its name, but I recall vividly going into the quaint old building at the bottom of Sheep Street with my parents around 1962 or 1963 while visiting Stratford from Birmingham. At the time, I was thirteen or fourteen years old and, from the age of twelve, had been collecting antique maps. In the shop, we were shown a first edition of Camden's Britannia of 1607 which was priced, I think, at £1,000 – an unthinkable amount to pay for a book. But, to this day, I've remembered that book and regretted that we couldn't buy it! Looking online, I see that a first edition is now selling for about £7,500, so perhaps it was just as well that we didn't, as it hasn't kept pace with inflation over the past sixty years. (£1,000 then is about £22,000 today.) But what a great treasure it would have been if we had bought it!

Margaret Cund

My late father Arthur Dumper (1907–1973) was a regular customer of the bookshop during the fifties and sixties and was quite upset when he learnt from your father that the lease was expiring and the shop would no longer be a haunt for him. Even worse, he learnt the news, probably through your uncle Aubrey Jaggard who he regularly played bowls with at FISSC, that any books not sold before the closure in 1964 were destined for the tip.

This resulted in him suggesting that I personally visit the shop to see if there were any books I wished to buy. I purchased a number of maths textbooks with answers all signed within by Leslie Watkins who had only recently retired as headmaster. The other gem I purchased again signed by Leslie Watkins is his *History of KES* published in 1953 which contains an acknowledgement to your father as being one of the persons who suggested he write the said history.

In 1970 I joined Three Counties Insurance Brokers.

Our office then was at 2 Chestnut Walk and a certain Bob Chambers, then living in Broad Street, came into our premises enquiring if we could arrange insurance for a new business venture. That was probably 1972 and his venture was the redevelopment of 4 Sheep Street.

I recall vividly what happened to the Shakespeare Press, all the old infill was taken away leaving for a short while just the original timber frame before new brickwork and utilities were added. The premises following the renovation opened as Diana Chambers Antiques and a separate antiques arcade shared the space. When Bob and Diana gave up the retailing in the 1980s, they then let the premises to the Vintner, the current occupant, and they became landlords.

David Dumper

CHAPTER 23 – *The Direct Descent*

WJ's Hypothesis for the Direct Descent

Page 6 – The last section of WJ's hypothesis for the Direct Descent

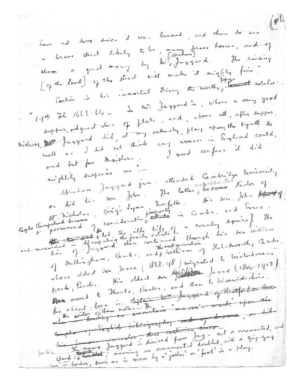

Note: After 'the idle squire' John of Steeple Bumpstead WJ just states, *"The line of Jaggard then continued through his son William of Dullingham and ('the next generation' – inserted) William of Stetchworth. This is incorrect, excluding John Jaggard (1791– 1843) entirely from the line of descent.*

The Jaggard Report – Patric Dickinson

<u>ANCESTRY OF JOHN JAGGARD (1791–1843)</u>

There can be no doubt that the ancestral line is fully established back to John Jaggard and his wife Mary Briggs but it might be helpful if I make a couple of comments on the transcript of the notes made by Captain William Jaggard about their children. One is that the child listed as Jack born in 1822 was in fact a daughter named Jael (in one or two online sources she is misidentified as a son named Joel). Also, she died not in 1837 but in 1852, being buried at Dullingham on 12th November 1852 aged thirty. Her brother Zephaniah, shown in the list as perhaps dying in 1870, in fact died in 1866 – he too was buried at Dullingham on 15th April 1866 aged thirty-eight.

In the 1841 census John Jaggard gave his age as forty-five. In that census, adults were required to state their age according to the last multiple of five years that they had completed. John must have thus been aged between forty-five and forty-nine in June 1841 and therefore born after June 1791. Since he was fifty-two when he died in October 1843, it seems safe to identify him as John, son of William and Elizabeth Jaggard, baptised at Dullingham 18th September 1791

His wife Mary, giving her age as fifty (i.e. fifty–fifty-four), is probably identifiable with Mary, daughter of John and Elizabeth Briggs, baptised at Stetchworth 2nd June 1788. This makes it all the more likely that she was the Mary Jaggard of Dullingham Ley buried at Dullingham 8th December 1844 aged fifty-six.

William and Elizabeth Jaggard were having children baptised at Dullingham from August 1783 and it therefore seems safe to identify them with William Jaggard and Elizabeth Clayton who were married there in May of the same year. Amongst the burials at Dullingham in the 18th century there is more than one William who might be him but the most likely contestant is William Jaggard, a widower of Burrough Green, who was buried 26th April 1828 aged seventy-one. We know that John and Mary Jaggard were living at Burrough Green between 1820 and 1828, so it seems at least plausible that William (a) joined them there when his wife died and (b) was brought back to Dullingham to be buried. There can be little doubt that Elizabeth was the Elizabeth Jaggard, wife of William of Dullingham Ley, who was buried at Dullingham 3rd March 1819 aged sixty.

William Jaggard's age at death does not fit perfectly with the baptism of William, son of Thomas and Sarah Jaggard, on 11th October 1758 but up till the mid-19th century it was nothing less than unusual for correct ages to be given at death, the generality being that the age of the deceased was often exaggerated. Often the next birthday was anticipated, a person of seventy being thought of as in the seventy-first year of his age and the age sometimes recorded as seventy-one. William would in fact have been in the seventieth year of his age in April 1828 but a discrepancy of this order is entirely normal. I would therefore be inclined to accept that he was the William baptised in 1758.

The list of baptisms at Dullingham supplied by Anthea Kenna includes Thomas, son of Thomas and Mary Jaggard, baptised in 1755, but according to at least three genealogical websites (Ancestry, Findmypast and Family Search) this baptism concerns Thomas, son of Thomas and <u>Sarah</u> Jaggard. The same website also lists the baptism of John, son of Thomas and Sarah Jaggard, at Dullingham on 28th September 1761 – an entry that does not appear at all in Anthea's list. Thomas and John were doubtless William's brothers. Since Thomas appears to be the eldest, it seems reasonable to identify their parents with Thomas Jaggard and Sarah Morley, who were married in 1754 at Dullingham.

I did notice that two children of a Thomas and Sarah Jaggard were baptised at Linton in the 1760s – Charles in 1764 and Susanna in 1765 – and it occurred to me that they might be the same couple as the Thomas and Sarah at Dullingham (especially as it rather looked as if Thomas's mother was named Susanna). Thomas Jaggard of Linton was a currier, who took an apprentice in 1776 and appeared as a freeholder on the electoral roll of West Wratting in 1780 (though actually living in Linton at the time). But he was himself apprenticed to Edmund Jackson of Linton, currier, in 1754, which makes him too young to be the Thomas marrying Sarah Morley the same year. So this Thomas and Sarah were evidently a different couple, quite possibly the Thomas Jaggard and Sarah Offord who were married at Great Chesterford, Essex in 1761. I mention this merely as an example of the possible confusions that can arise when scrutinising genealogical sources (yet another couple named Thomas and Sarah Jaggard were having children baptised at Cambridge in the 1760s).

A further indication that Thomas and Sarah Jaggard of Dullingham did in fact continue to live in that parish is provided by the fact that their son John was buried there in 1780. It therefore seems at least possible that they were the Thomas Jaggard, labourer, and Sarah Jaggard, widow, who were buried there in 1797 and 1803 respectively. It seems reasonable in turn to identify Thomas with Thomas, son of Thomas and Susanna Jaggard, baptised at Burrough Green in 1724 – and highly likely that Thomas's parents were the Thomas Jaggard and Susan Cornel married at Dullingham in 1721.

But I would be hesitant to accept without further proof that Thomas who married in 1721 was the Thomas Jaggard baptised at Withersfield, Suffolk in 1698. Whilst Withersfield is only six or seven miles from Dullingham, the parishes are not adjacent and in those circumstances there would need to be some corroborative evidence of the identification. By no means all parish registers have been transcribed and it therefore follows that online indexes of parish registers cannot be regarded as comprehensive. Nor is it the case that every single individual gets recorded in parish registers. Also, some registers were better kept than others and there were inevitable omissions from time to time. Moreover, it is important to remember that there were at any given time quite a few families who adhered to nonconformist sects (whose records tend to be sparse before the late 18th century). Such adherence could often be a temporary business, occurring perhaps in only one generation of a family's history. There are many reasons why the baptism of a particular individual is not to be found in a parish register.

For this reason, in the period before civil registration commenced and census returns existed, it is often necessary to explore a variety of sources to supplement the information found in parish registers. One of the most useful in this respect are probate records. Prior to 1858, wills were proved in ecclesiastical courts; those of Cambridgeshire folk are to be found in the records of the Consistory Court of Ely, to which there is a printed index covering the years 1449–1858. I am attaching scans of the relevant pages. Unfortunately, none of the entries is likely to assist in corroborating the ancestral line back to Thomas Jaggard and Susan Cornel or tracing back further. There are two listings for Jaggards of Dullingham, both called William, one an aledraper, the other a brick maker. The latter is evidently the William Jaggard of Dullingham Ley, widower, who was buried at Dullingham in 1826 aged sixty. The other entry dates from 1740 and is of potential interest but the individual concerned evidently died intestate because a grant of administration (rather than a will) was recorded. This would be unlikely to reveal very much other than the name of the individual to whom administration of the estate was granted – and his or her relationship to the deceased – but it might nonetheless be worth checking just in case it has any bearing on the line of descent.

The other thing worth doing would be to make a more complete list of the Jaggard entries in the Dullingham and Burrough Green parish registers. Anthea Kenna mentioned that she had extracted only some of the Jaggard baptisms at Dullingham, so I think they do need to be checked, especially as her list got the 1755 entry for Thomas Jaggard slightly wrong and omitted the John Jaggard who was baptised there in 1761. The original parish registers of Dullingham are held at the Cambridgeshire Archives in Ely but they have been fully transcribed and copies of the transcript are held both by the Cambridgeshire Archives and by the Society of Genealogists in London. I rather imagine that what Anthea Kenna consulted was a further copy held at the church. In the normal course of things, I would be able to look at the copy in the Society of Genealogists but they left their premises in central London last summer and have yet to occupy news ones in North London, which means that most of their material is inaccessible at the moment. The Burrough Green registers are also held at Ely where it is likewise possible to consult a transcript.

The fact that there are Jaggard entries in the registers of Dullingham and surrounding parishes back to the 1550s strongly suggests that your forebears lived in those parts from at least the early 16th century. The printer William Jaggard, on the other hand, was born in London and it seems that his father, born in the 1540s or earlier, was also a Londoner. It therefore seems highly improbable that the Dullingham Jaggards could have been descended from the printer. If there was any connection at all between the families (and there is no particular reason to suppose that there was), then it must have been several generations further back. Jaggard (together with its several variants, most notably Jagger) is by no means an uncommon name and it is just as likely that there was no connection at all between the printer and the Dullingham Jaggards.

P.L. Dickinson

22nd April 2022

BIBLIOGRAPHY

CHAPTER 1 – The Life and Death

Gerald Jaggard: *The Life and Death of a Stratford Bookshop (Unpublished book) c. 1974 Preface*

Gerald Jaggard: *Letter to Eric Jaggard – 10 March 1972*

CHAPTER 2 – The Shakespeare Press

Gerald Jaggard: The Life and Death of a Stratford Bookshop (Unpublished book) c. 1974

Historical Buildings - Grade 2 Listing - NGR SP2016654834

CHAPTER 3 – The First Folio and the Shakespeare Industry

Gerald Jaggard: *Letter to Eric Jaggard – 10th March 1972*

The First Folio – The Times Literary Supplement – Thursday April 19th1923

J. L. Garvin: Who Shakespeare Was? The First Folio Tercentenary – The Comedy of Doubt – The Observer –Sunday April 22nd 1923

Andrea Mays – The Millionaire and the Bard – Simon & Schuster Paperbacks

Peter Blayney W. M. – The First Folio of Shakespeare – Washington D. C. Folger Shakespeare Library 1991

Steve Newman – Shakespeare's Legacy – Internet Article

Johanne Stochholm – Garrick's Folly – The Shakespeare Jubilee of 1769 at Stratford and Drury Lane 1964

CHAPTER 4 – The Sixth William

Gerald Jaggard: The Life and Death of a Stratford Bookshop (Unpublished book) c. 1974

Jesse Jaggard – Ancestry website – 'Memory'

Mairi Macdonald – Shakespeare Centre Library and Archives – Handwriting Solves the Mystery of the Two William Jaggards – Stratford-upon-Avon Herald, 2005

CHAPTER 5 – "Bring it Over"

Gerald Jaggard – Stratford Mosaic – The Shakespeare Club and a Medley of Memories – Christopher Johnson Publishers Ltd 1960

Sidney Lee – The Lee Census – 1902

Leamington Spa Courier – Shakespeare in Folio – 25th February 1899

Stockton Herald – February 1899

Andy Jaggard – Walked Alone – Captain William Jaggard's Life – Entertainment for Shakespeare Club – May 2022

The Folger Institute Archives – 14 Letters and documents between Captain Wm Jaggard and Henry Folger - April – September 1903

CHAPTER 6 – A Farcical Tale

The Folger Institute Archives – 14 Letters and documents between Captain Wm Jaggard and Henry Folger – April – September 1903

Sidney Lee – The Lee Census – 1902

Eric Rasmussen and Anthony James West: The Shakespeare First Folio – A Descriptive Catalogue – 2012

Richard Noble – Rare Materials Cataloger, Brown University Library: The John Hay Library Copy

CHAPTER 7 – William Jaggard – Man of Letters All 2,000 of Them

Robert Bearman – Shakespeare Birthplace Trust Records Office William Jaggard – Man of Letters All 2,000 of them – Stratford-upon-Avon Herald, 2005

Captain William Jaggard: Office Letter Book, November 1907 – June 1909

Gerald Jaggard: The Life and Death of a Stratford Bookshop (Unpublished book) c. 1974

Captain William Jaggard: Gerald Jaggard Letters Collection

CHAPTER 8 – Piracy

Stanley Wells – Biography of William Jaggard (1568–1623)

Captain Wm Jaggard – The Passionate Pilgrim – Private Research Papers c. 1914–18

Gerald Jaggard – The Jaggard Story – Draft Manuscript – 1970s

Professor Alfred Pollard – The Mysterious "Volume of 1619" – The Sphere, 26th May 1923

R. Crompton Rhodes – An Unlikely Candidate – The Times Literary Supplement, 22nd March 1923

Captain Wm Jaggard – The Passionate Pilgrim & Sir John Oldcastle Piracy – Private Research Papers c. 1914–18

R.Compton Rhodes – William Jaggard and the First Folio – The Times literary Supplement – March 22nd 1923

CHAPTER 9 – City Librarian or Nothing

Gerald Jaggard: The Life and Death of a Stratford Bookshop (Unpublished book) c. 1974

Captain William Jaggard: Booklet of Testimonials

Captain William Jaggard: Gerald Jaggard Letters Collection

CHAPTER 10 – Life at 'Rose Bank' with WJ

Gerald Jaggard: The Life and Death of a Stratford Bookshop (Unpublished book) c. 1974

CHAPTER 11 – WJ's Missions and Making Enemies

Gerald Jaggard: The Life and Death of a Stratford Bookshop (Unpublished book) c. 1974

Captain William Jaggard: Gerald Jaggard Letters Collection

Nick Birch – Marie Corelli internet article – 2013

Captain William Jaggard: Shakespeare Bibliography – A Dictionary of Every Known Issue of the Writings of our National Poet and of Recorded Opinion Thereon in the English Language – Shakespeare Press, iv Sheep Street. MCMXI

Shakespeare Bibliography – Pamphlet of Independent Opinions – Shakespeare Press, iv Sheep Street. MCMXI

Gerald Jaggard – Stratford Mosaic – The Shakespeare Club and a Medley of Memories – Christopher Johnson Publishers Ltd 1960

CHAPTER 12 – WJ in the First World War

The Macdowell Club of New York City – Invitation Card – Shakespeare's Country from Roman Days to Now – Captain Wm Jaggard – March 3rd 1914

Unknown journalist: Twenty Years with Shakespeare – The Bibliographer – Descendent of Shakespeare's First Publisher, March 2014

Captain Wm Jaggard – Army Records Human and Humorous – in B.A.R. – Shakespeare Press, 1919

James Milne – Utopia in Bookland – The Graphic, July 19th 1924

Compiled in the Trenches – Many Misadventures of Massive Work, June 6th 1924

Captain Wm Jaggard – The Frauds and the Cranks – Private Research Papers, c. 1914–18

Captain William Jaggard: *Jaggard Jottings through ten centuries – Handwritten script c. 1914–1923*

Shakespeare Press

CHAPTER 13 – Gerald – Smitten by Shakespeare

Gerald Jaggard: *Stratford Mosaic – The Shakespeare Club and A Medley of Memories – Christopher Johnson – 1960*

Gerald & Aubrey Jaggard – Through the Ages – Historical Burlesque, c. 1921

Gerald Jaggard – Archie Flower – Man of Action – And of Dreams in Stratford Mosaic – The Shakespeare Club and A Medley of Memories – Christopher Johnson – 1960

George Bernard Show: *Speech – Proposal of 'The Immortal Memory' – Shakespeare Birthday celebrations 1925*

Gerald Jaggard: *The Life and Death of a Stratford Bookshop (Unpublished book) c. 1974*

Obituary for Marie Corelli – Stratford Herald – April 1924

CHAPTER 14 – The Housekeeper's Story

Richard Noble – Rare Materials Cataloger, Brown University Library: The John Hay Library Copy

The Ship's Register of Passengers Leaving from Southampton to New York on the 'Berengaria' – 24th March 1928

The Ship's Register of Passengers Arriving into the Port of London on the 'Ausonia' – 25th April 1928

1939 Census for the occupants of "Rose Bank", 180 High Street, Hildersham, Cambridgeshire

1939 Census for the occupants of "Rose Bank", 7 Tiddington Rd, Stratford-upon-Avon

Alan Harry: *Henry and Ellen Jaggard family tree snippet – Private family tree*

1911 Census for the occupants of the Pear Tree Inn, Hildersham

Hildersham Parish Electoral Roll 1935/Great Abington Electoral Roll 1945/50/60/65

Helen Greenland - Personal Testimonies, 2020/2021/2022

Henry and Ellen Jaggard's Family tree

1911 Census – Edith Parkin and Albert Edward Parkin, Stretford, Old Trafford, Manchester

1921 Census – Edith Parkin and Albert Edward Parkin, Charing Cross Road, London

CHAPTER 15 – Gerald's 'Lost Years'

Captain Wm Jaggard – Once a Printer and Bookman – Shakespeare Press, 1934

John Barnes – Notes about the life of Gerald Jaggard, 2003

Electoral Roll for 129 Loxley Road, Stratford-upon-Avon, 1930

Susan Brock and Sylvia Morris – The Story of the Shakespeare Club of Stratford-upon-Avon – Published by the Shakespeare Club, 2016

Leamington Spa Courier – A Great Attraction

Gerald Jaggard – Ilmington Awaits Her Cue – Leamington Spa Courier

Birmingham Daily Gazette – Queen of Shakespeare Land – May 1939

Nicholas Fogg – Stratford-upon-Avon – The Biography – Amberley Publishing 2014

Fred Wincote Story – The Stratford Auxiliary Fire Service 1943 – The Shakespeare Birthplace Trust Records Collection

Helen Greenland – Personal testimony – 2021

CHAPTER 16 – A Voice from the Dead

Gerald Jaggard: The Life and Death of a Stratford Bookshop (Unpublished book) c. 1974

Caroline Spurgeon: *Shakespeare Imagery and What it Tells Us 1934*

William Shakespeare: *The Rape of Lucrece – Lines 1667–73*

CHAPTER 17 – Forgery

Captain Wm Jaggard – The Poet's Enemies – Private Research Papers c. 1914–18

Captain Wm Jaggard – Shakespearean Frauds: the story of some famous Literary and Pictorial Frauds – Shakespeare Press 1911

? News of Books – Mr Jaggard Makes a Discovery, October 1922

Daily Mirror – Treasure Dug Up At Night – Judge Baffled by Way Expert was Deceived, March 1927

The Scotsman – Alleged Forgeries – Man Sent for Trial, November 27th 1927

The Henry Ireland Forgeries – The Huntington Library, Art Museum and Botanical Gardens

CHAPTER 18 – A Great Find

Adam Hooks: Selling Shakespeare Biography and Bibliography and the Book Trade – Cambridge University Press

Captain Wm Jaggard – Once a Printer and Bookman – Shakespeare Press, 1934

The Daily Mirror – Countess's Discovery – A Great Find – Shakespeare's Own "Ideas Book", February 1936

Professor G. B. Harrison – Countess Clara Eleanor Longworth de Chambrun – Preface to Shakespeare Re-Discovered

Boston Herald – A Shakespeare Discovery, November 5th 1936

The Sphere – Articles about Holinshed's Chronicles Discovery, 4th and 23rd April 1936

CHAPTER 19 – He Walked Alone

Helen Greenland Testimony

Obituary – Captain William Jaggard – Bibliographer of Shakespeare – The Times April 30th 1947

G. L. Riddell, Hon. Secretary: Letter with Resolution of Sympathy from The Livery Committee of the Worshipful Company of Stationers – 12th May 1947

Obituary – Eminent Stratford Bibliographer – Death of Captain William Jaggard – Unknown author

Gerald Jaggard: Stratford Mosaic – The Shakespeare Club and A Medley of Memories – Christopher Johnson – 1960

CHAPTER 20 – *Gerald's 'Shakespeare Press' – 1947–1960*

Gerald Jaggard: The Life and Death of a Stratford Bookshop (Unpublished book) c. 1974

Gerald Jaggard: Sheep Street – Birmingham Sketch – 1972

Steve Newman: Trinity Times – September 1997

Gerald Jaggard and Diana Salt: Letters following their engagement – April 1948

Rick Gekoski: How to Get Ahead or at Least Stay Afloat in the Rare Books Trade – July 2014

John Coleman: Pericles, Prince of Tyre at the Memorial Theatre, Stratford-upon-Avon, April 23rd 1900. Pamphlet Collated by Various Sources

Gerald Jaggard: Before the Curtain Rises – No. 23 – An Informative Pamphlet on William Shakespeare's Pericles

Gerald Jaggard: Before the Curtain Rises – No. 18 – An Informative Pamphlet on William Shakespeare's As You Like It

Before the Curtain Rises – No. 13 – An Informative Pamphlet on William Shakespeare's Macbeth (signed by Vivien Leigh and Laurence Olivier)

CHAPTER 21 – Gerald's 'Shakespeare Press' – 1960–1964

Birmingham Post: March 1st 1962 – Fight to Save 15th Century Stratford Bookshop

Birmingham Post: May 4th 1962 – 1,000 Protest Over Stratford Demolition

Birmingham Post: 6th September 1963 – Scheme to Restore Old Bookshop

Geoffrey Jaggard: Letter to Gerald – 1st January 1964 – Gerald Jaggard Letters Collection

Geoffrey Jaggard: Companion to Stratford – Shakespeare's Town as He Knew it – 1964

Birmingham Post: 21st December 1964 – Shakespeare Shop to Close

Gerald Jaggard: Letter to Stratford Herald 1962

Gerald Jaggard: Sheep Street – Birmingham Sketch – 1972

CHAPTER 22 – The Game is Nearly Up

Gerald Jaggard: Letter to Eric Jaggard – March 10th 1972

Captain William Jaggard and Gerald Jaggard: The Jaggard Papers

Captain William Jaggard: Jaggard Jottings through ten centuries – Handwritten script c. 1914–1923)

Gerald Jaggard: Type-written notes of speech to the Shakespeare Club for the 350th Birthday of The First Folio – November 1973

The Stratford Herald: First Folio Shown on its 350th 'Birthday' Celebration – And Descendent of its Printer Talks of Him and It – November 1973

Mr William Shakespeare's Comedies, Histories, and Tragedies, Published According to the True Original Copies – 1623 ('The First Folio')

Edwin Willoughby: A Printer of Shakespeare – The Books and Times of William Jaggard – 1934

CHAPTER 23 - The Direct Descent

Captain William Jaggard and Gerald Jaggard: The Jaggard Papers

Ancestry.co.uk: The Jaggard Family Tree – (1510 - 2023)

Eric Jaggard: Single sheet of notes – 'This is as close as I can come to the descent' c. 1947–1972

Captain William Jaggard: Jaggard Jottings through ten centuries – Handwritten script (c. 1914–1923)

Captain William Jaggard: John Jaggard (1791–1842) – Handwritten Research Notes on Direct Descent – 1903–1905

Captain William Jaggard: Jaggard Jottings from Olden Days – Article in B.A.R. – Shakespeare Press – 1921

Patric Dickinson: The Jaggard Report – 20th April 2022

POSTSCRIPT – Reflections on the Direct Descent

Gerald Jaggard: The Life and Death of a Stratford Bookshop (Unpublished book) c. 1974

Captain William Jaggard: Jaggard Jottings through ten centuries – Handwritten script (c. 1914 – 1923)

CHAPTER 24 – Loose Ends

Gerald Jaggard: Letter to Eric Jaggard – March 10th 1972

The Stratford Herald: First Folio Shown on its 350th 'Birthday' Celebration – And Descendent of its Printer Talks of Him and It – November 1973

Gerald Jaggard: The Life and Death of a Stratford Bookshop (Unpublished book) c. 1974

Image Captions

1. Sheep Street taken around 1908
2. The Shakespeare Press – Gable window – Restored by Wm Jaggard 1910
3. The Shakespeare Press 'founded 1591'
4. A print from WJ's collection of 'Treasures' – 16th Century Printing Shop
5. The First Folio
6. The octagonal rotunda for Garrick's Shakespeare Jubilee 1769
7. Andy as Gerald – 'Walked Alone' for Shakespeare Club – May 2022
8. Jesse Jaggard 'Poacher turned Gamekeeper'
9. Ex dono Willi Jaggard a Typographi 1623
10. WJ's letter to Henry Folger – April VII 1903
11. King Lear Quarto, showing original 1608 version, and 'False Folio', also 1608, but actually printed in 1619
12. WJ in stationer's costume – 'Rose Bank', Stratford 1930s
13. Marie Corelli
14. Shakespeare Bibliography – Wm Jaggard
15. Twenty Years with Shakespeare – The Bibliography-Descendant of Shakespeare's First Folio, March 1914
16. Jaggard family jottings, through ten centuries
17. The First Shakespeare Memorial Theatre, Stratford-upon-Avon
18. 'Supers' – Captain William Jaggard, and twins Aubrey and Gerald Jaggard
19. Destruction of the Old Shakespeare Memorial Theatre by fire – March 1926
20. The Berengaria Ship's Registry leaving Southampton for New York, March 1928

21. 1939 Census, 'Rose Bank', Hildersham
22. 1939 Census, 'Rose Bank', Stratford-upon-Avon
23. Edith E. Parkin (1879–1967) – Photo courtesy of Helen Greenland and Alan Harry
24. Edith Parkin in South Africa – Photo courtesy of Helen Greenland and Alan Harry
25. Albert and Edith Etta Parkin's memorial and headstone, Hildersham Parish Church – June 2021 – Photo courtesy of Helen Greenland and Alan Harry
26. The 'Berengaria' – First Class Lounge – C.F. Hoffman Southampton
27. The Stratford Auxiliary Fire Service 1943 Image courtesy of Shakespeare Birthplace Trust Records Office)
28. Clopton Bridge, Stratford-upon-Avon
29. Caroline Spurgeon's sketch of the 18th-century arch of Old Clopton Bridge
30. Mr Jaggard Makes a Discovery, 11th October 1922
31. Countess's Discovery – Great Find, Daily Mirror, February 1936
32. Edith Parkin by the lychgate, 'Rose Bank', Stratford, 1940s – Photo courtesy of Helen Greenland and Alan Harry
33. Obituary – Captain William Jaggard – The Times – 30th April 1947/ Resolution of Sympathy from the Livery Committee of the Worshipful Company of Stationers, 12th May 1947
34. Obituary – Eminent Stratford Bibliographer of Shakespeare
35. Captain William Jaggard – Photo courtesy of Helen Greenland and Alan Harry
36. Line drawing by Gerald Jaggard from Stratford Mosaic 1960
37. Diana Salt and Gerald Jaggard, shortly after they met in 1947
38. Anthea, Diana and Gerald, 'Avonhurst', December 1950
39. The Shakespeare Press, first floor, built c. 1490 (a WJ postcard)

Shakespeare Press

40. Gerald Jaggard in the Shakespeare Press 1960 – Stratford Mosaic
41. Speed County Map of Warwickshire
42. Pamphlet for Shakespeare's Play Pericles, Prince of Tyre at The Memorial Theatre, Stratford-upon-Avon – 23rd April 1900
43. Before the Curtain Rises, no 23 – Pamphlet for Shakespeare's Play Pericles devised by Gerald Jaggard
44. Before the Curtain Rises, no 18 – Pamphlet for Shakespeare's Play As You Like It, devised by Gerald Jaggard, signed by Vanessa Redgrave/Vanessa playing 'Rosalind' 1961
45. Before the Curtain Rises, no 13 – Pamphlet for Shakespeare's Play Macbeth, devised by Gerald Jaggard, signed by Vivien Leigh (Lady Olivier) and Laurence Olivier
46. Fight to save 16th Century bookshop, 'Old Curiosity Shop comes to Life'
47. No. 4 Sheep Street, the Shakespeare Press, 1964
48. The Shakespeare Press
49. First Folio shown on its 350th birthday, Stratford-upon-Avon Herald, November 1973
50. Jaggard family jottings through ten centuries by Captain Wm Jaggard
51. Captain Wm Jaggard research notes on John Jaggard (1791–1842/30)
52. "This is as Close as I can come to the descent"
53. Jaggard Jottings from olden days by Captain William Jaggard – Shakespeare Press

Printed in Great Britain
by Amazon